W9-AFP-988

HILLARY
RODHAM
CLINTON

MODERN FIRST LADIES

Lewis L. Gould, Editor

HILLARY RODHAM CLINTON

POLARIZING FIRST LADY

GIL TROY

UNIVERSITY PRESS OF KANSAS

© 2006 by the University Press of Kansas

All rights reserved

Published by the University Press of Kansas (Lawrence, Kansas 66045),
which was organized by the Kansas Board of Regents and is operated
and funded by Emporia State University, Fort Hays State University,
Kansas State University, Pittsburg State University, the University
of Kansas, and Wichita State University

Library of Congress Cataloging-in-Publication Data

Troy, Gil.

Hillary Rodham Clinton : polarizing first lady / Gil Troy.

p.   cm. — (Modern first ladies)

Includes bibliographical references and index.

ISBN 0–7006–1488–5 (cloth : alk. paper)

1. Clinton, Hillary Rodham. 2. Presidents' spouses—United
States—Biography. I. Title. II. Series.

E887.C55T76 2006

973.929092—dc22

2006013559

[B]

British Library Cataloguing-in-Publication Data is available.

Printed in the United States of America

10 9 8 7 6 5 4 3 2 1

The paper used in this publication meets the minimum requirements of the
American National Standard for Permanence of Paper for Printed Library
Materials Z39.48–1992.

To the next generation:

Aaron, Ariel, Aviv, Claire, Dina, Ezra, Joanna, Joshua,

Lauren, Leora, Lia, Naomi, Rachel, Rina, Ruth, Sarah, Yoni

With the hope that you will learn to find balance and wisdom

amid all the passions and seductions of the modern world:

Wisdom cries out in the streets . . . saying:

How long you thoughtless ones, will you love thoughtlessness,

how long will cynics delight in their cynicism,

and fools hate knowledge?

—Proverbs 1:20, 1:22

CONTENTS

EDITOR'S FOREWORD

As the last woman to occupy the position of the first lady in the twentieth century, Hillary Rodham Clinton was one of the most polarizing figures in the history of the institution. Her opponents attacked her even before her husband ran for president. Her defenders acclaimed her as both a loyal spouse and an example of how feminism could inform and improve public life. She became a U.S. senator and potential presidential candidate after her White House years, and controversy still follows her as her public career continues. Dozens of books have been written about Hillary Clinton, and more will appear should she embark on a race for the presidency.

Evaluating her tenure as first lady presents challenges for an historian in terms of balance and perspective. Much of the literature on Hillary Clinton is ideological and partisan in one direction or another. Gil Troy's narrative about Clinton's performance as first lady will not satisfy either her passionate critics or her staunch defenders. With his rich knowledge of the historical traditions surrounding the first lady as an aspect of the presidency, Troy places Hillary Clinton in the context of her predecessors and traces her activities during the turbulent decade that brought her to national prominence. His verdict is a mixture of praise and censure that will take the debate about Clinton's public role in a more sophisticated analytic direction. Readers will find incisive judgments about the first lady and her colleagues, new insights into such disputed terrain as the Whitewater episode, an original analysis of Mrs. Clinton's worldview and ideology, and fresh takes on the various controversies that swirled around the first lady. Troy is especially effective in his evaluation of the public responses to Clinton's years in the East Wing of the White House. She became a cultural icon as well as a public personage who was treated in much different fashion than those who had preceded her over the previous four decades. The result is a narrative that will renew in a lively and articulate manner the public colloquy about where Hillary Rodham Clinton stands in the continuum of modern first ladies.

Lewis L. Gould

PROLOGUE AND ACKNOWLEDGMENTS

In January 2005, with Democrats still reeling from George W. Bush's reelection triumph, Senator Hillary Rodham Clinton gave a speech marking the thirty-second anniversary of the Supreme Court's controversial *Roe v. Wade* decision legalizing abortion. Speaking to the New York State Family Providers, one of America's leading liberal Democrats predictably feared that the decision, which she again endorsed, was threatened. But the New York Democrat was careful to call abortion "a sad, even tragic choice" and America's abortion epidemic "a failure of our system of education, health care, and preventive services." Articulating a nuanced, centrist position in a normally polarized debate, Mrs. Clinton said, "The fact is that the best way to reduce the number of abortions is to reduce the number of unwanted pregnancies in the first place."[1]

"CLINTON SEEKING SHARED GROUND OVER ABORTIONS," the *New York Times* proclaimed.[2] The headline was doubly interesting because in New York in 2005, "Clinton" clearly referred to Senator Hillary Clinton and not her ex-president husband, Bill Clinton. The headline also fed those who saw Senator Clinton as the Democrats' great hope for 2008. In that spirit, the more critical *Washington Times* reported: "Sen. Hillary Rodham Clinton is staking out centrist positions on values issues that helped decide last year's presidential election, positioning herself to the right of her party's base on abortion, faith-based initiatives and immigration." Viewing the position more skeptically, the conservative paper also quoted Gary Bauer, president of the American Values organization and a former Republican presidential candidate, sneering—with just a hint of sexism: "I think what we're seeing is, at least rhetorically, the attempt of the ultimate makeover."[3]

Although this book concentrates on Hillary Rodham Clinton's rocky tenure as first lady from 1993 to 2001, it offers essential background to this exchange on many levels. The book explains how

Mrs. Clinton's personal and political passages in the 1990s helped set up the unprecedented move down Pennsylvania Avenue, from the White House to Capitol Hill. The book describes the public adulation and loathing Mrs. Clinton experienced and how she became one of America's most famous and controversial Democrats and one of the world's most famous and controversial women. The book traces Mrs. Clinton's ups and downs in the White House, showing how her often-searing experiences enhanced her popularity and her power. Being first lady transformed Hillary Clinton into a modern American icon, even as her dreams of reforming health care, revitalizing American values, and redefining the first lady as a copresident vanished. The book also roots Mrs. Clinton's centrism on the abortion issue—and others—not in the red versus blue political exigencies of today, but in an evolving philosophy that has elements that are far more traditional than either her liberal fans or her conservative detractors appreciate. By reading hundreds of Hillary Rodham Clinton's speeches and columns, it becomes easier to understand the kind of senator she has become—and the kind of American leader she wants to be.

Like it or not, love her or hate her, one thing is clear: Hillary Rodham Clinton is not likely to go away soon. Just as she sought to be the most powerful first lady since Eleanor Roosevelt, she is now on her way to becoming the most influential ex–first lady since Eleanor Roosevelt. Of course, as of this writing, with Democrats calling Hillary Clinton's Neo-Georgian Georgetown Mansion the "White House-in-Waiting" and "Fundraising Central," many supporters are actively hoping and planning to make Senator Clinton the first first lady and first woman ever to leap from a supporting role in the East Wing to the leading role in the West Wing.

As I researched and wrote this book, many friends, colleagues, and acquaintances asked the same four questions, repeatedly. Although I tell my students in class that there are no stupid questions, alas, all four persistent questions represent the sorry state of modern American political discourse and the particularly pathetic status of the conversation about Hillary Clinton. People want to know: "Where do you stand—do you like her or hate her?" This question reveals an unfortunate, high stakes, polarized, overly emotional, Ebert and Roeper, thumbs-up or thumbs-down approach to history and politics. Historians want to know what are her strengths and weaknesses, what were her successes and failures? Friends inquire: "Did you interview her," demonstrating a talismanic faith in journalistic techniques in our age of "mediaocracy," overlooking the limits of what interviews with well-practiced celebrities can achieve, and the corresponding historical distance lost. A more open, historical question would be: "What sources are available to understand who she is and what she has done?" Many wonder: "Is she a lesbian," betraying an addiction to sensational gossip to the detriment of serious discussion of political values. And almost all ask: "Will Hillary Clinton become president in 2008," reflecting a culture which speculates obsessively, perpetually handicapping the political horse race, looking for crystal balls, not historical insights.

This book is not a complete Hillary Clinton biography, but a book about what she did—and did not do—as first lady in the White House, as part of a broader intellectual project attempting to understand the modern presidency and the role of first ladies therein. I do not wish to read her mind. Rather, I want to measure her historical footprint. In search of the historical Hillary Clinton, trying to understand her tenure as first lady, this book considers her predecessors' experiences while assessing the historical forces shaping her life and times.

This study of Hillary Clinton's often frustrating, sometimes exhilarating, experiences as first lady could not have been completed without the assistance of numerous individuals. This book builds on my chapter on the Clintons in *Affairs of State: The Rise and Rejection of the Presidential Couple since World War II*, published by The Free Press of Simon and Schuster in 1997, and then published in an expanded and updated paperback by the University Press of Kansas in 2000 as *Mr. and Mrs. President: From the Trumans to the Clintons*. My thoughts on first ladies have also been presented in various formats, most notably in "Mr. and Mrs. President? The Rise and Fall of the Co-Presidency," *Social Science Journal* 37 (2000): 591–600, which was itself based on a paper presented to the Organization of American Historians annual meeting in Toronto in April 1999; a chapter in *The Presidential Companion: Readings on the First Ladies*, edited by Robert P. Watson and Anthony J. Eksterowicz, published by University of South Carolina Press in 2003; and in "Looking Back: Lessons for the First Lady—And Her Husband—From History," in the 2001 and 2005 editions of *Laura Bush: The Report to the First Lady,* edited by the indefatigable Robert P. Watson.

Without replicating the acknowledgments in *Affairs of State,* even though I remain deeply grateful to all mentioned therein, most especially my family, I must salute Fred M. Woodward, the patient and inspiring director of the University Press of Kansas, and his remarkable team, notably Karen Hellekson, Larisa Martin, and Susan Schott; Professor Lewis Gould, the editor of this First Ladies series, for his impressive work in the field as well as his insightful editing; Professors Allida Black, Alonzo Hamby, and Robert P. Watson, for valuable feedback on the above-mentioned writings that have helped shape my thoughts; McGill's principal Heather Munroe-Blum for her insights; and Deborah Bush of the William J. Clinton Library for her resourcefulness and prompt responses.

I also wish to thank two extraordinary students, Zak Miller, who volunteered his time one summer to research Hillary Clinton, and Bonnie Goodman, who has contributed much to this project with her zeal, insight, creativity, and skill. I could not have completed this project without them.

As always, and especially in this contentious field, I alone remain responsible for the book's errors—and what some no doubt will think its erroneous opinions.

HILLARY RODHAM CLINTON

GOSSAMER SHACKLES: THE FEMINIST FIRST LADY'S DILEMMAS

She glowed as a cover girl for the Christmas issue of America's top fashion magazine. Photographed in the Red Room, primly sitting beside a suitably imperial bouquet of roses, she was resplendent in a burgundy velvet dress Oscar de la Renta designed exclusively for her. Her ears glittered with Cartier pearl-and-diamond drop earrings. The Cristophe Salon had styled her dyed-blonde hair impeccably. The predictably breathless article about her "radiant peace" gushed about her American-as-apple-pie, properly feminine, and most first lady-like campaign "to restore decaying historical treasures."[1]

This was Hillary Clinton at the height of her popularity as first lady—in December 1998, as her husband faced impeachment. Just over a year later, in February 2000, Mrs. Clinton formally launched her Senate campaign. Now, Hillary!—as her posters called her—chose a businesslike look. Her tone was substantive. Her husband sat there, silently watching, in an historic role reversal.

What had happened to the Clinton copresidency? What had happened to Hillary Rodham Clinton's 1992 cry, "Two for the price of one,"[2] to her husband's remark, "If I get elected president, it will be an unprecedented partnership, far more than Franklin Roosevelt and Eleanor. They were two great people, but on different tracks. If I get elected, we'll do things together like we always have."[3] How was it that Mrs. Clinton could only find popular affection by morphing into Nancy Reagan—and could only find fulfillment by moving away from her husband and abandoning her post?

Clearly, the story of the emergence of what *Vogue* called "The Extraordinary Hillary Clinton" reveals much about the idiosyncratic sagas of both Mr. and Mrs. Clinton.[4] This metamorphosis also reflects the odyssey of modern American women, continually struggling to strike just the right balance, to convey just the right image, amid powerful competing forces. But the first lady's rise in popularity polls as her profile as a policy mover and shaker declined is rooted in a deeper phenomenon that has occurred repeatedly over the last few decades—and illuminates the peculiar nature of the position Mrs. Clinton occupied.

It is an article of faith among those who have served as first lady that the job is what you make it. Many women, including Hillary Rodham when she was the first lady of Arkansas, have believed the myth that policy making is a central part of the first lady's role and that by making policy, a first lady can embody and advance the cause of American womanhood. This perception comes from the first lady's centrality in America's celebrity-obsessed political culture, which confuses fame and power, image and impact, as well as the deplorable paucity of women in powerful positions in America today, which feeds a thirst for role models. Yet most descriptions of a policy-making first lady reflect wishful thinking, not historical reasoning.

Although the mistress of the White House enjoys some latitude and no one has dictated a job description, the first ladyship is a well-defined position with powerful constraints. Despite the justifiable longings of many women for a powerful voice in Washington, despite the enduring public fascination with first ladies, and despite reporters' constant pressure on first ladies to plunge into policy making, most Americans do not want the first couple sharing power in the White House. Moreover, the way the job of first lady has evolved over the past few decades actually hinders a first lady's effectiveness in the policy-making role. Presidential couples are supposed to work together on joint image making, not power sharing. Presidents have learned that a popular first lady can provide cheap and easy political points and is an essential prop in defining the presidential image; nevertheless, a controversial first lady can do a great deal more lasting damage.

During the 1996 campaign, Mrs. Clinton attributed the backlash against her to a sexist distaste for powerful women.[5] Indeed, first ladies have struggled with traditional double standards, the continuing collective confusion about feminine sexuality and destiny, as well as enduring sexist assumptions about women and power. Still, people tend to overlook the peculiarity of this particular position. The long-standing fears of anyone getting too close to the president, combined with millions of Americans' cultural need for traditional icons in the White House, make activist first ladies controversial. Proof of this enduring need for the first couple to offer Americans a traditional ballast also comes from the firestorm of criticism Betty Ford provoked with her candor about sex and drugs, as well as the chorus of hosannas both Barbara Bush and Laura Bush elicited with their respective warm, nonthreatening, literacy-minded public personae.

Before the 1930s, first ladies had much more freedom to define their own positions. Some first ladies were more famous or less famous (Dolley Madison versus Elizabeth Monroe); more controversial or less controversial (Mary Todd Lincoln versus Eliza Johnson); more influential or less influential (Edith Bolling Wilson versus Edith Kermit Roosevelt). But they had no ongoing policy-making role. Thanks to the governmental and presidential revolution Franklin Roosevelt unleashed, along with the pioneering role Eleanor Roosevelt carved out for herself in the New Deal, the myth of the policy-making first lady was born. Six decades later, Americans plunged into a particularly vigorous round of debates about the role of first lady, with America's first real feminist first lady, Hillary Rodham Clinton, at the eye of the storm.

Mrs. Clinton's tempestuous tenure had a mixed impact on the office itself. Like a meteor soaring through the sky, her ambitions, and the aspirations of millions of women whom she inspired, illuminated the role's great potential and the great hopes that a high-profile, visionary, ambitious, politicized first lady can generate. But these great dreams were meteoric—spectacular and fleeting. If anything, the first feminist first lady legitimized the low-profile, apolitical traditionalism of her immediate predecessor and successor, Barbara Bush and Laura Bush. By highlighting the position's constraints, and by causing too much tumult, Hillary Clinton's exhausting turn as first lady blazed the trail for the calmer and more calming Laura

Bush to follow. Mrs. Bush should be grateful to Mrs. Clinton for making the modern East Wing of the White House safer for less autonomous, less polarizing occupants.

Just who is Hillary Rodham Clinton? Since she first burst into the nation's consciousness in 1992 standing by her man while insisting, "I'm not some little woman standing by her man,"[6] Hillary Clinton has alternately fascinated, bedeviled, bewitched, and appalled Americans. She has consistently frustrated those who have tried to reduce her to one stereotype or another. She has charmed millions of women who see her as their champion, as their emissary, as their standard-bearer. She has enraged countless others who have demonized her as a power-hungry, heavy-handed, win-at-all-costs ideologue. Lawyer, policy wonk, partner, feminist, mother, wife, hostess, trendsetter, children's advocate, health care crusader, cover girl, icon, media sensation, Midwesterner turned Arkansasan turned New Yorker, senator, Democrat, and presidential hopeful, since 1992 Hillary Rodham Clinton has been bolstered by her friends, betrayed by her husband, cheered by Congress, interrogated by prosecutors, hounded by reporters, slandered by talk-radio hosts, accepted by senatorial colleagues, and lionized by women throughout the world.

Much of the criticism has dumbfounded Mrs. Clinton. As first lady, when speaking to one of the many women's groups that invariably gave her frenzied receptions, she often blamed the criticism on modern America's continuing discomfort with powerful women. This assertion is only partly true, as evidenced by the fact that as a senator, exercising power in her own right, she has generated far less controversy. A first lady is not just any powerful woman. Her unique position imposes particular constraints on her behavior and helps explain some of the venom—and some of the love—showered on her. Also, Hillary Rodham Clinton is not just any powerful woman. She has been uniquely controversial and contradictory since she first appeared on the national radar screen in 1992. Hillary Clinton, then, is triply fascinating—as one of the most powerful women in America today, as a representative figure who has faced many of the modern woman's challenges, and, by virtue of her tenure as first lady, as a member of one of the most exclusive and complicated sororities in the world.

From her birth in 1947, when Hugh and Dorothy Rodham gave their firstborn a unisex first name so she would not be limited by the straitjacket society imposed on women, Hillary Rodham Clinton has struggled with the modern woman's dilemma: how could she achieve fulfillment as a woman while thriving as an equal in what remains, in so many ways, a man's world? All married couples struggle with the connubial conundrum: the question of how to balance each partner's needs, and how to avoid the gravitational physics of most conventional marriages that means that when one partner is up, the other is often down. But when one partner is the president of the United States, the whole world scrutinizes the other's every move, and she is saddled with the oddly circumscribed yet undefined improvised throwback of a position we call "the first lady," resulting in dilemmas that are all the more intense, confusing, emblematic, and sometimes soul-crushing.

The first feminist first lady, the first presidential wife to come of age during the feminist era and embrace the movement unambiguously, Hillary Clinton has zigged and zagged in her attempt to resolve all these difficult questions. Like so many of her female peers, she has struggled to balance tradition and change, family and career, head and heart, and the yearnings to be a genderless, equal citizen of the world and her feminine identity. During the 1992 presidential run, the power-suit-wearing corporate lawyer of the primary campaign became the chocolate-chip-cookie-baking mom of the general election campaign. After the devastating 1994 failure of the health care reform plan, followed by the Democrats' loss of control of Congress, the crusading copresident who emerged in 1993 became the sensible and feminine junior partner. In 1998, Hillary Clinton helped save her husband's public career during the Monica Lewinsky humiliation by lambasting special prosecutor Kenneth Starr publicly and Bill Clinton privately. By 1999, frustrated by the many retreats and defeats, refusing to be pitied in public, the loyal stand-by-your-man woman struck out on her own to become the first first lady in history to run for the U.S. senate—or for any political office.

Today, Senator Clinton is one of Washington's most powerful Democrats, one of America's most influential leaders, and one of the world's most celebrated women. A key to Hillary Clinton's sanity, success, and incredible popularity among working women has been her elasticity. Rather than perceiving her as alternately betraying and fulfilling her ideals, she and her supporters have taken a broader view. Instead of treating life as a zero-sum game, as a series of either-or choices, Mrs. Clinton—like so many other working women—has tried to solve dilemmas by sidestepping them: by being a working woman *and* a mom, a pioneer *and* a traditionalist, a policy maven *and* a hostess, a feminist first lady *and* a feminine first lady.

In trying to explain the Hillary Rodham Clinton mystery, too many authors have tended to reduce her to a one-dimensional caricature, a power-hungry Machiavellian, an angry feminist, a hippie "McGovernik," a yuppie baby boomer, a noble crusader, the great liberal hope. It may be more illuminating to think of her as a combination of two central archetypes and ideologies in American public life, the Puritan and the Progressive. Bill Clinton is, in many ways, a synthesis of the Progressive liberal reformer and the Populist goods-delivering demagogue, in the sweaty, idealistic, big-government-oriented, bombastic tradition of William Jennings Bryan and Lyndon B. Johnson. Mrs. Clinton is different. Whereas her husband seems to have been born with near-perfect popular pitch, early on, she demonstrated a tin ear for populist appeals. Much of her crowd-pleasing behavior as first lady and senator seems learned rather than innate. But at her best, this Methodist feminist, this moralistic hippie preaching a gospel of individual accountability and governmental social responsibility, combines the sobriety, self-control and social discipline of the Puritan with the generosity, idealism and social engineering of the Progressive.

The cynical journalist who dominated the 1920s and 1930s, H. L. Mencken, may have overstated when he defined Puritanism as "the haunting fear that someone, somewhere, may be happy." And back in the pre-Revolutionary days, it was important to distinguish between Puritanism, Calvinism, and Methodism. Still, in our more secular times, perhaps the world's most famous Methodist can be rooted in America's broader Puritan tradition by dint of her zealousness, her search for moral purity, her rigor, her priggish side, and her sense of mission. Similarly, the value in defining one of America's leading liberals as a Progressive dodges some of the denominational and definitional arguments of the twenty-first century as to just what makes a good liberal, to focus on the essence of the late nineteenth- and early twentieth-century movement. That movement, combining the prim social engineering of a Jane Addams, the passionate muckraking of a Lincoln Steffens, and the expansive governmental interventionism of a Robert LaFollette, reflected a middle-class faith in the power of reason and the ability of government committees and programs to make society more rationale, reasonable, effective, and just.

Feminism itself, while clearly more connected to the Progressive impulse of American history, has a puritanical dimension as well. The convergence of the rise of feminism and the sexual revolution also bred an opposite impulse: a no-holds-barred libertinism. Still, in the 1980s, when some feminists found themselves awkwardly allied with Christian fundamentalists against pornography, the movement's primmer and more moralistic side dominated the headlines. Always faithful to her Methodist and traditionalist upbringing, Hillary Clinton resisted much of the excess of the 1960s unlike her husband. Always on the more socially conservative side of the feminist movement, by the 1990s, Hillary Clinton refused to cede all talk of morality to the right. Championing "family values," Democratic style, by talking about valuing families, she bluntly bemoaned young Americans' overreliance on abortion as a method of birth control. Mrs. Clinton did not see a contradiction between her calls for a moral reformation, a turn away from materialism, a return to community and family, and her faith in government and community as forces for social justice. At a time when liberalism often seemed to be degenerating into libertinism, her synthesis of Puritanism and Progressivism bolstered her husband's vision of a "third way" and kept the American left more moored to the mainstream.

This combination of Progressivism and Puritanism doubly reinforced Hillary Rodham Clinton's least appealing traits: her self-righteousness, her resistance to criticism, her ends-justify-the-means faith in all that she and her husband did to maintain power. At the same time, this dual tradition doubly reinforced her most appealing traits: her idealistic and moralistic vision for an American community combining collective social justice with individual responsibility, altruism with independence, modernity with tradition.

In fact, both Hillary and Bill Clinton's zeal for advancing their ideological agenda plunged them into another classic American tension, that between the pol and the goo-goo, the hard-nosed, power-hungry politico and the dreamy, pie-in-the-sky reformer. Perhaps best epitomized by the late nineteenth-century power struggles between the cynical but effective bosses of Tammany Hall and the lovely but ineffectual Mugwumps, this paradox feeds into the ongoing debate since the American Revolution between pragmatism and idealism. The bell-bottoms and jeans revolutionaries of the 1960s spent many a midnight "bull session," as they called it, "rapping" about how to reconcile power and righteousness, how to succeed without selling out, how to be a dreamer without being what they would call in the 1970s a "wimp." The feminist movement had an overlapping and parallel conversation about—and obsession with—power and the fear that compromising or becoming "good little girls" would prevent them from fulfilling their goals. The frustrations from enduring the Reagan revolution in the 1980s and seeing Democratic and liberal impotence, epitomized by Michael Dukakis's noble failure in the 1988 campaign, fed a win-at-all-costs idealism. The Clintons' aide George Stephanopoulos poignantly described this urge to "make history" and the way "raw ambition" and the refusal to "throw away" what they could "achieve" for the country led the Clintonites to overlook their own president's flaws and do anything to win.[7] It is fitting then, that Hillary Clinton would label Clinton's 1992 campaign headquarters "the War Room."

Part of the reason why critics found it so easy to hate the Clintons, and especially her, was because both Bill and Hillary Clinton conformed to a popular stereotype of the self-righteous baby boomer on the make. In American pop culture, this is the *Big Chill* crowd, which moved effortlessly from protest rallies to investment banks, from bell-bottoms to power suits, from attacking the Establishment to becoming the Establishment, while still mocking established values. All politics involves a volatile mix of high idealism and low cynicism. It becomes particularly vexing—and infuriating—when the two warring impulses are wrapped around each other so tightly that they blur together. The Clintonite will to power is as much a central theme of the Clinton story as the Clintonite desire to do good. Within these tensions lie the sources of their appeal and the secret of their survival, but at the same time, like characters in a Greek tragedy, the seeds of their sorrow.

Many more chapters remain to be written in Hillary Rodham Clinton's story. This book focuses on the nine critical years that introduced her to the American people—from her extraordinary, searing, post–Super Bowl *Sixty Minutes* interview in January 1992 at the start of the Clinton presidential campaign to the presidential transition from the Clintons to the George W. Bushes in January 2001, when the outgoing first lady was also the incoming senator from New York. During those years, Hillary Rodham Clinton lived out the central dilemmas of her life, often in painful and excruciatingly public ways. Her struggle to balance her identity as a woman and her need for equality made her an iconic figure. Her Puritanism tempered her Progressivism, feeding her husband's political redemption through centrism, only to see his sloppy behavior force her to sacrifice her Puritan ideals and reforming mission for the sake of their commitment to keeping themselves and those they deemed to be their fellow Progressives in power.

The Clintons could not have gone as far as they did, and Hillary Clinton could not have engendered the loyalty she did, without tapping into the dreams of a significant—and influential—segment of the America population. But that sense of realpolitik and a will to power that they needed to turn their dreams into realities also distracted them, undermined them, and continually threatened to consume them. Looking back on her struggle illuminates Hillary Rodham Clinton's own biography, the peculiarities of being a first lady, the challenges of being a modern American woman, and some of the central tensions defining the United States today. No matter what happens in the ensuing years, the story of Hillary Rodham Clinton as first lady will remain an important tale of turn-of-the-millennium Washington, America, and American womanhood.

On September 11, 2001, al Qaida terrorists rained destruction on New York, Washington, and a nondescript field in Pennsylvania. As with any transformative event, some reputations were made that day, and others were blackened. In yet another turn of the historic screw wherein the standing of presidents and their wives are often inversely related, as ex-president Bill Clinton saw people ask why he had not done enough to stop Osama bin Laden, Hillary Clinton's hold on her position as senator solidified. Although she was no Rudy Giuliani, Senator Clinton served as an important supporting player along with Governor George Pataki and Senator Charles Schumer in the heart-wrenching World Trade Center tragedy. She was there in her own right as New York's senator—not as Bill Clinton's wife, not as a former first lady, not as a token woman, not even as Hillary!

Such shifts are often palpable but not easily quantifiable. Still, it seemed that on that day—and during the immediate aftermath—Hillary Rodham Clinton emerged as a public figure on her own, dissipating the lingering cloud from her husband's administration, her last-minute move to New York, and her hard-fought campaign. "People now see her as a senator," said Bob Kerrey, the former Democratic senator from Nebraska who, like Mrs. Clinton, had also recently relocated to New York. Kerrey, settling in as president of the New School in New York City, could not resist comparing the two Clintons in the wake of 9/11: "He's become subordinate to her efforts. She has the power. He does not."[8] Preaching that "we're all New Yorkers now,"[9] the feminist first lady was now New York's senator, liberated from her dilemma-filled purgatory, empowered as a celebrity politician, released from the gossamer shackles of being the country's first lady. Responding to the greatest American trauma in decades, demanding extra funds for her newly adopted and now stricken state, Hillary Rodham Clinton was freer than she had been in decades to shape her own destiny—and, perhaps, that of twenty-first-century America.

CHAPTER 1

FROM PARK RIDGE TO LITTLE ROCK, FROM "GOLDWATER GIRL" TO "BILLARY"

By the time she ended her tenure as first lady in 1945, Eleanor Roosevelt had made her tale of overcoming childhood insecurity a part of her legend—and one of midcentury America's classic childhood sagas. The eventually triumphal story of this neglected daughter in an aristocratic family whose grandmother mocked her looks resonated widely. Although not quite a rags-to-riches story, the tale of the ugly duckling maturing into a world-famous swan reinforced many Ben Franklin–Horatio Alger ideals of overcoming adversity through grit, grace, and all-American goodness.

By the time she ended her tenure as first lady a half-century later, Hillary Rodham Clinton had made her childhood similarly iconic. She told a tale of the baby boomer growing up, daddy's little girl turned feminist, the "Goldwater Girl" gone Wellesley hippie, the Midwestern provincial blossoming into an idealistic advocate for children. This plot line provided a trendy, 1960s-oriented, consciousness-raising twist to the classic American narrative of local girl made good. In typical Clinton style—and reflecting a broader conceit that every baby boomer became a hippie (or even veered left)—in her memoirs, Hillary Rodham Clinton titled her chapter on growing up "An American Story."

Putting aside doubts of how broadly representative it might be, the Hillary Rodham Clinton coming-of-age tale is more complicated than the generational stereotyping suggests. Simply seeing Hillary's story as a story of a consciousness raised, a liberal born, a feminist unleashed, makes it far too ideological. Reporters often anxious to legitimize their own trajectories were far too happy to claim that "the radicalization of Hillary Rodham . . . traces the arc of her generation" and to quote her brothers' claim that at Wellesley College, Class of 1969, their sister discovered "a more compassionate way . . . of thinking about things."[1] In fact, again and again, Hillary Rodham Clinton made choices balancing ideology and pragmatism, liberalism and careerism, sexuality and individuality, feminism and tradition. According to her college boyfriend, she often insisted, "You can't accomplish anything in government unless you win."[2] To tell her story without acknowledging Hillary's ambition, will to power, and willingness to compromise is to reduce a three-dimensional biography into a two-dimensional poster. Such simplistic sloganeering is more suited to the annals of saints than the real-life chronicles of the politician Hillary Rodham Clinton was and became.

Hillary Rodham was born into America's postwar cornucopia on 26 October 1947. With both Senator Robert Taft and Governor Thomas Dewey confidently expecting to lead a Republican return to the White House, Democratic President Harry Truman was squabbling with Republicans about how to curb the inflation the postwar demobilization triggered. In Europe, the hero of the French resistance, Charles de Gaulle, was maneuvering to seize power. In the Middle East, Arabs and Jews were struggling over the pending UN vote to partition Palestine, and in Asia, Muslims and Hindus were clashing over the postcolonial arrangements in Kashmir.

In Chicago, where Hillary was born, newspapers experienced slowdowns that day because of the many postwar labor disputes afflicting America. Universities were full thanks to the GI Bill, and Europe was reconstructing thanks to the Marshall Plan. That autumn, on the heels of Jackie Robinson having broken the color barrier in baseball in the spring, Chuck Yeager broke the sound barrier in aeronautics, and Harry Truman, the New York Yankees, and the Brooklyn Dodgers burst through conceptual and technological barriers, when, on 5 October, Truman became the first president to address the nation on television, and the next day, the two baseball titans squared off in the first televised World Series.

Blessed by American freedom, prosperity, and confidence, Hillary Rodham enjoyed what she called a "*Father Knows Best* upbringing." It included a gruff, "opinionated," pulled-himself-up-by-his-bootstraps, small businessman father, a stay-at-home homemaker mother, two rambunctious brothers, and a two-story brick house with "two sundecks, a screened-in porch and a fenced-in backyard,"[3] all in a suitably suburban and Midwestern setting. Raised on "family, church on Sunday, respect your elders, do well in school, participate in sports," Hillary Clinton would remain committed to family, rejecting the "anti-image" denigrating the family when she became an adult.

For most of Hillary's childhood, Hugh E. Rodham, and most of the other dads, commuted from bucolic Park Ridge to downtown Chicago, eighteen miles away. Dorothy Rodham, and most of the other moms, spent days, her daughter recalled, "in perpetual motion, making the beds, washing the dishes and putting dinner on the table precisely at six o'clock." The Rodhams, Hillary Clinton would report, "were typical of a generation who believed in the endless possibilities of America and whose values were rooted in the experience of living through the Great Depression. They believed in hard work, not entitlement; self-reliance, not self-indulgence."[4]

Of course, closer scrutiny suggests that not all was placid in *Leave It to Beaver* land. Dorothy Rodham had endured a terrible, almost Dickensian, childhood, featuring parents who abandoned her, a four-day transcontinental train journey without adults when she was eight and her sister was three, and a "severe," abusive domestic arrangement for ten years with her grandfather and his cruel wife.[5] Remarkably—although, perhaps, more typically for that generation—Dorothy Rodham emerged from her traumatic childhood with a positive if driven personality, a deep love for her family, and an intense commitment to building a conventional middle-class life. Her husband, Hugh Rodham, was a fierce anticommunist with little tolerance for the beatniks of the 1950s or the hippies his daughter later would befriend and imitate. He was a "tough taskmaster, but we knew he cared about us," Hillary Clinton would recall of a father who, when his children excelled in school, usually mocked the school's easy grading standards rather than praising his offsprings' achievements.[6]

Her harsh father's high standards made his firstborn stoic and perfectionist. Her ambitious mother instilled in Hillary the confidence to aim high despite her gender, the ability to appear in public as level as a carpenter's bubble, and the determination never to divorce. Her parents gave her an androgynous name so her gender would not limit her. "I clearly expected to work for a living, and I did not feel limited in my choices," Hillary Clinton would later report gratefully. Her parents "simply encouraged me to excel and be happy."[7]

Hillary Clinton offered a glimpse into the emotional complexity of her world with her oft-told tale of being forced to confront the neighborhood bully when she was four. "Go back out there," Dorothy Rodham insisted. "And if Suzy hits you, you have my permission to hit her back. You have to stand up for yourself. There's no room in this house for cowards." Hillary Rodham apparently walloped her nemesis and impressed the locals. "I can play with the boys now!" she rejoiced.[8] Gradually bleaching the violence from the tale, in her 1996 ode to child rearing, *It Takes a Village*, Hillary Clinton wrote, "When they challenged me again, I stood up for myself and finally won some friends."[9] Seven years later in her memoirs, she simply remembered "return[ing] a few minutes later, glowing with victory."[10]

Anxious to please her demanding parents, Hillary Rodham was a smart, obedient, driven child, with something of a combative tomboy streak. She and many other young girls growing up with ambitious parents in the 1950s learned that success in the real world would require them to overcome their femininity and squelch their sexuality. This approach to sex and power made tomboys of ten-year-olds, but it also made them wrap their twenty- and thirty-year-old selves in a consciously masculine look. Perhaps it also imprinted a sense of sexual inadequacy that could express itself in a tolerance for a charismatic bad-boy husband who chased buxom blondes on the side.

Dorothy Rodham counted forty-seven kids living on their square block. Like so many of her peers, Hillary gained the security that came from viewing their neighborhood as their turf, trusting that conditions were safe, knowing that adults were always looking out for them. This prosperous, post–World War II suburban life was peppered with Fourth of July parades, Girl Scout cookie sales, reading assignments, Chicago Cubs heartbreak, and a stint as the president of the local Fabian fan club. Most definitely a good girl, Hillary Rodham seemed—like so many of her peers—form-fitted to America's conformist culture of obedience, a loyal, stable culture in which, Alan Ehrenhalt notes in his study of Chicago of the 1950s, "People just stayed married . . . , to their spouses, to their political machines, to their baseball teams."[11]

Hillary Rodham's ninth-grade history teacher, Paul Carlson, reinforced her father's take-no-prisoners Republicanism and Hillary's own Goldwater Girl tendencies. An ardent anticommunist and passionate libertarian, Carlson inspired Hillary to read Senator Barry Goldwater's manifesto, *The Conscience of a Conservative*. Hillary dedicated the term paper she subsequently wrote on American conservatism "To my parents, who have always taught me to be an individual." Hillary was entering her senior year in high school in 1964 when Goldwater ran for president. Knowing who she became, it is tempting to treat her "cowgirl outfit and straw cowboy hat emblazoned with the slogan 'AuH2O' " as a punchline.[12] But a shrewd chronicler of the 1964 campaign, Rick Perlstein, notes that Senator Goldwater hit a geyser of enthusiasm, especially among America's youth. Goldwater's "army of true believers" recruited a "record 3.9 million Americans who actively *worked* for the Goldwater campaign in some capacity." The incumbent and eventually winning president, Lyndon B. Johnson, "had half as many" volunteers, "from a voter pool half again as large."[13] Hillary shared in the excitement, even if she ultimately embraced the opposing side politically.

Goldwater Republicanism, however, was only one pole of influence. Hillary knew that underneath her mother's conventional, conservative, Park Ridge veneer was a passionate Democrat. The youth minister of Park Ridge's First United Methodist Church, Donald Jones, also sought to develop within Hillary a more Progressive outlook, thus intensifying this parental power struggle over Hillary's loyalties and identity.

Balancing passionate social activism with just a touch of the great liberal Reverend Reinhold Niebuhr's skepticism, Reverend Jones preached to the sheltered Park Ridge kids about "faith in action," challenging them to engage with what he called "the University of Life"—beyond the suburbs. Methodism preached a puritanical sense of mission, combined with a systematic—methodical—approach to morality, theology, and society. In a beautiful testimonial to the power of one teacher to revolutionize a student's world and the potential for religion to expand horizons, Hillary recalled, "Because of Don's 'University,' I first read e. e. cummings and T. S. Eliot; experienced Picasso's paintings, especially *Guernica,* and debated the meaning of the 'Grand Inquisitor' in Dostoyevsky's *Brothers Karamazov.* I came home bursting with excitement and shared what I had learned with my mother, who quickly came to find in Don a kindred spirit. But the University of Life was not just about art and literature. We visited black and Hispanic churches in Chicago's inner city for exchanges with their youth groups." Well aware of the competing influence of Hillary's "better dead than red" history teacher, Jones once told his prize pupil "that he and Mr. Carlson were locked in a battle for my mind and soul."[14]

Looking back as an adult in George W. Bush's "red" and "blue" America, Hillary Clinton would see that conflict "as an early indication of the cultural, political, and religious fault lines that developed across America" in the wake of the 1960s. But she would recall liking both mentors and said she "did not see their beliefs as diametrically opposed then or now."[15] This approach reflected the kind of centrist she wanted to be, but did not always succeed in being.

When Hillary boldly forsook the Midwest for a Northeastern women's college, Wellesley, in September 1965, she remained a rather conventional daughter of the Midwest. One classmate, Catherine Kennett, would recall that early on, Hillary dreamed of becoming "class president" and one day driving a "yellow Jaguar XKE convertible."[16] She occasionally ran into examples of what she would soon label "sexism"—most notably when a NASA form letter dashed her dreams of being an astronaut by saying no girls were being accepted into the program. As a "brainiac," she had noticed friends in high school "beginning to cut back on how well they did or the courses they took, because that's not where their boyfriends were. And I can recall thinking, 'Gosh—why are they doing that?'"[17] That kind of independence could be alienating in the conformist environment of the suburban high school, where Hillary was cruelly nicknamed "Sister Frigidaire."

Still, overall, Hillary Rodham was no radical, not yet even, in the author Miriam Horn's phrase, "a rebel in white gloves." But the members of Wellesley's class of 1969 were indeed plunging into a political, cultural, and ideological storm. They would be, in a far clunkier phrase of Horn's, "the monkeys in the space capsule, the first to test in their own lives the consequences of the great transformations wrought by the second wave of feminism," as well as the social tsunami that would be known simply as "the movement."[18] "We are, all of us, exploring a world that none of us even understands and attempting to create within that uncertainty," the first Wellesley undergraduate to speak at commencement would say when they graduated in the spring of 1969. "The only tool we have ultimately to use is our lives," said the speaker, Hillary Rodham.[19]

Baby boomers would be exceedingly self-conscious about their journey and their roles in transforming America socially and politically. The slogan shouted at Mayor Richard Daley's riot police outside the 1968 Democratic National Convention in Chicago, "THE WHOLE WORLD IS WATCHING," became a generational anthem—and aspiration. Hillary Clinton would echo the Wellesley truism from the time that it was a "girls' school when we started, and a women's college when we left."[20] Other campuses, and other individuals, including an engaging Rhodes Scholar and Georgetown University graduate named Bill Clinton, experienced the vicissitudes of the 1960s as well. But it is fair to say that for women, the changes were all the more wrenching, and even more so for students at a women's college shifting from the sensibilities of the 1950s to the 1970s seemingly overnight.

Hillary Rodham believed she got her money's worth at college; Hugh Rodham probably thought he did not. For years, he would say, only half-jokingly, that sending her to Wellesley had been a "great miscalculation."[21] Not only did his beloved firstborn come to look, sound, and dress like the hippies he detested, and not only did she start reading and believing the hated *New York Times*, but she also seemed to spend much more time talking about her friends, the trends, and the times than about her professors and classes. Blessed with one of the western world's finest—and priciest—educations, Hillary Clinton would later recall: "What I valued most about Wellesley were the lifelong friends I made and the opportunity that a women's college offered us to stretch our wings and minds in the ongoing journey toward self-definition and identity."[22]

Inevitably, as with so many of the most articulate—but not necessarily the most representative—members of her generation, Hillary Rodham's college memories are intertwined with some of the most momentous historical events of that time. As she tells the story of the Class of '69, the milestones stop being autumn homecoming and spring exams. Rather, she describes 1968 as "a watershed year for the country, and for my own personal and political evolution."[23] Rattled and radicalized by the North Vietnamese Tet offensive, the assassinations of Martin Luther King Jr. and Robert F. Kennedy, and the roller-coaster 1968 presidential campaign, Hillary and her set spent more and more time "arguing about the meaning of revolution and whether our country would face one." Especially decades later, in far more staid times, she would hasten to add, that she and her usual sparring partner "concluded there would not be" a revolution, and "even if there was, we could never participate."[24]

During the 1968 presidential campaign, Hillary Rodham wavered between the two major political parties, caught between her Midwestern past as a Goldwater Girl and her future as a leading Democrat. She volunteered for Nelson Rockefeller's Republican campaign, attended the 1968 Republican National Convention in Miami, and interned during the summer for the House Republican Conference. In yet another rueful glimpse into her lifelong conflict with her father, she would recall that her photograph with the House minority leader at the time, Gerald Ford, hung proudly in her dad's bedroom until his death. Yet that year Hillary also flirted with the New Left. She leafleted for Senator Eugene McCarthy's antiwar presidential run. She mourned Martin Luther King's death publicly and dramatically by wearing a black armband and marching in Boston. She witnessed the Democratic National Convention riots in downtown Chicago, and she spent the fall of 1968 campaigning for Vice President Hubert Humphrey. After Richard Nixon's victory in 1968, there was no turning back. Hillary Rodham emerged as an antiwar, pro-civil rights, anti-Nixon Democrat.

By this time, Hillary Rodham had also emerged as a political powerhouse on the Wellesley campus. One friend, Martha Sherrill, remembered thinking that "Hillary couldn't say no to a meeting. Get out the Robert's Rules of Order and she would come flying through the door."[25] To her great delight, Hillary was elected student government president, marking a dramatic turnaround from her hesitant, fearful freshman days. As a student leader, Hillary would be positioned to confront the Wellesley administration just as students were questioning the curriculum, the parietals, and the fundamentals of college life. Still, Sherrill would note, hers was mostly "a Hillary-style rebellion, methodical, rational, fair."[26]

Even in her academic work, Hillary Rodham remained fixed on politics and troubled by these conundrums regarding whether to change society dramatically or gradually, from the outside or from within. Her senior thesis on the community action programs of Lyndon Johnson's war on poverty included a look at the guru of community organizing, Saul Alinsky. This Chicago activist's rules for radicals fascinated Hillary, as did his calls for bold grassroots revolution. But ultimately, like her future husband, Hillary Rodham kept her cool and ensured her viability within the system. Her thesis adviser, Alan Schechter, would define her ideology as an "instrumental liberalism: using government to meet the unmet needs of the society to help those people who are not fully included within it."[27] Rodham acknowledged that she and Alinsky "had a fundamental disagreement. He believed you could change the system only from the outside. I didn't."[28] The legendary Alinsky actually offered Rodham a job after graduation. She disappointed him by attending Yale Law School instead. Hoping for change, she remained tethered to convention—and careerism.

Her now-famous finale at Wellesley replayed many of the dilemmas of her four years, showcased on a broader stage. Hillary Rodham's central role in student leadership and in rattling Wellesley's long standing status quo secured her the honor of delivering the first student commencement speech in the college's history. The blizzard of speech suggestions her fellow students sent demonstrated the great hopes so many invested in the moment—and in the movement's far-flung aims. Characteristically, Hillary triangulated. Her words were pointed enough to upbraid the black Republican senator who preceded her, Edward Brooke, as an Establishment apologist, guaranteeing media coverage. "SENATOR BROOKE UPSTAGED AT WELLESLEY COMMENCEMENT," the *Boston Globe* proclaimed the next day. "What a disrespectful young lady," some parents muttered, while some daughters predicted "she will probably be President of the United States someday."[29] But Hillary's attempt to "come to grasp with some of the inarticulate, maybe even inarticulable things that we're feeling," was itself somewhat incomprehensible, and certainly not a blueprint for revolution. Her tone and her moxie were bolder than her words or her vision. Even in the heat of the 1960s, Hillary Rodham's pragmatism led her to believe that "the challenge now is to practice politics as the art of making what appears to be impossible, possible."[30]

That spring, Dorothy Rodham was too ill to travel to Wellesley. At the last minute, according to Hillary's memoirs, her father swooped in and out of the hippie college "in typical Hugh Rodham fashion." And in typical Hugh Rodham fashion, his behavior was so subdued, his presence so muted, that years later, many students and professors were convinced that no one from the Rodham family had actually bothered to come witness Hillary Rodham's triumphal moment.[31]

Of course, for all the trendiness and all the countercultural pressure to conform to the new repudiation of convention, each individual blazed a particular path. Although she eschewed makeup, favored jeans, dodged beauty parlors, let her hair grow in all kinds of "unladylike" places, may have tried marijuana, and certainly, and rather publicly, cohabited with her future husband for years before they finally married, Hillary the Methodist good girl imbibed the 1960s' idealism more than its libertinism. Calling herself "a progressive, an ethical Christian and a political activist," she was well aware that she could only be "as outrageous as a moral Methodist can get." In corresponding with the Reverend Jones from college, she believed that one can "be a mind conservative and a heart liberal." She always wanted to balance "family, work and service."[32] Unlike many of her peers, during her Progressive awakening, she did not abandon her Puritan impulses, just as her growing idealism did not obliterate her Establishment-oriented ambitions. Even her taste in men ran to the political but conventional. One classmate, Kris Rogers, noted Hillary's penchant for "poli-sci, earnest-idealist, policy-activist, good-government types, not wild-eyed radicals."[33]

One of those boyfriends—Hillary Rodham's steady date for three years in college, Geoffrey Shields—told Bill Clinton's biographer, David Maraniss, that throughout all her ideological travels, "she was more interested in the process of achieving victory than in taking a philosophical position that could not lead anywhere."[34] Ultimately, like so many of her New Class peers, Hillary Rodham would figure out how to combine their newfound crusading spirit with more conventional pushes for professional success and careerist advancement. Yale Law School was a hothouse for such careerist-activists. There, Hillary Rodham burnished her credentials and furthered her ideological transformation. Acquiring the skills, prestige, and network to succeed as a superlawyer, she also secured the necessary knowledge, passion, contacts, vision, critical edge, and sense of alienation to feed her rebellion. Perhaps most important, she began to focus on one of the defining questions of her early career, namely "how the law affected children." In her push for children's rights, she began working with one of her most influential mentors, children's advocate Marian Wright Edelman.

In her first major article, "Children under the Law," published in the November 1973 *Harvard Educational Review*, Hillary Rodham sought, 1960s-style, to shift discussion about children from the realm of the personal and the familial into the political. In this analysis—and subsequent articles and speeches over the next two decades—Rodham argued that "child citizens" were "powerless individual[s]" who needed basic rights and should be treated with a presumption of competence rather than incompetence. Her integrated, government-centered, rights-oriented approach was radical enough—although, in fairness, John Leo of *U.S. News and World Report* would note in 1992 that her positions "were comparatively mild versions of what the children's rights movement wanted at the time."[35] And rather than simply theorizing along with so many of her comrades, Rodham would devote considerable energy over the next twenty years to adapting her ideas to the realities of children's lives in Arkansas and the rest of America. Still, looking back on the article, the historian Christopher Lasch would chide Rodham for undermining parents and having inordinate faith in government. "Criticism of parental incompetence has always been the child savers' stock-in-trade," Lasch warned.[36]

In her original 1973 article, explaining their powerlessness, Rodham described children as being in the category of people deprived of rights and "in a dependency relationship. . . . It is presumed under the circumstances society is doing what is best for the individuals," she wrote. "Along with the family, past and present examples of such arrangements include marriage, slavery, and the Indian reservation system." Law students make such comparisons all the time, seeking to identify common conditions that define a situation or status. Twenty years later, this statement would be a gift for opponents combing published records for dirt about the Clintons—a modern pastime partisans indulge in but resent when they are subjected to it. Hillary "equat[es] the family itself with slavery," conservatives charged unfairly.[37]

Researching the health and education of migrant children and becoming an activist for children's rights represented an interesting synthesis for this 1950s kid turned 1960s feminist. As one of 27 women in an entering class of 235, Hillary Rodham was entering a heavily male-dominated profession, and occasionally she would have to jostle for position as an equal at both law school and her eventual law firm. Moreover, Jane Addams–style spinsterish Progressivism was not for her. Hillary Rodham was choosing to be one of the lifestyle pioneers who would trailblaze for women professionals, postponing marriage and child rearing, creating new corporate mores for working women and career moms. And yet within the legal world, Hillary Rodham carved out a domain that was somehow womanly. Focusing on the question of children's rights was both feminine and feminist, both cutting edge in terms of some of the radical ideas she, Edelman, and others contemplated, and yet also somehow traditional, safe, and maternal. Even in this early, unformed incarnation, Hillary Rodham approached the woman's dilemma with some subtlety and more conventionality than she and others appreciated at the time. While plunging into what remained a man's world, Hillary Rodham—and many of her peers—remained highly identified with issues traditionally assigned to the woman's sphere.

Hillary Rodham entered Yale Law School something of a celebrity among her radical peers. Her commencement speech talking about the "trust bust" between generations and championing "the indispensable task of criticizing and constructive protest" had landed her in *Life* magazine featured with another activist, Ira Magaziner, from Brown University. In contrast to her start at Wellesley College, where she felt "overwhelmed," "out of place," and intimidated by the "girls who had gone to private boarding schools, lived abroad [and] spoke other languages fluently,"[38] Hillary now began Yale in the charmed circle of her law school class. The list of soon-to-be-famous people she met there, from Edelman and her husband Peter to Vernon Jordan and Robert Reich, will mislead generations of future Ivy Leaguers, who will assume that for them, too, simply being accepted into one of America's elite institutions will guarantee them entry to America's future power elite.

At Yale, Hillary Rodham also forged one of the most extraordinary partnerships in American history when she met Bill Clinton. She would remember this "Viking from Arkansas" as having "a vitality that seemed to shoot out of his pores."[39] Theirs would not be a storybook courtship. Even their first meeting would be shrouded in mystery and twisted by spin. Both Clintons described repeatedly how she, in proper feminist style, approached him first. The now-legendary encounter supposedly took place at the Yale law library in 1971, with Hillary telling Bill, "Look, if you're going to keep staring at me and I'm going to keep staring back, we should at least introduce ourselves." The more prosaic introduction story comes from their mutual friend Robert Reich, who introduced the two in the cafeteria the first week of law school, saying, "Bill, this is Hillary; Hillary, this is Bill."[40]

Reich admitted that the first meeting didn't take. The later one did. After their library meeting, they were attached but often at odds. He was glandular, she was controlled. He had a roving eye. She was a moralist. If he could have been a barfly in another life, she could have been a nun. Both were ambitious, strong-willed, and occasionally pig-headed. "All we ever do is argue," he would confide to an old friend shortly after she joined the University of Arkansas law faculty in Fayetteville.[41]

Still, time and again, observers would underestimate the intensity of their bond. He thought she was the smartest person he had ever met; she loved how "he combined an absolutely extraordinary mind with a huge heart . . . and we just started talking and never stopped."[42] They teamed up for a mock trial at Yale and in Texas for George McGovern's quixotic 1972 campaign, a defining mission for their social set. Years later, explaining why she pursued her beau in his backwater, this ardent feminist and accomplished lawyer would offer a simple and convincing explanation: "I had no choice but to follow my heart."[43]

Of course, student superstars like Hillary Rodham and Bill Clinton had many choices. Fresh out of law school, Hillary moved to Cambridge, Massachusetts, to work for Marian Wright Edelman at the Children's Defense Fund, then moved to Washington, D.C., to work for the House Judiciary Committee investigating the possibility of impeaching President Richard Nixon. By 1973, the "cancer" of the Watergate scandal had confirmed the movement radicals' worst impressions of America. The president of the United States appeared to be a liar and a schemer, actively involved in obstructing justice by covering up his and his subordinates' wrongdoing. "Never have I been prouder to be a lawyer and to be an American," she would say of her role in bringing down Richard Nixon.[44]

When nine months of nearly around-the-clock work ended abruptly with Nixon's resignation in August 1974, the ex-president wasn't the only one out of a job. Having passed the Arkansas bar exam (she failed the Washington, D.C., exam), having been invited to join Bill Clinton on the faculty at the University of Arkansas School of Law in Fayetteville, Hillary Rodham wavered. This twenty-six-year-old Ivy League lawyer activist with first-class credentials was eminently employable. New York, Washington, Boston beckoned—even Chicago, if she wanted to return home.

Meanwhile, her boyfriend, Bill Clinton, made his choice, rooting himself in his home state of Arkansas. He secured a job at the Fayetteville law school, and by March 1974 was running for Congress at the tender age of twenty-seven. Born just months before Hillary Rodham on 19 August 1946, Bill Clinton had a more tumultuous upbringing—one that would be seen as a harbinger of too many other stories of dysfunctionality that spread in the 1970s, rather than Hillary Rodham's flamboyantly conventional 1950s-style family life. Like his wife, Bill Clinton sprang from warring cultural heritages. Time spent in the Georgetown-Yale-Oxford stratosphere tempered but did not wipe out his Southern sensibilities. His family life compressed the pain of a William Faulkner epic or a 1960s antifamily screed into one short story filled with his own possible bastardy, his father's death, his stepfather's drinking and wife-beating, his mother's divorce and triple widowhood, and his own sexual compulsions. And yet his mother, who spent up to ninety minutes a day putting on her makeup, raised her son to maintain appearances. "Inside my head I construct an airtight box," she said. "Inside is love and friends and optimism. Outside is negativity, can't do-ism and any criticism of me and mine."[45] Bill learned his lessons well. Photos of Billy Blythe in his cowboy hat, or, after his stepfather moved in, Bill Clinton in his band uniform, did not reveal the tumult. His best friend in high school had no idea that the Clinton household was so volatile.

Naturally, Bill Clinton developed an elusive relationship with the truth. Even his great moment of self-revelation may have been imagined. Throughout his 1992 campaign, and more recently in his memoirs, Bill Clinton described a heroic confrontation wherein, once he had grown big and tall enough, he forced his stepfather to stop beating his mother when drunk. "I just broke down the door of their room one night when they were having an encounter and told him that I was bigger than him now, and there would never be any more of this while I was there," he told the reporter Joe Klein in January 1992—and repeated the story in his Democratic National Convention biographical video.[46] "When I was fourteen and in the ninth grade. . . . I grabbed a golf club out of my bag and threw open their door," the ex-president wrote in his memoirs. "I told him to stop and said that if he didn't I was going to beat the hell out of him with the golf club. He just caved."[47] This wish fulfillment contradicted young Billy Clinton's testimony during his mother's divorce proceedings when he was fifteen that Roger Clinton "threatened to mash my face in if I . . . went to my mother's aid."[48]

Bill Clinton's drive for success stemmed from his need to flee the humiliations of a drunken and abusive stepfather and a beaten and mercurial mother. He never lost his head amid the passions of his college years. He remained focused on the goal he articulated in his infamous 1969 letter to an ROTC colonel awaiting his recruitment: "to maintain my political viability within the system. For years I have worked to prepare myself for a political life characterized by both practical political ability and concern for rapid social progress."[49] Such a sober statement was typical of a man who later said, "I always wondered if I'd want to be sixteen when I was forty because I never felt like I got to complete my childhood."[50] This mix of prematurely aged child of dysfunction and perpetual adolescent explains his attraction to a sober, sometimes prickly, powerful, and well-bred woman dubbed "Sister Frigidaire" in high school. Both believed in the broad goals of the movement but remained ambitious enough to want to stay within the system while reforming it. Both were willing to compromise but remained convinced of their own righteousness—a distinguishing trait of their class.

From their first encounter, Bill Clinton and Hillary Rodham had an operatic relationship. The two forged an intense political and intellectual bond that could keep them mutually enthralled in hours-long talkathons. But their bouts also became the talk of Yale Law School, as did Bill's inability to remain faithful to Hillary. Despite his compulsive need to seduce other women, Bill Clinton proposed to Hillary Rodham when they visited England together in 1973, after they finished law school. "I was desperately in love with him but utterly confused about my life and future," Hillary Clinton recalled. "So I said, 'No, not now.' What I meant was, 'Give me time.'" Looking back, Hillary Clinton would say, "I realize how scared I was of commitment in general and of Bill's intensity in particular. I thought of him as a force of nature and wondered whether I'd be up to the task of living through his seasons."[51]

A year later, with Bill Clinton running for Congress, a torn Hillary Rodham made her fateful decision. "I chose to follow my heart instead of my head. I was moving to Arkansas."[52] "Are you out of your mind?" her Washington roommate Sara Ehrman snapped. "Why on earth would you throw away your future?" Ehrman would remember telling her friend "every 20 minutes" on the way down: "You are crazy. You are out of your mind. You're going to this rural, remote place—and wind up married to some country lawyer." "She'd been in the middle of everything, on the edge of everything," Ehrman would recall regarding Hillary Rodham in her twenties. "She was on the fast track to becoming a great legal star."[53]

Almost all the significant influences in Hillary Rodham's life urged her not to move to Arkansas. Hillary herself apparently assumed the move would be temporary. The political consultant Dick Morris would recall that both Clintons were "very explicitly focused on his ambitions, but Hillary regarded Arkansas as a place to go and then leave." Years later, Hugh and Dorothy Rodham's disapproval still stung in particular. After Bill Clinton became governor, Susan

McDougal would gush to his first lady, "Gee, your parents must be so proud of you, being married to a governor." "My parents don't even know where Arkansas is!" Hillary Clinton laughed. "They expected me to be doing something wonderful on my own in Washington."[54] In fact, when Ronald Reagan appointed Sandra Day O'Connor to the Supreme Court in 1981, Dorothy Rodham would be disappointed that Hillary had lost her shot at being the first female justice.[55]

Nevertheless, Hillary moved, Bill lost, and, a year later, on 11 October 1975, the two were married. It was a typical New Class baby boomer wedding. By then, they had known each other almost five years, had lived together during law school, and had been deliberating about marriage for over two years even as socially, the average age of first marriage was climbing, along with the average length of courtships and the number of couples cohabiting. She wore a gown hurriedly purchased off the rack. The dress was old-fashioned to please him, she said. Nevertheless, her Coke-bottle glasses and frizzy hair, and his wide tie and bushy hairdo marked them as children of the 1960s. Before the wedding, he told his mother that his bride would keep "her own name." His mother, who had changed her name for three husbands and would soon do so again, cried.

Disdaining convention, the happy couple did not plan a honeymoon. This her mother found intolerable. In the end, the newlyweds honeymooned in Acapulco with the Rodham family. He brought along *The Denial of Death* by Ernest Becker, which located man's natural "urge to heroism" in his fear of death.[56] The Pulitzer prize–winning tome, filled with references to Otto Rank, Søren Kierkergaard, and Sigmund Freud, exemplified many baby boomers' quest for meaning in abstractions. Becker proved particularly compelling to a young intellectual whose father died in a car accident three months before he was born.

The Clintons postponed having children to build their careers. The fertility rate had now dipped from almost four children for each woman of childbearing age in 1960 to less than two children. Fayetteville required some adjustment for Hillary Rodham. "There were simple small town/big town differences that she was getting used to," Diane Blair, a political science professor who befriended her, recalled. "Everybody knew her, knew who she was . . . there weren't many professional women here then, and she was The Lady Lawyer."[57] Years later, as first lady, "the Lady Lawyer" would remember both how much she stuck out in town and how intimate it all was. Once, when she called Information in an attempt to track down a student who had not appeared in class for a while, the operator not only told Mrs. Clinton the student's number but explained his absence. This "Mayberry RFD" life had its charms—and its suffocating limitations.

When Bill Clinton became the state's attorney general, the Clintons moved to Little Rock. By 1979, Bill Clinton, at thirty-two, was the nation's youngest governor. Hillary Rodham became the first woman partner in Little Rock's leading law firm, Rose Law Firm, and she established a national reputation by working with classic liberal organizations such as the Children's Defense Fund and the Legal Services Corporation. In fact, her continental crusading, her Wellesley-Yale pedigree, her impressive network of friends, and her powerful husband fed the myth of Hillary the legal superstar. Few could assess her lawyering skills, although some grumbled that they were exaggerated. "I was always mad at her for not doing more [legal work]," Joe Giroir, the Rose Law Firm's chief executive in the 1970s and 1980s, would recall.[58]

Among the embarrassing revelations that would pour out during the Washington years would be corrupt bank president Jim McDougal's claim that Bill Clinton, when governor, once asked McDougal about throwing some legal business toward his wife to boost her billable hours and take-home pay. McDougal added a telling detail to confirm his anecdote: the governor dropped by while jogging, leaving a sweat stain on the high-spending McDougal's new leather chair. And much of Hillary Rodham Clinton's defense during the Whitewater morass would be based on an inattention to the law, her clients, and her cases that, if true, suggested that she may have often risked malpractice.

Rounding the age of thirty, Hillary and Bill Clinton shared many of their peers' desires to build a family without abandoning either of their busy careers. They and many members of their generation were struggling with the mixed messages about work and family, the stressful, overscheduled nature of so much modern work for those who would soon be labeled yuppies, as well as the physical limitations of what was now called the ticking biological clock. In February 1980, at the age of thirty-two, after trying to get pregnant for a few years, Hillary gave birth. His mother had named him after his late father. Her parents gave her an androgynous name so her gender would not limit her. They named their daughter after a folk-rock ballad, "Chelsea Morning."

Hillary Rodham was certainly the leftist ideologue her conservative critics made her out to be. Time and again, she ingested and contributed to the New Left's cornucopia of statist and anti-Establishment reform ideas—at Wellesley, at Yale, as children's rights activist Marian Wright Edelman's protégé, as the chair of the New World Foundation, which funded civil rights crusaders and other New Left darlings, including the Palestinians. Yet she remained Hugh Rodham's daughter. Unlike many of her peers, she remained a churchgoer. Her Methodist upbringing opened her to the hip call for service while rooting her in traditional values of responsibility and temperance. Hillary tried to be an authoritative parent to her daughter with the flower child's name, rejecting both traditional authoritarianism and modern permissiveness. But she also exhibited the hyperintellectualism, self-consciousness, and awkwardness that would characterize so many of her fellow working mothers. "Chelsea, this is new for both of us," she would remember saying often. "I've never been a mother before, and you've never been a baby. We're just going to have to help each other do the best we can."[59]

Hillary Rodham's conflicting legacy made it easier to compromise, as so many of her friends did when they matured. She emerged as an odd amalgam, the family's breadwinner and a political wife, a pillar of the Northeastern instinctively liberal Establishment seeking to succeed in a Southern backwater, a Progressive with a Puritan streak. Superlawyer by day, managing complicated lawsuits and plunging into cutting-edge national issues regarding children's rights and legal aid by night, she was, she would ruefully recall, "also learning about the expectations and unspoken mores of life in the South. Wives of elected officials were constantly scrutinized." After Bill Clinton became governor in 1979, "the pressures on me to conform . . . increased dramatically." It was one thing to be "considered a little unconventional as the wife of the Attorney

General, but as First Lady of Arkansas, I was thrown into an unblinking spotlight. For the first time, I came to realize how my personal choices could impact my husband's political future."[60] Hillary Rodham resisted, trying to continue her Northeastern-style rebellion in the heart of the Old South. The results were disastrous politically and personally.

In November 1980, Bill Clinton and "that feminist in the governor's mansion" lost to Frank White and his wife, who campaigned constantly but silently by his side as "Mrs. Frank White."[61] After Chelsea's birth that winter, the Clintons had surprised cynics by keeping a low profile, rather than exploiting their new family status for political gain. Apparently Hillary laid down the law while Bill was feeling confident politically and was happily distracted by their new baby.

Campaign tensions only exacerbated tensions between the Clintons as the Republicans exploited Arkansans' discomfort with the governor's often-scowling, seemingly high-handed, too-Northern, too-feminist wife. "It took her a long time to pretend to like us," one local said of Arkansas' first lady.[62] Portending future moments of controversy during which Hillary Rodham's comments would make a bad situation worse, she told one interviewer that keeping her own last name made her feel more like a "real person."[63] The implied disdain for the 90 percent of America's married women who took their husbands' last names as their own seemed to confirm the criticism.

Losing the 1980 election devastated Bill Clinton. For months after the loss, he drifted professionally, loafed around despondently, and pursued women even more aggressively than usual. It was during this black period that a friend would report overhearing Bill Clinton playing with Chelsea within earshot of his wife, and singing "I want a div-or-or-or-orce, I want a div-or-or-or-orce."[64] Hillary Rodham became Mrs. Bill Clinton for the comeback campaign and Hillary Rodham Clinton thereafter. Her rationale that "it meant more to them"—Arkansans—"than it did to me" was the Clintons' all-purpose recipe for compromise as they kept ties with their old comrades but discarded many of their old ideals.[65]

Still, the makeover must have been wrenching. Rodham family lore had it that Hillary had decided as a nine-year-old to keep her last name when she married.[66] Her friend Eleanor Acheson remembered that "to her," keeping the name "was an act of self-worth."[67]

Now, to mollify Arkansan Neanderthals, Hillary Clinton streaked her brown hair blonde, stuck contact lenses in her eyes, and began dressing for success in the way she and her sisterhood detested. Radical feminists particularly resented such blonde, peppy "ladyness" as "a reflection of gender power and the invisibility that marriage brings to women."[68] Ultimately, Hillary Clinton's feminism proved as elusive as her husband's liberalism—she returned to this set of first principles when convenient, sacrificing even core ideals when it seemed necessary.

In the media's simple world, Bill Clinton's compulsive womanizing meant that the Clintons' marriage could not be good. More accurately, the Clinton marriage combined aspects of a frontier marriage and a peer marriage. Hillary Rodham had been raised to appeal to her man's head more than his heart, but such a strategy had its limitations and frustrations. When Bill's mother first met Hillary, she recoiled from this Yankee know-it-all with "No makeup. Coke-bottle glasses. Brown hair with no apparent style." Virginia Cassidy Blythe Clinton Dwire Kelley had raised Bill to desire "beauties in the classic Hot Springs beauty-pageant mold." Bill chided his mother, "Look I want you to know that I've had it up to *here* with beauty queens. I have to have somebody I can talk with."[69] "Sister Frigidaire" would civilize "Elvis" Clinton, as a lady should. Like so many others, this marriage would be based on a mutual devotion to the head of the household. "Hillary loves Bill, and Bill loves Bill,"[70] the Clintons' political guru Dick Morris would explain. "It gives them something in common."[71]

At the same time, the Clintons built a "peer marriage" where he could relinquish the "provider role" and the two could share a "deep friendship."[72] "The woman I marry is going to be very independent," his friend Carolyn Yeldell Staley remembers Bill saying. "She needs to have her own interests and her own life."[73] Whereas other women worshipped Bill and never left him alone, Staley noted that when Bill and Hillary enter "a room, they go their separate ways. She . . . never drew her identity from him."[74]

Such equality and familiarity between spouses often dulled passion. Pop psychologists preached, "Nice is not romantic."[75] Bill Clinton said he often told Hillary Rodham when they were courting, "I would like being old with her"—an asexual tribute to a girlfriend.[76]

Married to a feminist madonna, Bill Clinton still chased sex goddesses. This pattern seems to have begun when Bill Clinton and Hillary Rodham started dating. It intensified after he became the Boy Wonder governor. "This is fun," his Whitewater partner Susan McDougal recalls Governor Clinton saying. "Women are throwing themselves at me. All the while I was growing up, I was the fat boy in the Big Boy jeans."[77] Sadly, Hillary Rodham Clinton ended up as one of those "Smart Women" who made "Foolish Choices," in the words of the 1985 bestseller.[78] These bad-boy types made exciting boyfriends but difficult husbands. Her cohort gradually, painfully, rediscovered the bourgeois strictures against adultery and divorce.

The Clintons' bouts were legion and legendary. "You couldn't sustain that level of irritation if it were an arrangement," one friend winced.[79] The Clinton marriage endured at least two major crises, when Bill lost the governorship in 1980, amid attacks on his hippie wife and gossip about his womanizing, and after the four-term governor aborted his presidential run in 1987 because of his "Gary Hart problem."

In 1987, the leading Democratic contender for the 1988 Democratic nomination, Senator Gary Hart, had already been hounded out of the race because reporters caught him keeping company with a blonde model who was not his wife. With the race wide open, key players in the extensive network of contacts the Clintons had developed, which would be known in the 1990s as FOB, "Friends of Bill," had flown into Little Rock from all over the United States. Reporters and photographers had also gathered, expecting Governor Clinton to launch a presidential campaign. But Bill Clinton's trusted aide, Betsey Wright, had gathered a too-long list of Bill Clinton seductions. She urged her boss to avoid humiliation and remain the Arkansas governor. Bill Clinton had prepared his wife for what she might hear from Betsey Wright. Still, when he defied expectations and abruptly announced, "I need some family time; I need some personal time," his tough wife cried.[80]

Four years later, on *60 Minutes*, Bill Clinton said, "If we had given up on our marriage . . . three years ago, four years ago, you know . . . I wouldn't be half the man I am today."[81] A week later, Hillary Clinton told *Newsweek*, "If Bill Clinton and I had been divorced three or four years and he were running for president, no one would ask him anything."[82] These coincidental hypotheticals suggest the depth of the crisis. Dorothy Rodham's trajectory from broken home to reasonably happy homemaker shaped her daughter. "My strong feelings about divorce and its effects on children have caused me to bite my tongue more than a few times during my own marriage and to think instead about what I could do to be a better wife and partner,"[83] Hillary Clinton later admitted.

For all the talk about her retreat on the last-name issue, Hillary Clinton did not retreat into obscurity. She could have hidden behind her need to mother Chelsea or work full-time at the Rose Law Firm as excuses to stay out of the public eye and away from her husband's career. She did not.

In her second incarnation as Arkansas' first lady, Hillary Clinton was blonder, peppier, and more conventional, but by no means a silent partner. Placing Bill's career before hers, she took a leave of absence from the law firm to help run his comeback campaign in 1982. She often defended her husband publicly and aggressively. She chaired critical initiatives such as the fifteen-member Education Standards Committee, which plunged into doubly treacherous waters by proposing a hike in the sales tax and imposing competency tests on teachers as well as students. She took great pride in introducing HIPPY to Arkansans. The Home Instruction Program for Preschool Youngsters was a program developed in Israel for underprivileged youth that Mrs. Clinton transplanted to Arkansas after reading a newspaper description while visiting in Miami. And she spoke frequently and publicly about "we," not "he." In February 1985, Mrs. Clinton celebrated the transformation in infant mortality rates that, thanks to another Clinton program, changed Arkansas from having one of the highest rates of dying babies among the fifty states to having one of the lowest. Unabashedly speaking of her husband's administration in the plural, she rejoiced: "We made it one of our priorities. . . . It is a soluble problem, and we have, in five years, dramatically improved our services."[84]

"Billary," this flamboyantly public interdependent partnership, generated its own mythology. After Mrs. Clinton gave an impassioned speech about education reform to a joint session of the Arkansas Senate and House of Representatives, Representative Lloyd George from rural Yell County proclaimed: "Well, fellas, it looked like we might have elected the wrong Clinton."[85] Both Clintons were savvy enough to see through such compliments as potentially undermining of the governor. And Mrs. Clinton was careful to focus her agenda on more traditionally feminine areas such as health care, education, and infant mortality. Still, both also found such talk exhilarating and would enter the 1992 campaign boasting about their political "blue light special" of "two for the price of one," or "buy one get one free."[86]

In more contemplative moments, Bill Clinton acknowledged just how much his wife sacrificed for his career—and if he forgot, Hillary Clinton was always there to remind him. *Newsweek* would report that in the summer of 1991, Bill Clinton "agonized over asking Hillary to 'once again sacrifice' her career for his political ambitions. Clinton thought it would be better to wait four years 'and let her shine.'" The argument that his wife would also be able to advance her agenda swayed him. Predictably, Hillary Clinton herself was more skeptical, some reported, even speculating that she ultimately agreed "only because she thought it would be a training run."[87]

In Arkansas, as in New Haven, Hillary indeed emerged as the tougher character. The alternate in their moot court competition at Yale, Robert Alsdorf, told David Maraniss that although Hillary never worried about stepping on anyone's toes, Bill "would massage your toes."[88] Similarly, in Arkansas, Governor Clinton did not mind using his first lady as a lightning rod sometimes, and many perceived her as the more liberal of the two, the less compromising of the two, and the harsher of the two.

While the two continued to duke it out—both publicly and privately, about personal issues and policy issues—the two Clintons shared a lot philosophically and strategically. Both were pragmatic Progressives. They were, as Hillary said in college, "heart liberals" who would do almost anything to win. In Arkansas they demonstrated a willingness to fight hard, to stretch the rules, to rationalize the most aggressive tactics by pointing to the nobility of their aims and their enemies' iniquity. As members of America's increasingly established liberal power elite, they spoke a language of reform suffused with a disdain for capitalism and the Establishment. But as members of Arkansas' power elite, they flourished in a culture of cronyism, back-scratching, sweetheart deals, and get-rich-quick schemes. Don Tyson, the Arkansas chicken billionaire and a master of back-room Arkansas finagling, defined his state's politics as "a series of unsentimental transactions between those who need votes and those who have money."[89]

Thanks to Tyson and others, both Clintons were sucked into the Arkansas miasma with surprising ease. Blessed by a strange coincidence neither admitted to thinking about too much, as Bill Clinton's power grew, financial opportunities for the Clinton family appeared. On the eve of Bill Clinton's first gubernatorial election, an attorney for Tyson Foods, Jim Blair—who was also a close friend of both Clintons— steered Hillary Rodham into the complicated, treacherous cattle futures market. Within a year, she had parlayed $1,000 into $100,000—a 10,000 percent profit. Unlike standard investors, Arkansas' new first lady never had enough money on deposit to cover her investments had they soured rather than soared. "Nobody called and asked me for anything," she later explained innocently.[90] At best, the move reflected a naive faith in Blair, a willful ignorance of the market, and an amateurish insensitivity to propriety. At worst, Tyson's people had manipulated the market as a welcome-to-the-governor's-mansion present for Arkansas' new first family.

Another investment opportunity that opened up at that time proved much less successful on all levels. Jim McDougal, another friend of the Clintons, but a far shadier character than Blair, arranged for the Clintons to buy some land with him and his wife on the White River. McDougal wanted to subdivide the area, build vacation homes, and make a killing by selling off the now-developed plots individually. Although they were equal partners, somehow the Clintons did not have to put up an equal stake. Not only did this Whitewater project lose money, it would permanently stain the future Clinton administration. The mismanaged project raised questions of tax fraud, bank fraud, and perjury. Jim McDougal's subsequent moves as a savings and loan swindler and Hillary Rodham's client besmirched both Clintons. As other, far more tangential charges would stick, nevertheless, many Clintonian sins and many more hysterical allegations would be clumped together under that accursed title: Whitewater.

Still, approaching her forty-fifth year in 1992—and her husband's go-for-broke campaign for the presidency—Hillary Rodham Clinton could look back on a seemingly unbroken chain of successes. She had joined the nation's intellectual elite, had moments to bask in glowing media coverage, and had a string of impressive achievements in her five-page CV, from having chaired the National Legal Aid Society under Jimmy Carter, to having been named one of America's 100 most influential lawyers, twice by the *National Law Journal*. She was a player in certain circles in the nation's capital and a powerful force in her adopted state of Arkansas. She had a famous husband and a lovely daughter—and she had moved her parents down to Little Rock to join her new life.

Alas, the success had come at a cost. Again and again, Hillary Rodham had been forced to make difficult choices. She had situated herself in alien, if not occasionally hostile, territory. She sacrificed many personal sensibilities as well as philosophical stands and professional aspirations to support her husband's career. She was not the mousy, intimidated, entering freshman she feared she was when she entered Wellesley; nor was she the powerful, independent, uncompromising reformer she had dreamed of being when she left Yale. Hillary Rodham Clinton had a tough streak and an anger that may have been rooted in these frustrations. Like so many women, like so many of her peers—but in a much more dramatic, public, and possibly painful way—Hillary Rodham Clinton had discovered that life in middle age, and life in the 1980s and early 1990s, was more complicated, and often more sobering, that it had appeared during those heady youthful days in the late 1960s and early 1970s. Little did she realize how much more complicated it was about to get.

CHAPTER 2

THE 1992 CAMPAIGN: "I'M NOT SOME LITTLE WOMAN"

It was supposed to be a campaign of sweet vindication. After the frustrations of having to play by Southern belle rules in Little Rock. After the pressures to change not just her look but her name, her very identity. After the traumas from so many marital ups and downs, so many deceptions and betrayals. After the humiliation in 1987 of having their closest friends and family members gathered in Arkansas, waiting for Bill Clinton's campaign launch, only to have the presidential quest derailed by a too-long list of girlfriends. The 1992 campaign was the great opportunity to make it all right, to return to the national stage, Hillary Rodham Clinton's more natural turf, and wow America. Instead, while defying the odds and securing the White House, she—and her husband—would be forced to confront and relive many of their biggest mistakes, most horrible moments, and most agonizing marital misadventures. This searing roller-coaster ride, this odd mix in 1992 of epoch-making political success and unbearable personal mortification, would characterize much of the Clintons' years in the presidential spotlight. This toxic combination of tremendous political power and monstrous personal anguish would mark and mar both Bill Clinton's presidency and Hillary Rodham Clinton's tenure as first lady. Specifically for her and for the odd role she would fulfill, the horizons glimpsed, the plans contemplated, the possibilities imagined would frequently be far more satisfying and uplifting than the gritty realities.

Bill Clinton spoke with amazement about the amount of time his mother devoted every morning to putting on her "public face"—the rouge, the eyelashes, the lipstick. Bombarded by indignities, Hillary Clinton, too, had to put on her own public face. Just as any winning presidential campaign serves as a rehearsal for the subsequent administration, Hillary Clinton's 1992 campaign would try out many of the stratagems and rationales she would rely on as first lady to survive the trials she endured. Sometimes tough as nails, sometimes so pliant as to lack any real definition or principles; sometimes articulating a radical feminist critique explaining away the attacks, sometimes watering down her definition of feminism to make it indistinguishable from apple pie; Hillary Clinton's defenses helped her get by but also fueled the vitriol.

Some of Mrs. Clinton's critics attacked her, somewhat paradoxically, both for being a radical leftist ideologue and a slick pol willing to say anything and do anything to seize power. But as first lady–to-be and first lady, Hillary Clinton lived that paradox for nine years. Sometimes she stood on principle, even at the risk of being too stubborn. This ideological rigidity would be most pronounced during the denouement of the health care debate, when Mrs. Clinton's refusal to compromise helped doom what had been the most viable and bipartisan attempt to reform America's medical system in a generation. Yet sometimes she jettisoned core ideals in the struggle for political survival and the never-ending quest for public approval, as would be most apparent during the Monica Lewinsky scandal when rivers of rhetoric about marriage, feminism, and traditionalism evaporated in defending President Clinton and demonizing the special prosecutor, Kenneth Starr.

When Bill Clinton began his run for president in October 1991, he promised "a new kind of leadership." He introduced Hillary Clinton as "my wife, my friend, and my partner in our efforts to build a better future for the children and families of Arkansas and America."[1] Governor Clinton pitched his unique partnership as part of the appealing baby boomer package he was peddling to get America moving again. On the stump, he exulted, "buy one, get one free!"[2] She crowed, "If you vote for him, you get me."[3] Their peer marriage heralded an era of joint leadership and reform.

The Clintons' modern, baby boomer partnership was supposed to highlight the criticism of President George H. W. Bush as being out of touch, emphasizing that it was time for a change. President Bush's poll ratings had been so high after the Persian gulf war victory in January 1991 that many of the leading Democrats did not even bother mounting a presidential campaign. But subsequently Bush's domestic policy had stumbled and his poll ratings had tumbled. The first major recession in a decade saw 4.5 million Americans lose their jobs as unemployment soared to 7.8 percent.[4] Bush's summer 1990 decision to raise taxes to cut the deficit split the Republican Party and allowed Democrats to mock Bush for breaking his pledge: "Read my lips. No new taxes."[5] The videotaped police beating of Rodney King in Los Angeles, a large, drunken African American motorist, exacerbated racial tensions that would explode in four days of riots in April 1992. And as America floundered economically, George Bush himself seemed strangely passive and adrift, leaving himself vulnerable to a young, dynamic leader eager to trigger a changing of the guard.

Yet by March 1992, the Clintons' generational crusade was stalled, their marriage mocked and pitied. In surveys, only 28 percent viewed Hillary Clinton favorably. Over half thought the Clintons had a "professional arrangement" rather than a loving marriage. Most Americans first met the Clintons in a fifteen-minute post–Super Bowl *60 Minutes*. Bill Clinton acknowledged causing "pain" in the marriage, and Hillary Clinton huffed, "I'm not some little woman standing by her man like Tammy Wynette."[6] Since then, revelations of promiscuity, draft dodging, and marijuana usage had burdened Bill Clinton with the major sins of his generation.

It may have marked the strangest national debut in the twentieth century. On one of America's secular holy days—Super Bowl Sunday—the Clintons took advantage of the huge lead-in audience to try to put to rest all the gossip about his womanizing. Given his obscurity, Bill Clinton recognized that, in his first encounter with a mass audience, he was simultaneously exposing millions of Americans to the rumors about his marital problems while trying to minimize them. And here was Hillary Clinton, superlawyer, child crusader, and indispensable political partner, forced to make her debut on the national stage by publicly cauterizing this embarrassing personal wound, which once again threatened their joint political aspirations. The Clintons' advisers, however, had convinced them that this public ordeal offered the only shot at salvaging the campaign. Both had agreed, somewhat reluctantly, although they were united in their refusal to utter the "a-word," adultery, or anything more specific than a general reference to Bill Clinton's having "caused pain" in the marriage.

The interviewer, Steve Kroft, asked pointed, persistent questions. Kroft challenged Governor Clinton to define his relationship with the blonde, well-coifed, part-time singer Gennifer Flowers and confirm or deny whether he had violated his marital vows, as she claimed. The questions elicited the Clinton bob-and-weave, a grab bag of evasions, lawyerly formulations, and quick-witted counterattacks that, at the time, saved his campaign—but by 1998 would elicit groans of recognition from weary reporters. Regarding Flowers, Kroft said, "She's alleging and has described in some detail in the supermarket tabloid what she calls a 12-year affair with you." Clinton responded: "It—that allegation is false." Years later, when he confirmed sleeping with Flowers, he would still be able to claim "that allegation" was "false" as long as he found one inaccurate detail in the tabloid account. Seeking clarity, Kroft asked, "I'm assuming from your answer that you're categorically denying that you ever had an affair with Gennifer Flowers." Clinton replied "I've said that before and so has she"—which only recycled denials.[7]

Regarding the broader question of whether or not he was an adulterer, Clinton made his evasiveness sound principled, setting himself up as a precedent-setting martyr, an idealist trying to take the high road despite reporters' hounding. "Look, Steve, you go back and listen to what I've said," Clinton insisted. "You know, I have acknowledged wrongdoing, I have acknowledged causing pain in my marriage. I have said things to you tonight and to the American people from the beginning that no American politician ever has. I think most Americans who are watching this tonight, they'll know what we're saying, they'll get it, and they'll feel that we have been more candid. And I think what the press has to decide is: Are we going to engage in a game of gotcha?" When Kroft pointed to a poll showing "14 percent of the registered voters in America say they wouldn't vote for a candidate who's had an affair," Clinton shot back: "That means 86 percent of the American people either don't think it's relevant to presidential performance or look at whether a person looking at all the facts is the best person to serve."[8]

With his finely tuned political antennae, Bill Clinton had sensed that Americans were fed up with aggressive reporters. Many wanted to fall in love with a candidate. Clinton was implicitly asking how many talented, idealistic Gary Harts and Bill Clintons were the American people willing to sacrifice on the altar of journalistic intrusiveness. Clinton was inviting voters to take a leap of faith and trust him, using his wife as the guarantor of his integrity and worthiness.

Although she was no Pat Nixon staring in silence for a full half-hour as her husband Richard Nixon gave his 1952 Checkers speech, Mrs. Clinton let her husband do most of the talking. Early on, Mrs. Clinton, feeding the notion of reporters as predators, talked about consoling women who had been falsely accused of having affairs with her husband: "I felt about all of these women, that, you know, they've just been minding their own business, and they got hit by a meteor. I mean, it was no fault of their own." Introducing a theme she would repeat throughout her White House years, Hillary Clinton sought the American people's sympathy, saying, "There isn't a person watching this who would feel comfortable sitting on this couch detailing everything that ever went on in their life or their marriage. And I think it's real dangerous in this country if we don't have some zone of privacy for everybody."[9]

Hillary Clinton uttered her infamous remarks denigrating a beloved country music icon two-thirds of the way through the tense interview. Kroft, responding to Bill Clinton's complaint that divorcés are not scrutinized and couples who have stayed together despite marital strife are harassed, said, "I think most Americans would agree that it's very admirable that you had—have stayed together, that you've worked your problems out, that you seem to have reached some sort of an understanding and an arrangement."[10] The governor, who later confessed that he wanted "to slug" Kroft,[11] insisted: "You're looking at two people who love each other. This is not an arrangement or an understanding. This is a marriage." And Hillary Clinton plunged in saying, "I'm not sitting here like some little woman standing by my man like Tammy Wynette." Explaining herself, she added, "I'm sitting here because I love him and I respect him and I honor what he's been through and what we've been through together. And, you know, if that's not enough for people, then, heck, don't vote for him."[12]

Bill Clinton's honey-smooth, good ol' boy Bubba persona softened his go-getterish ambition and Ivy League credentials. Unfortunately, his wife demonstrated an unerring ability to stumble at the treacherous intersection where class and gender fears met. Sounding like a snotty Seven Sisters Northeastern intellectual, Hillary Clinton missed the female power many lower-class women recognized in Wynette's 1969 hit about the difficulties of being a woman. "Oh, you'll have bad times, and he'll have good times, doing things that you don't understand," Wynette sang ruefully but wisely. "Hey, but if you love him you'll forgive him, even though he's hard to understand."[13] Not only had that song inspired millions, it actually described Hillary Clinton's approach to the flawed man she loved and defended.

Although the *60 Minutes* encounter resurrected Bill Clinton's campaign, it engulfed Hillary Clinton in her first major media firestorm. "Mrs. Clinton," a furious Tammy Wynette wrote. "You have offended every woman and man who love that song—several million in number. I believe you have offended every true country music fan and every person who has 'made it on their own' with no one to take them to a White House."[14] Hillary Clinton quickly apologized, but the remarks, with their seemingly snobbish contempt for everyday Americans, dogged her for years.

The 1992 campaign was supposed to be the "Year of the Woman" —not the little woman. As the campaign began in October 1991, Professor Anita Hill accused President George H. W. Bush's Supreme Court nominee—and her former boss—Clarence Thomas of sexual harassment. A defining, galvanizing moment for many feminists came when the all-male Senate Judiciary Committee grilled Hill, treating the accuser as the guilty party. Women activists cried that the men in Congress just didn't get it—and reporters gleefully echoed the claim. As a result, groups such as EMILY's List, working to elect women to Congress and other offices, saw their membership grow more than 600 percent.

Still for all the rhetoric, the emotion, and the congressional successes, 1992, like the feminist movement itself, would be a mixed bag for women. By 1992, feminism had succeeded in revolutionizing American life, but the movement had also alienated millions of American women. Feminist leaders struggled with one characteristic mark of a movement's success: the core ideas and values had been integrated so successfully into American life that few gave the movement credit anymore for its considerable achievements. So many women had entered the workforce, enrolled in universities, and demanded equality at home and at the office, that feminism's breathtaking achievements became commonplace. As a result, much of the public conversation about feminism focused on its flaws.

In 1991, the feminist journalist Susan Faludi complained of a "Backlash" against American women, and it was only partially true. The movement had lost élan and momentum. There were female critics, such as Professor Christina Hoff Sommers, complaining that feminism had been stolen, that "women" had "betrayed women" by going beyond the women's liberationist "equity" agenda to push an angry, radical, either-you're-with-me-or-against-me "gender" crusade.[15] There were lower-class women, continuing a complaint rooted in Betty Friedan's suburban sensibility in 1963, that feminism was too oriented toward the upper class. Many women insisted, as Professor Elizabeth Fox-Genovese would write, that "feminism is NOT the story of my life."[16] Despite the women's movement's considerable achievements, Hillary Clinton's seeming contempt for unenlightened country women hit nerves that were already sensitive because of the turn in the national conversation about women, which tarnished the movement's reputation.

Moreover, as Hillary Clinton emerged in all her complexity, as a professional woman, political activist, and feminist ideologue who was also betrayed by her husband, forced to service his career, and now sought power though him, her messy mélange of symbols would confuse the public and the activists. As members of EMILY's List and other feminists would take credit for electing "four new pro-choice Democratic women senators and 20 new congresswomen" with $6.2 million raised from more than 23,000 members,[17] they would have to cope with the Clintons' more headline-grabbing, contradictory, often undermining legacy.

Bill Clinton gambled his future on the celebrity culture's protocols. The daily exposés of *Entertainment Tonight,* the weekly scandals in the *National Enquirer,* inured Americans to the sins of the rich and famous. The assumption that "they're all guilty of something" promised redemption, after a confession. The unfaithful politician Gary Hart and baseball's compulsive gambler Pete Rose had suffered as much for not apologizing as for any initial sins. Anyone who tried stonewalling reporters learned who was boss. Besides, in a polity where, according to the yuppie prince of darkness, *thirtysomething*'s advertising boss Miles Drentell, history was last week's cover of *People,* sins were quickly forgotten. "They don't have pictures," a shameless Bill Clinton bragged to Gennifer Flowers, unaware she was taping him.[18] In January 1992, he told *Time,* "I wish I could find a way to get all these stories out early so I don't have to deal with them after I'm nominated, when they can be so distracting."[19] Days later, Flowers obliged him by describing their "twelve-year affair."

The battle-scarred vassals of Clinton's formidable war room sprang into action. Frustrated by their party's years in the presidential wilderness, convinced that Reaganism and Bush's follow-up threatened the country, these Democratic operatives vowed to recapture the White House by whatever means necessary. The manic Cajun consultant James Carville, his Jesuitical partner Paul Begala, the profane New York reformer Harold Ickes Jr., Clinton's Girl Friday George Stephanopolous, and the advertising whiz Mandy Grunwald led a formidable team that understood that Gennifer Flowers—like all their enemies—had to be destroyed. Flitting in and out of the team was Hillary Clinton's brash New York lawyer friend, Susan Thomases, the first of many aides in the broader Clinton political family more loyal to the candidate's spouse than the candidate himself.

Over the next nine years, Clinton's aides would struggle to save the great seducer from himself. They mastered singular techniques that would come in handy time and again—and become one of Clinton's most enduring legacies to American politics. With the hair-splitting skill of Talmudists, with the brutality of Huns, Clinton's samurai warriors mastered a brilliant jujitsu whereby no attack went unanswered, accusations were turned on the enemy, and the viciousness of the cross fire numbed the American people. Truth to Clintonites was malleable, severing the weakest link in a story invalidated it all. When Clinton read Gennifer Flowers's account of their affair, "Every time he spotted a detail he knew was wrong, he seized on it, even squeaking out a laugh when he found charges he knew he could disprove," Stephanopolous later recalled. "I was happy to make a list of the details that were false, but I didn't press Clinton to say which ones were true." Dozens of scandals and hundreds of lies later, a now disenchanted Stephanopolous would regret his behavior. "I wanted to believe that it was all malicious fiction, to see Clinton as he saw himself—the target of unscrupulous enemies who would try to destroy him personally because they opposed his policies," Stephanopolous later confessed. "And I needed Clinton to see me as his defender, not his interrogator, which made me, of course, an enabler."[20]

While his minions wallowed in the mud— even spending tens of thousands of federally provided campaign dollars to hire private investigators and silence potential "bimbo eruptions," Clinton floated along the high road. "Try to make some chicken salad out of this chicken s—t," his aides urged their scandal-plagued candidate before he appeared on ABC's *Nightline* on 12 February. "Get on your economic message and ride it as far as you can."[21] Clinton perfected a high-flying rhetoric that shamed any questioners who dared to interrupt his lofty discourse by questioning his base behaviors. "You know, Ted, the only times you've invited me on your show it was to talk about a woman I never slept with and a draft I never dodged," Bill Clinton chided *Nightline* host Ted Koppel, using a line Mandy Grunwald supplied.[22] The fact that Clinton had slept with that woman and had at least monkeyed around with his draft status was irrelevant. By the time Clinton and his people finished spinning, parsing, browbeating, blackmailing, blast-faxing, defaming, denigrating, maligning, scolding, preaching, and pontificating, reporters were chastened, Clinton's poll numbers were rising, and Gennifer Flowers's reputation was mud.

Hillary Clinton cleverly redirected her fury from her husband toward reporters. Then and later, she was able to defend Bill Clinton's behavior in public by denouncing their most vitriolic enemies. Still, the revelations took their toll on Mrs. Clinton—and her own reputation, not just her husband's. Watching Hillary Clinton run damage control strategy sessions regarding the Flowers allegations, imagining what private words the two exchanged, George Stephanopolous wondered: "Is this what they bargained for? Was there a deal between them?" The young aide "admired their ability to sacrifice privacy and pride for the chance to do some good—but wondered if I should be appalled. Is it about power's potential or just power? When is the price too high?" Mostly, however, Stephanopolous recalled, "I just felt sorry for them."[23]

On 8 March 1992, *New York Times* reporter Jeff Gerth uncovered the Clintons' money-losing stake in that Whitewater land deal connected to a failed bank. "CLINTONS JOINED S & L OPERATOR IN AN OZARK REAL ESTATE VENTURE," the headline charged. Here, at the start of what would become the Clinton years' defining scandal, came the first of many holograms. From the angle of the Clintons' defensive nitpick brigade, the very headline was misleading. Jim McDougal only became an "S & L operator," running Madison Guaranty Savings and Loans, five years after the Clintons and McDougals made their money-losing investment. Besides, no crimes occurred; the Clintons were never indicted. From the angle of the critical slash-and-burn squad, here was the start of the money trail, the first thread that could unravel the Clintons' back-room crimes. Moreover, many charged that even if the initial deal was legal, eventually it caused tax fraud and other crimes, especially once Hillary Clinton began representing Jim McDougal and other shady characters before McDougal's financial house of cards collapsed.

The truth was somewhere in the middle. The Clintons' business relationship continued with the McDougals through the high-flying, corrupt S&L years, meaning that the governor of Arkansas was doing business with a crook whose business the state regulated—and who could benefit from greater access to the office. Governor Clinton had authorized McDougal to arrange loans for the Whitewater Corporation in the Clintons' name; the Clintons then claimed ignorance of the loans. At the Rose Law Firm, Mrs. Clinton had worked on Madison Guaranty–related transactions that ultimately proved fraudulent, meaning that, at best, she incompetently provided unwitting legal cover to crimes. Moreover, the S&Ls had become a central and expensive symbol epitomizing the Democratic critique of Republican misrule. An estimated one thousand savings and loans institutions, 40 percent of the industry, went broke, mostly after wild spending triggered by deregulation. The cost at the time was well over $100 billion—with fears it could reach $500 billion. McDougal's bank bailout alone cost taxpayers $73 million.

The stench of sleazy connections, this complex of possible improprieties, the whiff of greed, and the need for pedantic, mealy-mouthed, legalistic defenses clashed with the Clintons' public posture as idealistic, Kennedyesque, do-gooder reformers committed to public service and rejecting Reaganite gluttony. After all, Bill Clinton launched his presidential campaign by charging: "The Reagan-Bush years have exalted private gain over public obligations, special interests over common good, wealth and fame over work and family. The 1980s ushered in a gilded age of greed, selfishness, irresponsibility, excess, and neglect."[24] And at the end of the day, the office of the independent counsel would convict twelve others in Whitewater-related offenses and find much circumstantial evidence suggesting that both Clintons—Yale Law School's finest—had flouted some laws, knowingly or unknowingly. But the Clinton critics would overstep in using exaggerated language, blowing the misdeeds out of proportion, treating low-level improprieties and possible misdemeanors as high crimes and felonies, while monopolizing public attention for far too long.

That spring of 1992, the timing was particularly bad for the Clintons. Aides feared another scandal would knock out their "Comeback Kid," especially one striking the core of the Clintons' political identity. Hillary Clinton and her Rose Law Firm cronies began covering up the paper trail linking the Clintons with James McDougal and his Madison Guaranty Savings and Loan—or at least minimizing the ties that, if exposed, would make the Clintons look guilty in the 1990s' "gotcha" culture.[25]

At the next Democratic candidates' debate, former California Governor Jerry Brown attacked Bill Clinton's "electability problem" and his "conflict[s] of interest," including "funneling money to his wife's law firm."[26] Bill Clinton and his aides had prepared for that moment. "The minute you hear the word *Hillary,* rip his head off," George Stephanopolous advised Clinton. "Don't let him finish the sentence."[27] On cue, Clinton, who always did anger well, responded. "I don't care what you say about me," Bill Clinton exploded, his

Southern accent thickening, "but you should be ashamed of yourself for jumpin' on ma wife." The next day Hillary Clinton snapped: "I suppose I could have stayed home and baked cookies and had teas. But what I decided to do was pursue my profession, which I entered before my husband was in public life."[28]

Despite his unfortunate phrasing, Bill Clinton's vigorous defense of his wife proved that this New Age man and policy wonk was not a wimp. Periodically over the next decade he would burnish his image with similarly overheated defenses of her. "Bill: stop trying to have it both ways," William Safire of the *New York Times* would taunt; "you cannot be gallant about a feminist."[29] Yet even while accepting new mores, most Americans still relished such husbandly chivalry.

Hillary's self-defense was less successful. Since Jackie Kennedy had warned Lady Bird Johnson about the perils of "tea poisoning" in the White House, each first lady had vowed not to limit herself to serving tea, a symbol of a lady's gossamer shackles. Yet coming from Hillary Clinton, the vow sounded like a declaration of war on the American home. This savvy pol, perhaps fearing the exposure of her financial schemes, confirmed the mainstream's worst stereotype of a career woman. She seemed self-righteous and contemptuous, like Glenn Close in the 1987 film *Fatal Attraction*. With Bill already the candidate of sex, drugs and rock-'n'-roll, Hillary became, as the *New York Times* put it, "the overbearing yuppie wife from hell."[30]

One of Bill Clinton's political consultants, Paul Begala, would remember thinking immediately, "People are going to take that out of context. They're going to suggest she doesn't care about stay-at-home moms." Begala warned Mrs. Clinton: "You know, Hillary, you've got to go restate this. People are going to think that's an attack on stay-at-home moms." Convinced, as usual, of her own goodness, Hillary Clinton was shocked. "And she had the most wounded and naive look on her face," Begala recalled. "She said, 'No one could think that.'" She said, somewhat disingenuously, overlooking her own ambitions and demons, "I would have given anything to be a stay-at-home mom. My mother was a stay-at-home mom. I just didn't have a choice because Bill was making $35,000 a year and we needed to support the family." Sure that Begala was misreading the situation, she assured him, "Oh, you worry too much."[31]

Hillary Clinton was trying to highlight her own dilemmas. She deflected many of the attacks on her, no matter how personal, by viewing them in a broader context. "While Bill talked about social change, I embodied it," she later recalled. "I represented a fundamental change in the way women functioned in our society. . . . I was being labeled and categorized because of my positions and mistakes, and also because I had been turned into a symbol for women of my generation."[32]

Yet the Clintons were not facing generational tensions as much as a class war. Bill and Hillary belonged to an elite subset of their generation that had been universalizing their experiences and presuming to speak for their peers for decades. In the 1970s, neoconservatives attacked this New Class; twenty years later, the historian Christopher Lasch would deride the "new elites . . . the new aristocracy of brains [that] tend[s] to congregate on the coasts, turning their back on the heartland and cultivating ties with the international markets in fast-moving money, glamour, fashion, and popular culture."[33] As always, the media shorthand was most telling: the 1960s' hippies shaved, traded their dashikis for designer suits, and became yuppies.

Yuppie,[34] the derisive term for "young urban professionals" that spread in 1984, made explicit the class tensions that sparked when college students clashed with Richard Nixon's blue-collar "silent majority." Yuppies were defined by their *lifestyle*, the trendy term itself encapsulating the disdain many felt for these self-indulgent and often self-loathing brats who pursued moneymaking as zealously as they had advocated revolution. In retrospect, millions of bystanders would say they belonged to the movement—even though only a quarter of the white population went to college, and only 28 percent of that elite admitted in 1969 to participating in any kind of demonstration.[35] Yet although millions more indulged in some aspect of the yuppie lifestyle, few admitted it. Offering the kind of pedantic sidestep characteristic of her peers—and of the future Clinton White House—Hillary Clinton would say, "I'm too old to be a yuppie."[36]

Hillary Clinton was not too old to be a feminist—or to be burdened with the frustrations millions felt with that movement. Her tea-and-cookies quip bespoke the elitist disdain for homemaking many sensed from feminists and which the conventional wisdom blamed for destroying the American home. One woman wrote that "the women's movement started off on the wrong foot because it ranked women's paid work over unpaid work."[37] Hillary Clinton's phrase also reflected the presumption that paid work was a matter of choice, a step toward self-fulfillment, rather than the economic necessity it was for most of America's 56 million working women. Now, Republicans gloated, the real Hillary Clinton had emerged.

The demonization of Hillary Rodham Clinton had begun. The Clintons' class baggage fed an anxiety about the duo that they, and especially she, clumsily exacerbated. "She has a housekeeper. She doesn't understand," one sixty-nine-year-old rural Pennsylvania woman would declare, confident that if Bill Clinton lost the presidency, "she'll dump him."[38] The Clintons posed as the most open public figures since Jimmy Carter—Bill shared the pain of his showdown as a fourteen-year-old with his violent stepfather to connect with his countrymen. Once in office, he would say he preferred briefs to boxer shorts, and the first lady would often tell a too-vivid story about her baby spitting up breast milk from bad breast-feeding technique. Yet while sacrificing their dignity to create a false intimacy on TV, both conveyed a sense that they were holding back, that they were somehow insincere.

Questions proliferated about this McGovern organizer turned New Democrat, this Southern governor who boasted about his generation's idealism yet refused to admit he dodged the draft or smoked pot, this Yale lawyer and Rhodes Scholar from one of the two most primitive states in the union—Arkansans often said, "Thank God for Mississippi." With the spouse considered a window onto the candidate, many of these questions settled on Hillary Clinton: how could a feminist relinquish a career in the megalopolis and her last name for her man? How could a 1960s liberal who came to fame when *Life* quoted her commencement speech rejecting the "prevailing, acquisitive and competitive corporate life" go corporate?[39] How could any woman put up with her Bubba's tomcatting? It was easier to indulge the traditional fear of powerful women, to deem the marriage a sham, to caricature Hillary as an avenging feminist, than to try to understand the enduring, if imperfect, bond uniting these two complex people.

Shrewdly, the Clintons made the campaign a referendum on George Bush's mudslinging in 1988 and his incompetence at the helm. As a candidate of questionable moral fiber, Bill Clinton had to focus on "the economy, stupid." Remembering the Republicans' demagogic commercials in 1988 accusing the Democratic nominee Michael Dukakis of letting black murderers roam free, Hillary Clinton called the attacks on her man "the daughter of Willie Horton." "We are banking on the fact that the voters will care about jobs, the economy, and what happens in this country—not on our marriage,"[40] she said. Bill Clinton defined addressing issues as a mark of character. Only policy fidelity counted.

Traumatized by Michael Dukakis's haplessness in 1988, both Clintons were determined to counterpunch. Hillary Clinton redirected her anger from her husband toward the Republicans—and the press corps. Conceding nothing, she preferred attacking their enemies to defending her husband or her actions as a lawyer. Early in the campaign, Richard Nixon, in his guise as an elder statesman, once again slighted his own wife when he warned, "If the wife comes through as being too strong and too intelligent, it makes the husband look like a wimp."[41] Months later, Mrs. Clinton claimed that her old nemesis Nixon "was the first one to start it. I think I might have said to Bill that Richard Nixon never does anything without a purpose. Either he was getting even with me because I was on the impeachment staff—because he has a very long memory—or it's because he's laying the groundwork for an attack on me, which has turned out to be the case. . . . It all goes back to Nixon's comments."[42]

Hillary Clinton condemned the double standard that spread her husband's inner life onto the nation's media yet covered up allegations of a George Bush affair. In the language of the 1960s, she told journalist Gail Sheehy that "the Establishment—regardless of party—sticks together. They're gonna circle the wagons on [Bush's alleged girlfriend] Jennifer Fitzgerald and all these other people." When *Vanity Fair* published the interview in May, it rendered the quotation as "Jennifer——."[43] Never before had a presidential candidate's spouse attacked her husband's rival so directly and so viciously.

Jennifer Fitzgerald was a trusted Bush aide whose closeness to the vice president fed rumors. Had Fitzgerald been a Democrat or a Clinton aide, Hillary Clinton would have led the feminist charge, crying sexism at the assumption that a senior man working with an attractive, intelligent junior female was necessarily intimate with her. In fact, throughout the nine years of the adultery wars, when it suited them, Hillary Clinton and the other Clintonites would frequently betray a remarkable insensitivity to the sensibilities of many women placed in awkward positions, feeding rumors about Republican infidelities while threatening or libeling women who might reveal Bill Clinton's infelicities.

Hillary Clinton's nuclear attack on campaign protocols injured both the Clintons and the Bushes. Her claim that she had been speaking "off the record" with a well-known reporter perpetuated her reputation as a viper and as an unguided conversational missile. In this ugly attack, Hillary Clinton exposed the will to power that motivated her, drew Bill Clinton to her, and kept her with him, despite the humiliations. In undercutting Bush's claim to be a family man, damning him with modern America's everybody-does-it ethic, Hillary Clinton gave reporters the opening they needed. Headlines screaming "HILLARY'S REVENGE," "HILLARY GOES TABLOID," "BILL'S WIFE DISHES THE DIRT" put Bush's "mistress" on the media map.[44] The story focused on the Clinton charges without having to document Bush misbehavior. Although even the personality-obsessed journalist Gail Sheehy called them "rumors that have never been proved,"[45] they now circulated enough for respectable reporters to detail them.

At first, the Clintons promoted Hillary Clinton as Bill Clinton's greatest political asset. "If I get elected president, it will be an unprecedented partnership, far more than Franklin Roosevelt and Eleanor," the governor averred. "They were two great people, but on different tracks. If I get elected, we'll do things together like we always have."[46] "We care about the same issues and values and concerns," Hillary Clinton proclaimed. "We are a partnership." She did not believe that the first ladyship was "a job" and insisted: "We ought to let individuals have the right to be who they are."[47]

Though the Clintons dismissed talk of a copresidency, Republicans used the term, knowing that it triggered fears about designing women. They gleefully skewered "the Lady Macbeth of Little Rock," "the Winnie Mandela of American Politics." As a result, 40 percent of voters viewed Bill as a "fast-talking" "wishy-washy" pol and his wife as "being in the race for herself" and "going for the power." In their pseudoscientific argot, Clinton's polling gurus, who were constantly monitoring voters' reactions with focus groups, reported that "the mean line usually dropped down when Hillary appeared on the screen."[48] Stan Greenberg and Celinda Lake reported that "using Hillary actually alienates women voters who say 'Stop trying to promote your wife in order to discredit the sex scandal.'" The pollsters quoted one admittedly "harsh" but representative respondent who snapped: "Put Hillary in the kitchen or the PTA and leave running the country to the President."[49] Other political activists noted a generalized disdain for her, with Texas Democrats reporting, "We don't like Hillary. . . . We don't like her type of woman."[50] Rumors had it that the Republican operative Mary Matalin's office featured a poster of Mrs. Clinton that proclaimed, "We've got to get this evil woman."[51]

At the same time, Hillary Clinton proved remarkably popular with the Democratic base, most especially with career women who, like her, spent their lives juggling professional aspirations, family concerns, individual desires, their husbands' demands, the expectations of tradition, and the ambitions of feminism. In 1992, Hillary Clinton would start down the path that would make her one of the Democratic Party's most effective fund-raisers. One luncheon in Boston became a post–Republican Convention pep rally for Hillary Clinton, crowding 1,300 people into the Park Plaza ballroom and netting $500,000 for the campaign. In states like Massachusetts, Mrs. Clinton would enjoy rock-star status. In the fall, a *Boston Globe* and WBZ-TV poll would find Hillary Clinton the most popular figure among the presidential candidates and their wives, with a 62 percent popularity rating statewide, even though her national favorability rating was 38 percent. Mary Anne Marsh, a Democratic consultant, explained, "Women in Massachusetts respect women who stand up for things," speculating that the outspokenness that alienated others charmed many Bay State women.[52]

When it came to managing the Hillary problem, candidate Clinton displayed both his superhuman capacity for denial and a lovably human imperviousness to his wife's flaws. When confronted with polling data showing Hillary's unpopularity, Clinton sighed, "Oh, man, they don't like her hair." George Stephanopolous and James

Carville rushed out of the meeting and "collapsed in hysterics." In thinking about it, though, Stephanopolous remembered it as "just a sweet moment,"[53] a glimpse into the bond uniting the two Clintons. Soon the campaign needed to go retro. To do so, it needed Hillary Clinton's help. The political strategists' top-secret "Manhattan Project" in the spring of 1992 advised greater cooperation between Hillary's people and Bill's people. The "campaign must recognize the central importance of Hillary's communication to what people believe about Bill Clinton as a prospective president," Greenberg, Carville, and advertising strategist Frank Greer reported in late April."[54] *"The core problem of the Clinton candidacy is Clinton's essentially 'political' nature"* [emphasis in original]. Americans did not trust Bill Clinton. Unfortunately, Hillary Clinton only exacerbated the problem. Clinton's consultants proposed "a lower profile [for Mrs. Clinton] in the immediate short term, as we try to reintroduce Bill Clinton" alone, followed by "events where Bill and Hillary can 'go on dates with the American people.'" Hillary Clinton dutifully traded in her power suit for an apron and challenged Mrs. Bush to a chocolate-chip-cookie-baking contest.[55]

It was a stunning and painful about-face. At the Republican Convention, both Marilyn Quayle, the vice president's wife, and Barbara Bush, the first lady, would address the crowd. Hillary-bashing, as it came to be known, would be the order of the day, with Mrs. Bush calling Mrs. Clinton the "cocandidate," and the conservative columnist and Republican renegade Pat Buchanan sneering about a "Clinton & Clinton" ticket, calling Bill Clinton's wife his "lawyer-spouse."[56] Just before the convention, the party chairman, Rich Bond, said the Republicans' head fund-raiser had America's "second-toughest job," because "The first-toughest, is the person in the Clinton campaign who is charged with keeping Hillary Clinton under wraps."[57] Meanwhile, at the Democratic Convention, Hillary Clinton kept a respectful distance from the podium—and what must have been a frustrating silence.

At the Democratic Convention, Bill Clinton found a new, more legitimate governing partner, vice presidential nominee Al Gore. In choosing another young Southern baby boomer, Clinton was emphasizing the generational divide between the vital virile Democrats and the aging anachronistic Republican president. In finding an experienced Washington hand, a forty-four-year-old who had already served four terms in the House of Representatives and two terms in the Senate, Clinton was forging a strong peer partnership. Although never a copresident, Bill Clinton's vice president would be a formidable presence in the campaign and, eventually, in the White House.

For a supposedly rigid ideologue, Hillary Clinton proved remarkably elastic. In what was billed as the "Year of the Woman," this woman—and her man—would do anything to win. As the consultants rewrote her lines, Hollywood stylists from her friend Linda Bloodworth-Thomason's sitcom *Designing Women* redid her look. One cartoon showed Chelsea clutching her mother's side as Mrs. Clinton yammered: "Hi there! I'm Hillary Clinton—the *new* Hillary Clinton! Do you want a homemade cookie? Do you like my new hair style? Do you want to hear about my family values?"[58]

Just as John F. Kennedy in 1960 had both been bemused and appalled by reporters' fascination with his full head of hair and how he combed it, Hillary Rodham Clinton found the scrutiny of her look both insulting and infuriating. But like Kennedy, she knew to take it seriously. What could be called the case of the disappearing headband symbolized her maturation in the public eye to some, whereas others saw an eager-beaver willingness to do anything for public approval. Disingenuously concealing just how seriously she took the criticisms and the various makeovers, as first lady, Mrs. Clinton would frequently joke, "I figure that if we ever want to get Bosnia off the front page, all I have to do is either to put on a headband or change my hair and we'll be occupied with something else."[59]

When convenient, and in front of the right audience, Hillary Clinton was happy to locate her troubles at the complicated nexus between feminist politics and the generational shift from the George Bush GI Joe generation to the Clintonite baby boomers. "That whole transition [of women in the workplace] has been played out at every level in the public and private sector except the presidency," Mrs. Clinton argued during the campaign. "And it's because Bill and Al [Gore] are the first of the postwar generation to be nominated for this job. So our lives are different from our parents'. So it hasn't had a chance to be acted out on the presidential stage." Echoing that thought, and throwing an elbow at the Republican attack machine,

Bill Clinton accused the Republicans of trying to "make it a Willie Horton thing against all working women, trying to run against them in a way that I really think is lamentable."[60]

And yet, when pressed, Hillary Clinton would retreat into an apple-pie definition of feminism that would have satisfied Nancy Reagan. When a reporter asked whether President Bush might brand her a feminist, Mrs. Clinton smiled, added a smidge of a Southern accent, and drawled: "It could be, and I just keep telling people to look in the dictionary, 'cause at least in my big fat 'ol dictionary at home, it says a feminist is someone who believes a woman ought to have the same social, economic and political rights as a man. . . . But the word will be twisted."[61]

As slippery as they were, the Clintons protected their daughter from much of the hoopla. When Chelsea was younger, they had inoculated her against mudslinging by imitating the Clinton critics at the dinner table. After Chelsea watched the *60 Minutes* interview, Bill Clinton asked tentatively, "What did you think?" "I think I'm glad that you're my parents," the twelve-year-old responded. Feeling compelled to soften their image, the Clintons posed with their daughter for a convention-eve *People* cover story, marched her to and around Madison Square Garden for the convention, and allowed her to appear in the Clinton campaign film saying, "What I would like America to know about my mother and father is that they're great people, and they're great parents."[62] Still, the Clintons vetoed the consultants' attempts to showcase Chelsea too much. During the administration, the Clintons would also show remarkable restraint and skill in maintaining the teenager's privacy, even though they did deploy Chelsea when absolutely necessary.

Hillary Clinton's retreat advanced Bill Clinton's cause. By June, Stanley Greenberg noted that voters were "more neutral about Hillary"—which was an improvement. Even more important, the trend lines of potential "switchers" "begin to move up when Hillary talks about 'a good marriage partnership.'"[63] The polls were trending higher; the Clintonites had neutralized the Hillary problem, for now.

The Clintons' "two for the price of one" pitch and Hillary Clinton's makeover blurred the cultural battle lines. Some feminists, like Letty Cottin Pogrebin, acknowledged, "When we elect a President we get a governing couple; more precisely, when we elect a man we give his wife power. . . . I count a smart First Lady as a bonus."[64] Others, like former congresswoman and feminist firebrand Bella Abzug, mourned Hillary's retreat, saying, "We ought to have reached the stage where we accept women for what they are, not try to put them in some cookie cutter."[65] Andrew Sullivan of the *New Republic* snapped: "On her own, she'd never be elected president of the United States, and her attempt to get there by virtue of her marriage is not only an insult to all the women candidates who have the temerity actually to run for office but a worrying sign of a creeping Clinton court."[66] Most voters agreed. Only a quarter wanted to see Hillary Clinton in the Cabinet, as her husband once contemplated, 58 percent wanted a traditional first lady, and 66 percent approved of her continuing her law career.

The polls suggested that most Americans accepted the two-career couple. When it came to the presidency, however, they wanted perfect and perfectly traditional couples. The "Republican mother" remained more alluring than a "first feminist." A first lady could have a project or a profession, but not power. Reporters acknowledged that "this is no Nancy Reagan, obsessed with the man. This is a woman who lives and breathes social welfare policy, who has a résumé that would have put her on transition team lists had Bill Bradley . . . been elected President, who was a key player in her husband's campaign."[67] Still, "there are lines not to cross," the *Christian Science Monitor* editorialized after the campaign.[68]

Feminist author Karen Lehrman mourned Hillary Clinton's descent into the "Harriet Nelson role." Warning that feminism is not "nepotism," Lehrman condemned Clinton's "betrayal of feminism" and admitted that feminists would have been much less indulgent if "she were less liberal and intelligent," let alone pro-life. Hillary Clinton should have remained an independent career woman and continued to practice law, a choice two-thirds of Americans would have applauded, according to some polls. "By cynically repackaging her as a suburban housewife, however," Lehrman complained, "the Clinton campaign has not only shown disturbing signs of condescension (who do they think they're kidding?) but has missed a great opportunity to present a new genre of First Lady: articulate, highly educated, career oriented, has her own passions and ideas and acts independently of her husband."[69]

Although Hillary Clinton continually impressed people with her poise, ultimately, she was too poised. Her refusal to acknowledge any conflict, any sacrifice, any sense of loss, appeared disingenuous and did not help a husband whose sincerity was already in doubt. Denying any makeover but continuing her counterattack, she said she was sure Republicans would make her image an issue: "I'm sure they will; they have nothing else to talk about," she said.[70] Anxious to prove that she was not a passive, pathetic political wife, she went overboard. Saying "as far as I'm concerned, the main reason I'm interested and involved in this campaign is because of the issues I'm involved in" lacked credibility unless she was indeed a Lady Macbeth.[71]

Further attempting to soften Hillary Clinton's image, and feeding this notion of the happy baby boomers ready to seize the reins, the Clintons and the Gores often campaigned together on a bus. With 130 journalists in tow, this seemingly old-fashioned technique exploited the latest celebrity-focused trends. Bill and Hillary Clinton, along with Al Gore and his wife Tipper, seemed to be having a grand old time. Many Americans enjoyed feeling that they had an inside glimpse at the candidates and their wives, and they delighted in being part of this upbeat, youthful, glamorous attempt to revitalize America. Bob Schieffer of CBS gushed: "Seeing them out there on the campaign trail, they seem young, and vibrant, and full of energy. . . . I think this bus tour that they are on right now is one of the great political innovations of recent years. I mean, finally, a candidate is getting out, and actually talking to real people. You see them out there—You can tell they are having a lot of fun. I think that it is really creating a lot of energy."[72]

Still, during the general election campaign, amid all the scrutiny, both Clintons emerged as shape-shifters, each varying his or her respective image as the enterprise demanded—but never appearing fully human. Bill Clinton projected opposing archetypes well enough that enough voters overlooked the inconsistency. One day, the good ol' boy bragged about his '65 Mustang and imitated Elvis. The next night, he might be the New Age feminist, calling attacks against his wife "an attack on women who are independent, strong-minded and who work for a living."[73] Hillary Clinton also ranged widely. One morning, she would play the homemaker on ABC's *Home Show*. In the afternoon, she would appeal to "all working women" by talking about being "engaged in the same kind of juggling act that most women I know are." That night, she might be the power networker, raising millions from adoring women professionals. In the short term, in an increasingly fragmented media world where the big three networks no longer dominated, such shapeshifting worked.

Bill Clinton's victorious election campaign fused the old politics with the new. The focus on the economy, combined with the call to "Put People First" and the commitment to win at all costs, mimicked Franklin D. Roosevelt's hard-headed, crowd-pleasing, big-government synthesis of Progressivism and Populism. Clinton's New Covenant, like the New Deal, made the Democrats the party of government programs engineered to help the "forgotten man," now the forgotten person. Bill Clinton, like Franklin Roosevelt, attracted devoted aides who were willing to bully opponents. Watching Clinton work a crowd, making eye contact, shaking hands, slapping backs, glistening with sweat, glorying in the people, evoked images of Huey Long, William Jennings Bryan, and other great American populists.

Yet this old-fashioned demagogue was a carefully packaged commodity fluent in the visually driven patois of television.[74] He was a celebrity prompted by consultants, stage-managed by advertising executives, advised by the Ivy League aristocracy, blessed by Hollywood royalty. A son of the television age, a product of the consumer culture, the first president raised on *Howdy Doody* and Crest commercials, he knew that the way to reach Americans was to entertain them. This modern sorcerer confessed on *60 Minutes,* played saxophone for the hip talk show host Arsenio Hall, and bared his soul at the Democratic National Convention. Fittingly, he was best known not for a phrase but a gesture, the way he telegraphed empathy by thoughtfully, mournfully, biting his lip. In Arkansas, his skills as an old pol earned him the nickname "Slick Willie"; his identity as a yuppie prince was inextricably linked to his wife and earned the sobriquet "Billary."

Hillary Clinton also offered up an alluring and paradoxical fusion of the new politics with the old. This hippie turned yuppie, this Wellesley feminist, this crusading lawyer demanding legal aid for indigents while serving the Arkansas powers that be, embodied many of the *Big Chill* stereotypes of how the 1960s kids became corporate sellouts in the 1980s. Pictures of Hillary the brunette hippie with her Poindexter glasses, feminist nonhairdo, and flower-power bell-bottoms seemed jarring next to Hillary the blonde yuppie, with or without her controversial, on-again–off-again headbands. But for all her New Class rhetoric and ways, Hillary Clinton remained a churchgoing Methodist, a devoted daughter, a doting mother, a long-suffering and self-sacrificing wife.

In 1992, Hillary Clinton first saved Bill Clinton's remarkable campaign, then repeatedly endangered it. Unlike Barbara Bush, she never offered her husband an easy wellspring of mass support. At the end of the campaign, 50 percent in a Gallup poll approved of Mrs. Clinton and 29 percent disapproved. She was a polarizing figure, with 42 percent saying she came closer to their values and lifestyle than previous first ladies and 41 percent disagreeing. A quarter feared she would play too big a role in the Clinton White House. Hillary Clinton proved particularly popular with college-educated women, urbanites, minorities, and eighteen- to twenty-nine-year-old women. These would be her core supporters throughout the Clinton years. Only 41 percent of the women in her own generation felt closer to her lifestyle and values; 47 percent of those born between 1943 and 1962, the baby boom cohort, did not.[75] Class identity had proved more powerful than a media-generated fantasy about a cohesive generation rising to power.

By the general campaign, a pattern that would operate throughout the Clinton years had emerged. When Hillary Rodham Clinton felt comfortable or popular, she acted in a way that some reporters called "Hillary I"—the presumptive copresident; when besieged and needing to revive her public standing, "Hillary II" emerged—the happy homemaker and cookie baker.[76] Mrs. Clinton's aides insisted that their boss had not changed; "the American people are just getting to know her better." But the Hillary Clinton of fall 1992 was far more cautious and disciplined than her earlier incarnation that winter. Now, when she talked policy, she preferred to talk about "being a voice for children in the White House," without endorsing any specific programs and without dreaming too boldly—at least in public.[77] Now, the *New York Times* noted, she was careful to talk about "my husband" and reserve the pronoun "I" for women's issues, such as keeping the streets safe. "I'm sick and tired of children being shot going to and from school, being shot as they stand on the play-grounds, being caught in random gunfire," Mrs. Clinton declared at one gathering of Methodist ministers. Occasionally, and preferably off camera, Hillary Clinton catered to her base, plunging into the abortion debate and appearing at rallies with Kate Michelman, the president of the National Abortion Rights Action League. "I think she's struck a happy balance," Mary Rose Oakar, a Democratic con-gresswoman from Cleveland, believed. "Maybe she was a little ex-treme in being self-assertive early on. But she's extremely comfort-able now. She's being who she is."[78]

By late October, when Mrs. Clinton visited Cleveland, it seemed clear that the Clintons were well on their way to the White House. Just who Hillary Clinton was, and just how much she could truly be who she wanted to be, was by no means settled—and, in fact, was far less clear than it had been at the start of Bill Clinton's quixotic, but surprisingly successful, quest for the presidency.

CHAPTER 3

COPRESIDENT: "IT'S ELEANOR ROOSEVELT TIME"

It is easy to forget that Hillary Rodham Clinton's first few months in office were triumphal. She helped shape the new administration's strategy and vetted appointments. She assembled a crack staff of aides devoted to her and her issues. The media coverage was adoring. Her influence on personnel and policy seemed unlimited. Passage of *her* health care package looked assured. In fact, it was Bill Clinton, not his wife, who stumbled at the beginning, continuing a recurring pattern among first couples wherein when one thrives, the media often perceives the other one as failing.

Despite the Clintons' strategic turn away from the "two for the price of one" rhetoric in the 1992 campaign, Bill Clinton encouraged his wife to play an unprecedentedly active role as first lady. That mandate affected how Mrs. Clinton organized her office, linked her work to her predecessors, and positioned herself regarding the public. Seven Sisters and Ivy League intellectual that she was, she began her tenure by studying the histories of previous first ladies. Unfortunately—Mrs. Clinton would say typically—this historical inquiry ended up as fodder for late-night comics, thanks to the *Washington Post* reporter Bob Woodward's caricature of her channeling Eleanor Roosevelt's spirit. Still, it was clear from the start that the Clintons were playing to the bar of history, looking at this pioneering role for a first lady as part of a broader—and long overdue—transformation and modernization of the White House, the American government, and the United States of America.

Although Bill Clinton only won 43 percent of the popular vote, the Clintons felt vindicated. They believed they had a mandate to emphasize issues over character, to stiff-arm the press, to restore Democratic leadership, to create a new generational tone, to reclaim the "zone of privacy" Hillary Clinton demanded on *60 Minutes,* and to establish a copresidency.[1] The term *copresidency,* which was mentioned in one article in 1987, would appear over 92,000 times in 1993.

Whereas the Clintons embraced the term at first, Hillary Clinton's predecessor, Barbara Bush, recoiled from it. On moving into the White House in 1989, Mrs. Bush had made clear that she wanted to repudiate the trend intensified by Betty Ford, Rosalynn Carter, and Nancy Reagan toward a first lady's more active involvement in American politics and policy. "I do not speak out on issues because I am not the elected official. When I am an elected official," Barbara Bush chuckled, "I will speak out and I hope George Bush will do for me what I have done for him."[2] Echoing Mamie Eisenhower's classic 1950s line, "Ike runs the country and I turn the lamb chops," the Bushes embraced the traditionally separate spheres distinguishing the home and the office, the woman's domain and the man's. Barbara Bush said of her husband, "I don't fool around in his office, and he doesn't fool around in mine."[3] Her concerns were "running the house, listening to my children's problems, passing them on to George if they're important." She would not be "a wavemaker." Going in, she vowed that she would not "lobby George" or his subordinates.[4] And during one of many combative interviews, when Mrs. Bush resisted reporters' entreaties to take specific stands on issues, she reminded PBS's Judy Woodruff, "I'm not a co-president."[5]

The Bushes saw themselves as exemplars of their generation. George and Barbara Bush were the seventh presidential couple whose identity had been forged amid World War II. Whereas John Kennedy had entered office in 1961 promising to apply the GI's can-do spirit, the Bushes were fighting a rearguard action, trying to preserve a world that observers now derided as "conservative kitsch . . . an ideal past that never existed."[6]

In fact, the Bushes could not resist creating a copresidency—or more accurately, a joint image-making project. George Bush needed his wife to help embody his values and provide symbolic cover when his policy, or the nation's pocketbook, would not suffice. Barbara Bush became George Bush's most prominent and most effective cheerleader. She acknowledged the absurdity of her position at the start of her nationally televised "conversation" with the American people during the 1992 Republican Convention, at a time when her rival Hillary Clinton was nowhere near the Democratic Convention microphones. "There is something not quite right here," the first lady said, acknowledging the august company she found herself in; "speeches by President Ronald Reagan, President Gerald Ford, Secretary Jack Kemp, Senator Phil Gramm—and—Barbara Bush?"[7] This was the kind of modesty so essential to her success. Barbara Bush had seven minutes to demonstrate compassion for "crack babies and babies with AIDS," uphold "family values . . . however you define family," and praise "the strongest, the most decent, the most caring, the wisest—and yes, the healthiest—man I know."[8]

Ironically, the Bushes' reluctance to govern together as a couple and Barbara Bush's reticence enhanced the first lady's popularity and power. Although Mrs. Bush did not dictate policy, she helped shape public perceptions of the Bush administration. Barbara Bush's emergence as copresident in her limited, more symbolic, less policy-oriented way, would reveal the unspoken but compelling forces that mobilized modern first ladies—and that fed Hillary Clinton's great expectations.

Barbara Bush learned from Lady Bird Johnson's example to keep her major project as first lady "useful" and noticeable, and to make sure that "it reflects well on your husband."[9] The first lady's most successful stunt for literacy was the publication of *Millie's Book,* a runaway best-seller in 1990.[10] The book was similar to *C. Fred's Story,* which sold 15,000 copies when George Bush was vice president. For Mrs. Bush, ghostwriting for a dog was easier than exposing her writing directly. With 136 pages of text and dozens of glossy color photographs, the book offered a dog's perspective on White House life—the spirited Bush grandchildren, the visiting dignitaries, the servants, the tourists, the beautiful decor. *Millie's Book* revealed just what Barbara Bush wanted to about the Bushes' life. It was filled with charming frills that united Americans. This was the copresidency at its most alluring, its most queenly, its most benign.

In publishing the book, Barbara Bush demonstrated that she had also learned from Nancy Reagan how to harness popular culture for the public good. However, whereas Mrs. Reagan had made a guest appearance on the sitcom *Diff'rent Strokes* as part of her antidrug crusade, Mrs. Bush refused to appear on the geriatric comedy *Golden Girls*. Barbara Bush was more comfortable filming public service announcements than risking the dignity of her husband's office on a sitcom.

Now, in 1992, and unlike his predecessor, the young new baby boomer president had big plans for his wife. He said that the one person he wanted in the room when key decisions were made, his Bobby Kennedy, was "Hillary." Close friends agreed. "He married a brain trust; it would be very wasteful not to use it," said Linda Bloodworth-Thomason, the creator of television's *Designing Women*. *Newsweek* reported that Bloodworth-Thomason, along with eight other close friends, celebrated Hillary Clinton's birthday in October 1992 by giving the first lady–to-be a "circle of friends" gold bracelet, with their initials engraved on the links, along with letters from each of them articulating their dreams for Hillary Clinton's tenure.[11]

At their best, Hillary Clinton and Bill Clinton each brought out the best in each other. "He's more spontaneous and creative," one staffer observed. "Can you imagine if he married someone just like himself? His life would be a disaster. And if she married someone just like her, no one would have dinner at her house. People would be too intimidated."[12]

The Clintons contemplated Hillary Clinton as chief of staff or "principal domestic adviser." Ultimately, she feared that in Arkansas, her independent identity had been eclipsed by her husband's commanding presence. Years earlier, John Robert Starr, a veteran Arkansas columnist, had asked, "Hillary, what do you want to do?" Wanting to make her mark, on her own, she replied, "I want to run something."[13] In the heady days after the election, she speculated with friends and advisers about taking on a history-making and identity-affirming job: attorney general, secretary of state, chief of staff. Others argued, "You can't do that. It'll destroy her. It'll destroy us. It'll mean she's co-President."[14]

A joke circulating at the Bush White House Christmas parties had Mrs. Clinton applying for various administration jobs, with

Barbara Bush applying to fulfill the traditional first lady job for an-other four years. Mrs. Clinton, however, made it clear that she wanted both portfolios. Already fearful of speaking publicly on the "Hillary" question, pro or con, one "key adviser" told the White House corre-spondent Kenneth Walsh, anonymously, "She wants to get deeply in-volved in policy-making, and I wouldn't limit it to children's issues or women's issues. I wouldn't limit it to anything." Characteristically, her husband agreed, saying, "I think she can easily do what she's supposed to do as first lady and still have time and energy to be involved in some of these specific areas that I think she's so good at."[15]

Clearly, during the three-and-half-month transition, a new Hil-lary Clinton emerged—or more accurately, the old Hillary Rodham from Arkansas and the campaign "blue-light specials" returned. In a mid-December interview with the *Wall Street Journal,* the incom-ing president said he hoped Mrs. Clinton would sit in on Cabinet meetings. "She knows more about a lot of this stuff than most of us do," he said.[16]

"I think that whether Hillary Clinton sits in on Cabinet meetings or not, she will have something to say," Wendy Sherman, a Demo-cratic political consultant insisted on CNN. Trying to normalize the situation, Sherman explained, "She is a friend of her husband's. She is his wife. She is an attorney and a smart, competent, capable woman in her own right. She will be a voice that he will listen to, and I don't think she needs to sit in on a Cabinet meeting to do it. I don't think that's the point at all."[17]

Still seething from the campaign, Hillary Clinton did not want sweeping proclamations about her role; nor did she want to get per-mission from the press or the public to serve in her husband's admin-istration. When ABC's Diane Sawyer interviewed both Clintons on *Primetime Live* a week before the inauguration, Hillary Clinton de-nied she had her own agenda. She would play on the president's team. "No, it'll be what I've done here [in Little Rock], which is to support the agenda that Bill is putting forward, which I think is the right agenda," she said humbly, cautiously. As she had been doing since her Yale days, she tried to soft-pedal her trailblazing by rooting herself in the women's sphere. "I mean, what we need to do for chil-dren and families in this country is what he's outlined," she contin-ued. "And what I want to do is what I've done here—to try to play a role in making that happen, whether it's in immunizing children or providing better health care or improving schools so that all children do have the best education available to them, or making some of these systems that government runs, like the foster-care system, work for people instead of causing problems."[18]

When asked directly about sitting in on Cabinet meetings, first Mrs. Clinton said, "I'm going to do what my husband asks me to do on these issues," and then, "It depends upon what he decides." Sawyer asked, "Is it a tricky passage?" Mrs. Clinton responded, "Well, I think it is, because our society's going through a tricky passage about men's and women's roles and appropriate partnerships between husbands and wives, and I've said many times in the last year that what is being played out in the homes and workplaces of America is now being played out in the White House." The incoming president disagreed, insisting, "If the issue is, what is best for the American people, it's not tricky at all for me. It's easy. In all these years that Hillary and I worked together on education issues or children's issues here, she was practicing law and earning most of the money for our family. Now she's not going to do that anymore. She has more time, more energy, and more ability, and I know it—some of it may be tricky, but I would be derelict in my responsibility to the people of this country if I didn't have someone of her ability and character and devotion working on things that we all care about."[19]

In truth, they were both wrong. Bill Clinton deluded himself in believing that relying on his wife would not be politically treacherous. In focusing on the first lady only as a symbol of American women, Hillary Clinton overlooked Americans' traditional fears of anyone seemingly unaccountable getting too close to presidential power, as well as the complexities inherent in the unelected, undefined, "wife of" role.

Ever the good student, Mrs. Clinton read biographies of her forty-three predecessors, paying particular interest to Eleanor Roosevelt. The incoming first lady, along with so many modern chroniclers of first ladies, was particularly interested in first ladies who had been activist, trailblazing, and policy oriented, acting as essential partners, not decorative appendages. Hillary held imaginary "conversations with" Eleanor, asking "How did you put up with this?" "Eleanor" would "answer": "You're just going to have to get out there and do it, and don't make any excuses."[20]

Hillary Rodham Clinton refused to disappear into the policy-making woodwork or into a traditional ladylike role. Flexing her muscles, she became one of the five people, including vice president-elect Al Gore, and the secretary of state-designate Warren Christopher, to vet major appointments, perhaps the most important and daunting task a new administration faces. "Friends of Hillary" would be as prominent in the administration as "Friends of Bill." Her old boss from the Nixon impeachment proceedings, Bernard Nussbaum, became White House counsel. Nussbaum's top assistant would be one of her two closest friends from the Rose Law Firm, Vince Foster. Hillary Clinton and Foster were so close that some Arkansas gossips claimed the two were having an affair. Her other comrade, Webster Hubbell, became the number two man at the Justice Department. These appointments extended the first lady's zone of influence by creating a network of people throughout the executive branch more loyal to her than to the president, who were committed to keeping her informed.

Ultimately, reporters would count at least eleven top positions—and dozens of lower-level but highly influential policy postings—as "Hillary's choices." In crucial domestic policy areas such as health, welfare, and justice, many of these appointees came from the pool of talent Hillary Clinton knew best—the network of social activists involved in Marion Wright Edelman's Children's Defense Fund and other liberal social advocacy groups. These people included Donna Shalala, the secretary of Health and Human Services; Carol Rasco, the White House domestic policy adviser; Ricki Seidman, deputy communications director at the White House; Ed Acheson, head of policy development at Justice; and Marion Wright Edelman's husband, Peter Edelman, a lawyer, as Shalala's special assistant.[21] While Bill Clinton was developing a centrist philosophy he would call the "third way," his wife was hiring more traditionally oriented Great Society advocates who still had great faith in big government. In fact, on the eve of the 1996 Democratic Convention, when the president would push through his major welfare reform, Peter Edelman would resign in protest.

Moreover, moderates blamed Mrs. Clinton for the "diversity jihad" that held up many appointments in the search for women and people of color. Hillary Clinton's close friend, Susan Thomases, served as the first lady's enforcer, demanding enough "EGG"—ethnicity, gender, and geographical diversity—in appointments.

As a candidate, Bill Clinton had demonstrated that he was a New Democrat by distancing himself from the toxic politics of special interests and tokenism that had hurt Walter Mondale's 1984 campaign for the presidency, among others. Since the 1960s, the Democratic Party had become home to—critics claimed hostage to—activists asserting an African-American agenda, a Hispanic agenda, a feminist agenda, a union agenda. Clinton's most dramatic break from that dynamic occurred when he appeared at one of the Reverend Jesse Jackson's Rainbow Coalition events during the campaign. Clinton embarrassed his host by objecting to the presence of the rap singer Sister Souljah, who had said after the Los Angeles riots, "If black people kill black people every day, why not have a week and kill white people?" Clinton, happy to impress whites and look courageous by confronting blacks in front of a black audience said, "If you took the words 'white' and 'black' and reversed them, you might think [the notorious former Klansman] David Duke was giving that speech."[22] Yet now, entering the White House, the Clintons' search for a Cabinet that "looks like America" made the president look like a hostage of the special interests, especially of women's groups, and helped derail his attempt to have the entire Cabinet confirmed by inauguration day.

The haste and the harsh behind-the-scenes politicking contributed to the first major appointment fiasco, when the president, at Hillary Clinton's urging, nominated Zoë Baird as attorney general. Baird was the general counsel of Aetna Life and Casualty. She lacked a national profile, but both Clintons knew her from the Renaissance Weekend, the yuppie think tank and New Year's "happening" at Hilton Head, South Carolina, they attended annually. Besides, although her choice meant the Clintons had placed a woman in one of the top four Cabinet spots (the other three being State, Defense, and Treasury), Baird was not the women's groups' favored candidate. This pleased the president, who by late December resented the feminist pressure to hire a woman and the press obsession with Clintonite "bean counting."

Unfortunately, Baird and her husband had hired two illegal aliens to serve as their chauffeur and nanny in 1990, and had not paid Social Security taxes for either. Baird reassured the transition team her lawyers were working out the problem. Her aides compared the infraction to an unpaid parking ticket. The head of the Senate Judiciary Committee, Joseph Biden, a working-class kid with no trust fund, disagreed. Demonstrating better political instincts about how Americans would perceive the yuppie finagling of a woman earning hundreds of thousands of dollars a year who wanted to become the nation's chief law enforcement officer, Biden said, "No, this is like a wreck on a Los Angeles freeway."[23] Biden was right. The Clinton administration, on its first days in office, ran directly into the class and gender resentments Hillary Clinton had stirred up a year earlier with both her Tammy Wynette and stay-at-home-and-serve-tea cracks. Eleanor Clift on CNN called the illegal hiring "an elitist crime," saying, "it was women in steno pools across the country who did her in. They were the folks who wrote in and called in."[24]

To make matters worse, just before the White House announced the next nominee, but after news of the pending appointment had already leaked, it turned out that Judge Kimba Wood and her husband had also employed an illegal alien as a nanny. Many in the elite media, such as the *New York Times,* would view "Nannygate" as a women's issue. Worried that professional women who had to hire nannies to advance their careers were being unfairly targeted, the novelist Erica Jong wrote in the *Times,* "We should be marching down Fifth Avenue waving banners that say 'I hired an illegal alien.'"[25] To most Americans, this was a class issue and a law-and-order issue. Talk radio crackled with denunciations of the privileged yuppies who thought they were above the law. In the more plebeian—and Republican—*New York Post,* Amy Pagnozzi would snap, "On a $600,000-a-year family income, Zoë Baird could have hired one of those Mary Poppins status-symbol nannies who not only have a green card but can tutor a kid in French."[26] Eventually, the Clintonites found an unmarried woman without children, Janet Reno, to serve as attorney general, although she and Mrs. Clinton had neither deep connections nor a particularly warm relationship.

Although White House insiders blamed Mrs. Clinton and her people privately, publicly, Nannygate became one of the many political fumbles that marked President Clinton's rocky start. Considering the power of both Mrs. Clinton and the Democrats in Congress in torpedoing Baird, a *Wall Street Journal* columnist, Paul Gigot, joked, "None of this would be happening if Bill Clinton [*sic*] were still president."[27]

Hillary Clinton's power within the White House continued to grow. In the ever-delicate tug-of-war over office real estate, Mrs. Clinton and her chief of staff, Maggie Williams, received precious office space in the West Wing, in addition to the traditional first lady suite of offices in the East Wing. Soon, more moderate Clinton staffers were grumbling that the first lady's offices, on either side of the building, were simply the "Left Wing."

Reporters pointed to Hillary Clinton's new role as indicative of a broader pattern that would dog the administration. By inauguration day, one columnist for the *Atlanta Constitution* sniffed, "I don't know why we're so surprised about all these promises, made in the heat of election passion and now scattered around broken like the debris of a messy divorce. It was clear from the start that Bill Clinton is the Great Seducer."[28] Two days later, on CNN's *Crossfire*, even Michael Kinsley, the host from the left, complained that Hillary Clinton's new prominence represented "a reversal" of Bill Clinton's "campaign themes." Kinsley's guest, Eleanor Clift, said, "Well, it's an adjustment for the American people." Unknowingly anticipating eight years of such wordplay, the host from the right, John Sununu, interjected, "Euphemisms for broken promises, huh?"[29]

During those first few weeks, while the president appeared overwhelmed and uncertain, the first lady became focused and passionate. According to Bob Woodward's insider account, at a Camp David retreat for the entire Cabinet and senior White House staff the weekend of 30–31 January, Hillary Clinton invoked the Clintons' Arkansas experiences to advocate a bold, visionary approach to governance, linking their many policy proposals to a broader story that the public could comprehend. When Secretary of State Warren Christopher suggested narrowing the mandate down to a few priorities, Mrs. Clinton disagreed vehemently: "Why are we here if we don't go for it?" she thundered.[30]

Wisely advised to avoid giving his wife a formal, additional, title, the president instead assigned her his biggest challenge, just as he had done in Arkansas when they tackled the school system. President Clinton said Hillary Clinton would chair his Task Force on National Health Reform, with six Cabinet members reporting to her, because "she's better at organizing and leading people from a complex beginning to a certain end than anybody I've ever worked with in my life."[31] Hillary Clinton later said that her husband wanted the operation "run out of the White House . . . instead of having to referee fights" over "turf."[32] Like Richard Nixon, Bill Clinton mistrusted Cabinet government. With more power flowing into the White House, it was only natural to divert some to the president's life partner.

The elite media approved. This approach was "more honest" than lurking behind the scenes, the *New York Times* editorialized. "She will stand *with* her man, or maybe ahead of him."[33] Many women, especially professionals, toasted Hillary's rise. Her new job, and her West Wing office, close to the president, "is not just breaking a glass ceiling but knocking down a thick wall," Eleanor Clift rejoiced in *Newsweek*.[34] *Ladies' Home Journal* praised Hillary for ushering in "the age of the smart woman."[35] "Hillary is all of us," Sally Quinn claimed in a *Newsweek* cover story, yet again reflecting the simplistic notion that the question of a first lady's role only had to do with women's roles.[36] "Can she do it? Can we do it? That's the question."[37]

As a mark of this newfound confidence, the East Wing press secretary, Lisa Caputo, said her boss would be known as Hillary *Rodham* Clinton. The "ladylike" phase was over. Hillary Rodham Clinton had arrived. "If the person that has the last word at night is the same person who has the first word in the morning, they are going to be important," Clinton's campaign consultant James Carville unapologetically told the *New York Times*. "You throw in an IQ of a g'zillion and a backbone of steel, and it's a pretty safe assumption to say this is a person of considerable influence."[38]

Such arrogance was dangerous. Although polls now showed that 63 percent of those surveyed liked Mrs. Clinton, 59 percent opposed a major policy role for her. A vast majority, 70 percent, wanted a "traditional First Lady."[39] Inaugural celebrations of "the Dynamic Duo"[40] eclipsed campaign warnings about Mrs. Clinton's image as "an empowered Nancy Reagan."[41] "The voters aren't getting what they were told they were getting," Mickey Kaus complained in the *New Republic*. Addressing Hillary Clinton's cheerleaders—including 57 percent of women under forty who applauded her power grab—Kaus warned: "Nepotism is not feminism."[42]

Hillary Clinton and her thirteen aides established what would be known as "Hillaryland." Throughout much of the twentieth century, the first lady had a social secretary and a handful of aides and typists, with much of the office work focused on keeping up with correspondence and arranging state dinners. When Rosalynn Carter entered the White House in 1977, she found the East Wing to be chaotic, demoralized, and ineffectual. An average of 100 invitations and 1,000 to 2,000 letters arrived each week. An entourage of 50 to 115 reporters usually accompanied the first lady on her travels. Jimmy Carter's transition team concluded that the office of the first lady had to be modernized and adapted to Mrs. Carter's "needs."[43] Four decades after the Eleanor Roosevelt revolution, and a decade after Richard Nixon tried to assert more centralized control, the East Wing was not yet integrated into the White House bureaucracy. Merging the East Wing and West Wing correspondence sections would improve coordination. The social entertainment office was reduced to accommodate the Carters' desire for a "working White House." Shifting clerical jobs to the West Wing freed "precious physical space in the East Wing" and provided cover for staff increases in press relations, advancing "substantive First Lady projects."[44]

The reorganization distanced the first lady's office from its roots as an ad hoc center for social affairs and family support. Maintaining the tradition of Lady Bird Johnson's press secretary Liz Carpenter and Betty Ford's spokesperson Sheila Weidenfeld, Mary Hoyt combined the jobs of press secretary to the first lady and staff coordinator. Hoyt and the Carters had more "substantive" concerns for "an active and popular First Lady."[45]

Funding for the East Wing had evolved haphazardly, in small, improvised grants buried in larger congressional allocations for running the White House. It was continued out of tradition. But officially, lawyers concluded, Rosalynn Carter's seventeen aides and the vice president's wife's four staffers were "illegal employees." Federal employees were not allowed to "work for private citizens."[46] Only on 2 November 1978 would a short amendment to a bill finally authorize "assistance and services . . . to be provided to the spouse of the President in connection with assistance provided by such spouse to the President in the discharge of the President's duties and responsibilities."[47]

These changes invigorated the East Wing while expanding it. In his zeal to establish his wife's credibility, Jimmy Carter, the man who was depomping the West Wing by carrying his own luggage, would be criticized for making the East Wing more imperial. Headlines pronouncing "ROSALYNN CARTER WANTS BIGGER STAFF" embarrassed the Carters. East Wingers would also have a hard time explaining that their demand for perks and salaries commensurate with their West Wing peers was a matter of respect, not a grab for power. No longer a bureaucratic outlaw, the office of the first lady still lacked legitimacy.

Fifteen years later, concerned about the budget, especially for the East Wing, the Clinton White House operations subsumed many minor functions to limit the number of aides assigned to the first lady. Throughout the White House, whereas previous administrations distributed photographs of the president and the vice president, the Clintons distributed photographs of the president and the first lady in various poses. In "Hillaryland" East and West, the photographs tended to be solo shots of the first lady.

This enclave included an unprecedented three staffers honored with White House commissions; the vice president's staff had one. The first lady considered her chief of staff, Margaret Williams, as equal to the president's chief of staff. Characteristically, Williams had previously worked for the Children's Defense Fund, and Lisa Caputo, the press secretary, had worked for various Democratic congressmen and candidates. The deputy chief of staff, Melanne S. Verveer, worked for two of the most effective liberal lobbies, Common Cause and People for the American Way. The common backgrounds and ideologies also facilitated the camaraderie among these activists devoted both to the first lady and to their Progressive, programmatic, big-government approach to problem solving.

Feeling safe among her loyal aides, Hillary Clinton could indulge her softer, girlish, and Midwestern "okey-dokey artichokey" sides. She mothered her assistants, found them dates, fixed their collars, celebrated their birthdays, and joked frequently. "Hillaryland" was a calm island in a tempestuous White House notorious for infighting and staff turnover. After three years, only two of the original staffers had left, one because her mother took ill.[48]

Hillary and her staffers originally conceived of their "shop" as a policy-making center oriented toward health care and children's issues. But as Margaret Williams acknowledged in one of her many

Whitewater depositions, the staff ended up focusing on "press work," not policy matters, given "the press interest in Mrs. Clinton, from the hats that she wears to what she says on health care."[49] As the controversies multiplied, the office would function more like a war room than a think tank.

Initially, the first lady and her staff were overwhelmed by the president's promise to submit health care legislation "within one hundred days of our taking office."[50] The Clintons claimed that some 36.6 million Americans were uninsured and a comparable number probably lacked adequate insurance. They estimated that health care was an $800 billion industry, involving as much as one-seventh of the American economy, that was desperately in need of repair.

On the campaign trail, both Clintons had emphasized health care reform as a priority. In his Democratic Convention acceptance speech, Bill Clinton offered what could be considered the Clinton haiku: "Jobs. Education. Health Care. These are not just commitments from my lips. They are the work of my life." There and elsewhere, Clinton envisioned "an America in which health care is a right, not a privilege. In which we say to all of our people: your government has the courage—finally—to take on the health-care profiteers and make health care affordable for every family." At the presidential campaign launch, back in October 1991, Clinton had "pledge[d]" that "in the first year of a Clinton Administration we will present a plan to Congress and the American people to provide affordable, quality health care for all Americans."[51]

The Clinton critique diagnosed America's health care system as too expensive, too hit-and-miss, too bureaucratic. Too many Americans were not covered by health care insurance at all, endangering their family's financial health if their actual health suffered. At the same time, too many of those covered were held hostage to the whims of midlevel cost-conscious managers with MBAs, not MDs, who were micromanaging what medicines Americans received, what procedures they needed, and how many days' recovery in a hospital their particular ailments merited.

Protecting the "60 million Americans" who lacked "adequate health insurance," the Clinton-Gore campaign manifesto *Putting People First* mourned that "the United States is the only advanced county in the world without a national health-care plan. . . . No

American family should have to go from the doctor's office to the poorhouse." Fleshing out the plan, the Democrats promised, "We are going to preserve what's best in our system: your family's right to choose who provides care and coverage, American innovation and technology, and the world's best private doctors and hospitals. But we will take on the bureaucracies and corporate interests to make health care affordable and accessible for every American."[52] This statement helps explain the ultimate failure of reform. The American health care system indeed had many strengths that millions of Americans appreciated—and would fight to retain. Millions of working people, for example, enjoyed the best medical care in the world, thanks to their union or corporate insurance. Blaming "the bureaucracies and corporate interests" was demagoguery, not policy; it might work as a short-term campaign strategy, but it offered no long-term solutions to the serious health care conundrums. Still, health care reform had been a useful campaign rallying cry. After the summertime conventions, a Kaiser Family Foundation–Harris poll estimated that Americans trusted Governor Clinton over President Bush to provide affordable health coverage for all Americans by a margin of 55 percent to 27 percent.[53]

Once in office, the Clintons struggled with the fact that twelve years after Ronald Reagan' inauguration, they now lived in a Reaganized America. Clinton was not quite ready to say it, as he would in 1996, but the era of big government was over; America's governing ideology no longer assumed that every big, complicated social problem had a big, comprehensive government solution waiting to be funded. Only 20 percent of the electorate trusted the federal government "to do what is right" always or most of the time. This historic low contrasted with the more than 70 percent of the population who had great faith in the government in 1958.[54]

Ronald Reagan had delivered a triple blow to modern government. Reagan's rhetoric made tax hikes seem like stickups while focusing American attention on the failures of Great Society programs and the idea that "guvmint," as he called it, was the problem, not the solution. At the same time, the Reagan-era budget deficits made any massive government program politically and economically perilous. Throughout the 1992 campaign, Texas billionaire Ross Perot had personified these new fears, warning that out-of-control deficit spending was "robbing future generations of their inheritance." That message resonated with the voters: Perot won nearly 20 percent of the popular vote.

Thus, Hillary Rodham Clinton tried to solve a seemingly insolvable problem in an environment that was doubly skeptical: there were doubts about her sense of propriety, and her political ideology reinforced the generalized suspicion toward government. The Clinton administration's internal polls in the spring of 1993 showed that even as Americans harbored great hopes for health care reform, 53 percent of those polled were more concerned that the government would "create new problems," versus 41 percent who most worried about inaction which would lead to higher costs and Americans continuing "to have problems with insurance."[55] Tracy Hedleten of Blue Ash, Ohio, a participant in a *Washington Post* focus group, would ask three weeks after the Clintons launched their health care plan, "When have you ever seen the government involved in anything that wasn't more red tape?"[56]

Sensitive to these risks, the Clintons recruited a collaborator for the first lady from their A-Team, an FOB (Friends of Bill) yuppie prince who had also mastered the meritocracy with a résumé as stellar as theirs. Ira Magaziner was featured with Hillary Rodham as another leading campus rebel in the 1969 *Life* magazine portrait, and like Bill, he was a Rhodes Scholar. Magaziner was a hit at the 1991–1992 Renaissance Weekend, where the Clintons and other members of the yuppie elite networked, partied, and pontificated. An über Progressive with a zealot's faith in commissions and programs, Magaziner had never met a complex system he didn't love—and didn't believe he could improve. A campaign volunteer in 1992, Magaziner had outdone both Clintons in the one important realm where they continued to feel inadequate. As a business consultant who started his own firm, he had earned millions of dollars. Explaining this appointment in retrospect, the president would explain that Magaziner "was one of the few people I knew that I thought understood the health care system and could render it intelligible to people who weren't in health care. Secondly, because he worked with me in the campaign, he understood what I thought had to be done. Thirdly, I thought Ira understood big systems, because he made quite a lot of money, several million dollars, advising corporations about what kind of changes they ought to make to meet the demands of the global economy."[57] Magaziner knew the task was daunting. He would recall bantering with the first lady about the project: "We just kind of joked about how crazy we both were to try it." Despite his misgivings, Magaziner said, "when the President of the United States says, 'I want you to do this,' you do it."[58]

A Washington novice, Magaziner worked behind the scenes, coordinating the 28 committees and 500 experts. The labyrinthine process had "working groups," "tollgates," and "clusters" established to keep the information flowing in a way that only a social reformer turned millionaire business consultant could love. Meanwhile, the first lady focused on the big picture and the political marketing. As she breezed in and out of meetings, barking orders, decisions were made too hastily. "After the meeting last evening, I talked for a moment with the First Lady to try to underline the key importance of the purchasing cooperatives," Princeton professor Paul Starr told Magaziner in early February. "And before I could finish a sentence, she said, 'But we need cost containment.' And then she ran off. . . . We need some time to talk this out." Even with the haste, the hundred-day deadline proved impossible. Spring dragged into summer and summer into fall as anticipation, frustration, and deprecation grew.[59]

Altruism and ambition fueled Mrs. Clinton's efforts. George Stephanopolous noted that this "sweeping" reform program "would save lives and prove to the world that a first lady could be a fully public presidential partner."[60] Tackling health care was ambitious. The scale of the industry, the complexity of the issues, the decades-long track record of failure to solve the problems, and Americans' newly Reaganized distrust of big government or more taxes would have scared off most poll-driven or success-oriented politicians. And the president, master politician that he was, did seem less enthusiastic about entering the morass than his wife, who was deeply committed to solving the problem. The mother in her mourned as she heard stories about kids deprived of basic treatment. The egalitarian in her bristled as she saw the inequities in the system, wherein 80 percent of Americans had access to perhaps the best health care ever offered and 20 percent were shut out. The Puritan in her disapproved of the unseemly profits the drug companies and many health care professionals enjoyed. The visionary in her shuddered while anticipating a system that would become increasingly more inefficient and expensive. And the Progressive social crusader in her trusted that a rational group of experts could design a system that would be fair, cost-effective, equitable, viable, and popular.

Yet even as Mrs. Clinton attracted praise for her mastery of detail and her poised presentations, her role complicated an already Sisyphean endeavor. David Gergen, a Republican "wise man" recruited to help stabilize the White House, found the "three-headed system for decision-making," meaning Vice President Al Gore, along with Mr. and Mrs. Clinton, inefficient and unnerving at best. All too often, "Bill people" skirmished with "Gore people" and "Hillary people."[61] Moreover, as in a dysfunctional family with three parents rather than two, decisions, once made, could be unmade by revisiting the question with one of the other principals.

This unworkable system was even more complex with the health care effort because of the fragilities of the Clinton marriage. In selecting Mrs. Clinton to head the effort, Gergen would later write, for all the president's respect for the first lady, "does anyone doubt that he also wanted to placate her?"[62] And given the seesaw dynamics between them, wherein when one soared, the other often was eclipsed, in launching Hillary Clinton, once "on top," she was "not as tethered to the other," as she should have been. "For all her idealism, she needed his political genius to succeed." Finally, all too often, people bowed and scraped around her. "She was like an extremely wealthy person with many suitors who can never be sure who is telling the truth."[63]

When she first convened the task force, Hillary acknowledged the awkwardness: "I don't want you to think because I'm the president's wife it's not OK to tell me what you think. I want everything on the table."[64] But her zeal, her temper, and her status inhibited subordinates. Too many aides wondered, "Do I want to take on the President's wife?"[65] In an era of brittle gender relations, the ambitious liberal men working for the Clintons feared that disagreeing with a woman would seem antifeminist. As a result, the leading critic among the economic advisers was the head of the Council of Economic Advisers, Laura D'Andrea Tyson, despite her relatively low standing in the pecking order. "She was one of the only people who could speak up because of the gender thing," one aide noted. "The others just felt, 'Why should we get into this?' "[66]

Less subtly, the first lady's ambiguous legal status caused trouble even before Bill released their 1,364-page Rube Goldberg scheme to restructure one-seventh of the American economy. In February, opponents filed suit charging that the first lady's presence made the task force a Federal Advisory Committee forced by a 1972 law to conduct business in public. She, after all, was not a government employee—hiring her would have violated the "Kennedy rule" against nepotism. At the same time, another federal law prevented "unpaid consultants" from serving at all.

Typically, the Clintons tried to argue both ways. The Justice Department claimed that Congress's authorization of offices and staff made the first lady the "functional equivalent of a federal government employee."[67] The president's lawyers also noted first ladies' "longstanding tradition of public service" as "advisers and personal representatives for their husbands." Yet when Republicans challenged Mrs. Clinton's health-related investments, White House counsel Bernard Nussbaum said, "the First Lady, like the President, is not covered by the conflict-of-interest statutes and regulations" applied to government workers.[68]

Republicans enjoyed their revenge. They had endured twelve years of ethical nitpicking brought on by the adversarial culture's hostility to the Establishment, the media's penchant for scandal, the Democrats' take-no-prisoners opposition to the Reagan and Bush administrations, and many Reaganites' greed or insensitivity to the changing mores about money and influence. Recalling Clinton's search for an attorney general who employed legal domestic help, one conservative jeered that "Bill Clinton, of all people, may have problems with an undocumented worker"—Hillary Clinton.[69]

The first lady's status confused the courts. In March, a federal district court judge chided the president for "precipitat[ing] a constitutional confrontation" and ruled that "the First Lady is not an officer or employee of the Federal government."[70] In June, the Washington, D.C., Court of Appeals reversed the lower-court ruling, finding that the law funding the East Wing treated "the presidential spouse as a de facto officer or employee." The president had an "implicit authority to enlist his spouse in aid of the discharge of his federal duties."

Therefore, the sunshine law did not "apply to the Task Force merely because Mrs. Clinton is a member." The court did not say whether she was subject to conflict-of-interest laws.[71]

The litigation was distracting and demoralizing. Magaziner's crafty attempts to distinguish the working group from the task force almost earned him a contempt of court citation and a perjury conviction. The ambiguous nature of the first lady's position, the new tendency to criminalize political conflict, and the Clintons' instinctive refusal to address such difficult issues directly worsened the strain. Hillary Clinton wanted the deliberations closed to the press because she remained bitter about the 1992 campaign. "In retrospect, I think that was a mistake, because it was the most inclusive legislative process in modern history," the president later said.[72] Even though the task force met with 572 different organizations in three months, frustrated reporters blasted the "secret" process. The reform-friendly *New York Times* complained that this "exercise in policy-making that affects virtually every major constituent, interest group and business . . . is largely taking place in endless meetings of working groups behind closed doors."[73] More pointedly, Mary Hinds, who worked on "opposition research," seeking dirt on Hillary Clinton for President George Bush's reelection campaign, labeled Mrs. Clinton "the Oliver North of this administration. . . . Here we have an unelected official who has no responsibility to anyone, who can make public policy in secret."[74]

"Sooner or later Hillary & Co. will have to choose: Is she Betty Crocker or Eva Peron?" one *Boston Globe* columnist teased after the District Court decision.[75] In fact, few observers in the early days of the administration doubted the copresident's power. She had a prominent seat at all key meetings. The president asked repeatedly, "What do you think, Hillary?"[76]

Hillary Clinton was supposedly Bill's backbone, the only person people feared in a White House that was charmingly nonhierarchal but infamously disorganized. "If I didn't kick Bill Clinton's ass every day, he wouldn't be worth anything," she had told one press secretary back in Little Rock.[77] Aides joked about "Hillary's Alzheimer's . . . forget everything else but remember the grudge."[78] Among the president's men—and often with the president—the overworked first lady was brisk, even ferocious. Vicious shouting matches in the middle of meetings, blurring the political and the personal, embarrassed staffers. In Arkansas, some of the state troopers who guarded the Clintons later told reporters they had hated working for Mrs. Clinton, whom they considered imperious and foul-mouthed. Rumors that the first lady threw a lamp at her husband perpetuated her reputation (although some insisted it was only a briefing book). Still reeling from the campaign, always too fearful of "the Establishment," Mrs. Clinton demanded that aides plumb the leak. The resulting White House paranoia alienated the Secret Service, accelerated a ham-handed purge of the travel office, and may have prompted a review of confidential FBI background reports that would have Republicans in 1996 scolding the Clintons for their "enemies list."[79]

Hillary Clinton, of course, dismissed the rumors and poohpoohed claims that she had much influence. She never contradicted her husband publicly and rarely acknowledged her power. "I kind of view myself in some ways as a citizen representative" on her own task force, she said, claiming she would not have a say on the final proposals—a claim that changed, of course, when she was negotiating with Congress.[80] One time in Texas, PBS's Bill Moyers asked her, "What is it like to govern?" She answered "It's been exhilarating, frustrating, eye opening." Pausing, she added, "Just to set the record straight, I'm not really governing either." Governor Ann Richards guffawed: "If you believe that, I've got a bridge I'd like to show you." And the acerbic Senate Republican leader, Bob Dole, simply called the first lady "Mrs. President."[81]

Hillary Rodham Clinton's image during those first hundred days—steely, principled, efficient, and shrewish—came straight from what one feminist scholar called the "dauntingly homogeneous bank of imagery to be drawn on whenever women look like they are stepping into the political arena."[82] It contrasted with the stumbling, temporizing, ineffectual impression Bill Clinton made. As usual, one stereotype fed off the other. As reporters mocked the president for backtracking on allowing gays to serve in the military and deserting controversial appointees, the legend of Hillary the powerhouse grew. Although she was too shrewd to admit it, on some level, Mrs. Clinton had to enjoy newspaper claims that "Hillary Rodham Clinton's first 100 days in the White House were not as rocky as her husband's, and she generally gets higher marks for her professionalism and political savvy than he does."[83] Shrewd observers worried that Mrs. Clinton's focus on health care reform "disrupted the delicate balance between the couple. Because Hillary has a real job, she cannot devote the time she once did to her husband's problems. And he has suffered as a result."[84] Feeding the legend, the president confirmed the oft-published tale that when Chelsea took ill, she told the school nurse to call her father, not her mother. Wags had Chelsea saying, "She's very busy working on health care and all sorts of other important things"; the president acknowledged he was easier to reach by phone.[85]

Intoxicated by her success and sobered by her father's stroke in March, Hillary Clinton seized her "white glove pulpit" to try to reshape American values. At the University of Texas in Austin, she demanded a "Politics of Meaning." After the Reagan-era paroxysm "of selfishness and greed . . . all of us face a crisis of meaning," she said.[86] She sought "a new ethos of individual responsibility and caring . . . a new definition of civil society which answers the unanswerable questions posed by both the market forces and the governmental ones."[87] This gambit to heal the social consequences of the 1960s revolt without repudiating its ideals culminated in May, when the cover of the *New York Times Magazine* featured an ethereal first lady dressed in white. Michael Kelly's article about her "new Reformation" was titled "SAINT HILLARY."[88]

Hillary Clinton's fusion of 1950s nostalgia, Methodist altruism, and 1960s cultural critique answered her husband's call for a "third way" between liberalism and conservatism. In college, she had wondered about being "a mental conservative and a heart liberal." Her "politics of meaning" showed that the rebels of the 1960s were moralistic, and, like most radicals, were suffused with their own nostalgic conservatism. "There's a very strange conservative strain that goes through a lot of New Left, collegiate protests that I find very intriguing because it harks back to a lot of the old virtues, to the fulfillment of original ideas," Hillary Rodham suggested in her Wellesley College commencement address in 1969.[89]

In two commencement speeches she delivered that May 1992, the first lady continued to challenge the contemporary American values system. Reflecting back on her Wellesley commencement speech's "idealism," she ruefully noted "that at 21, I was perhaps unable to appreciate the political and social restraints that one faces in the world." Still, she called for more "balance" in people's lives, more of a concern for the "we," not just the "me."[90] At the University of Michigan, she harked back to the Progressive communalism and virtuous sense of mission that shaped John F. Kennedy's call, at that university, for a Peace Corps.

At the University of Pennsylvania, Mrs. Clinton echoed Philadelphia's Ben Franklin on the issue of good citizenship, saying, "The noblest question in the world is, 'What good may I do in it?'"[91] Some, including the syndicated Hearst columnist Marianne Means, favorably compared Hillary Clinton's challenging, substantive remarks to the supposedly soporific, status quo–oriented commencement speech Barbara Bush gave as first lady at Wellesley in 1990.[92] In fact, much as her successor would do, Barbara Bush had also tried to show modern Americans how to live creatively, boldly, and morally. "You need not, probably cannot, live a 'paint by number' life," Barbara Bush had said in her address, after weeks of controversy over whether a stay-at-home mom and passive first lady was a suitable role model for modern Wellesley students. Mrs. Bush urged the graduates to "believe in something larger than yourself," to live lives filled with "joy," and "to cherish your human connections: your relationships with friends and family."[93]

Despite the scattered applause, many more in the media mocked Mrs. Clinton's flirtation with metaphysics. Many who found a kind of roguish charm in having a president who flirted with sin found a saintly first lady too priggish, too preachy, too ethereal, too grandiose. This search for a meaningful framework and the proper balance between individualism and the community, which was so important to the first lady, struck a rare flat note for her those first few months. Fast learner that she was, she retreated from that kind of rhetoric in the future, or covered it better.

This first lady fascinated reporters. *Parade* focused "an issue on one person . . . for the first time"—Hillary Clinton.[94] In May, a *People* cover story on how "Hillary Clinton—mom, wife, policy wonk—redefines the First Lady," pictured a whimsical first lady stretching back from the White House balcony—the same pose a *Time* cover story celebrating Nancy Reagan's rise used in 1985. *People* also gave Mrs.

Clinton the high compliment Mrs. Reagan only earned after four years, calling her "Her Own Woman."[95]

The White House PR people were anxious to emphasize the first lady's softer, more maternal, nonideological side. They wanted to present an average mom representing everyman—and every-woman—in the White House. "If she's considered a feminazi, then people aren't going to trust whatever her group puts out," a Democratic consultant told *Newsweek*.[96] Learning from 1992, Mrs. Clinton's people wanted to avoid the class baggage with which the first lady had been saddled. Traveling to Nebraska and Montana, an aide explained, would "assure people this is not some Eastern effete thing that's been cooked up."[97] Many of these profiles recycled a story about the first lady scrambling some eggs in the executive mansion kitchen for a sick Chelsea Clinton one night, although the ubiquity of that one story made some observers fear that it was the exception worth publicizing rather than a typical moment for this superwoman.

Hillary Rodham Clinton was too much her own woman. In public, the first lady often neglected her primary task: supporting the president. Her "politics of meaning" speech, her *New York Times Magazine* star turn, barely mentioned Bill Clinton. One poll would find that 52 percent believed she had more input into "her" health plan than he did, only 4 percent said he had more than she did; other polls would find twice as many Americans deeming her smarter than him than the other way around.[98]

Still, by dramatic margins of 72 percent to 19 percent, Americans expressed more confidence in Bill Clinton's credibility on the health care issue than in congressional Republicans.[99] Given Hillary Clinton's identification with the issue and her growing popularity in polls, this confidence reflected a joint mandate. Celinda Lake, a Democratic pollster, concluded in the spring that "voters are enormously reassured to have her in charge." "From the outset, it's been Hillary Clinton's task force," said Geoffrey Garin, another Democratic pollster. "The credibility of the plan and her credibility are now very closely tied together."[100]

The buildup culminated in September, when Mrs. Clinton testified before Congress for the still-to-be-released health care program. "This is as big as it comes. This is Eleanor Roosevelt time," one aide exulted.[101] In over 130 meetings with legislators, she had hewed to the script, "search[ing] for consensus," as Ira Magaziner put it, and emphasizing "security, cost control, prevention, quality, choice: these are non-threatening, non-aggressive middle-class themes."[102]

The first lady played the gender card. She began by saying she was "here as a mother, a wife, a daughter, a sister, a woman." She mentioned her mother and Mrs. Roosevelt repeatedly.[103] Her authoritative, fawning, and charming performance prompted a rare standing ovation. When Hillary had testified for the Clintons' Arkansas education reforms back in 1983, one legislator had smirked, "It looks like we've elected the wrong Clinton."[104] A decade later, national legislators were equally condescending. The crusty Democratic Congressman Dan Rostenkowski said, "I think in the very near future the President will be known as your husband."[105] The first lady smiled politely. Such accolades led the *New York Times* to rejoice, in a telling choice of words, that the first lady "captivated and dominated two usually grumpy House Committees."[106]

The legend of Hillary the powerhouse grew. Radio stations played a parody of Helen Reddy's "I Am Woman," anthem: "I am Hillary, hear me roar, I'm more important than Al Gore." The Speaker of the House, Tom Foley, introduced Mrs. Clinton at one event at Statuary Hall in the Capitol, saying, "This room saw the inauguration of five presidents—Madison, Monroe, Jackson, Adams and Fillmore, so first ladies have been in this room before, but none has ever brought such an important product and result of her efforts and work. None has had so large a role in the public policy of our country."[107] And, in perhaps the ultimate compliment, reporters began speculating about the first lady as a potential president.[108] A USA Today/CNN/Gallup poll asked whether Hillary Clinton seemed qualified to be president. Even though most did not want her running, a majority of baby boomers between the ages of thirty to forty-nine agreed she was qualified. "No woman has been deemed sufficiently well-known, qualified or campaign-tested for the ultimate political responsibility," a columnist for Hearst newspapers wrote. "But in a few years we will have that woman. And she already sleeps in the White House."[109]

Hillary Clinton's first year in office certainly had its traumas. In the spring, her father's stroke, extended hospitalization, and death pulled the first lady from Washington, helped delay the health care reform, and added one of life's great traumatic transitions onto an already trying transition year. In July, the shocking suicide of her close friend and trusted counsel, Vince Foster, was the kind of public-private ordeal peculiar to White House life, which so blurs the two, usually more distinct, spheres. Foster's depression, although clearly rooted in deeper personal demons, seems to have been intensified by Washington's toxic atmosphere, where, as he wrote in a note that he tore up that was found in his briefcase, "ruining people is considered sport."[110]

Either stunned by the blow, buffoonishly incompetent, or fiendishly trying to cover up the Whitewater and Travelgate messes, the first lady and her aides spent the next few days mourning their friend and mishandling the papers entrusted to him as their personal lawyer and White House counsel in ways that would haunt the Clintons for years. Conflicting stories emanated from secretaries and Secret Service personnel about who entered or did not enter the office, how long they stayed, and whether they exited with files or not. The aides themselves often gave conflicting and sometimes implausible explanations, suggesting, for example, that a rapid sequence of thirty-second and one-minute phone conversations were attempts to offer emotional support to each other rather than quick attempts to pass on messages about how to proceed. Once again, right-wing critics would exaggerate and treat allegations of misconduct like proven felonies, and the Clintons' defenders would be blind to the sloppiness and improprieties that fed the fantasies. These and other strains made the fawning cover stories and the rising polls all the more satisfying.

The president was also on a roll that autumn. In August 1992, his $496 billion deficit reduction package squeaked by Congress. In September, days before Hillary Clinton testified, Bill Clinton pitched the health care plan to Congress. When the TelePrompTer first fed him the wrong lines, his eloquent improvisation enhanced his legend as a master salesman who was smarter, swifter, and more sincere than Ronald Reagan. In November, Clinton muscled the NAFTA treaty through the Senate and rendered a moving tribute to Martin Luther King Jr. in Memphis, calling on African Americans to help stop the violence in America's cities. Bill Clinton had discovered the president's bully pulpit. He too could play politics with old-fashioned virtues.

It was, in fact, a rare moment of balance for the couple, with the two thriving and playing off each other. The Clintons planned to celebrate their triumphs at thirty-two Christmas parties in December. On 10 December, *People* interviewed the first couple for its year-end issue. The president listed all his accomplishments. Both laughed at the talk of a copresidency. Bill Clinton blasted opponents who "don't want to take on my policies, so they think they can hurt me politically by acting like Hillary has too much power or too much influence."[111] *People's* editors selected photographs of an ebullient couple at work and at play, dancing cheek to cheek under a gleaming chandelier. With Bill Clinton's popularity pushing 60 percent, and with Hillary Clinton's at nearly 70 percent, his presidency had finally hit its stride. Looking back on that period, Hillary recalled, "We thought we had a real window." She did, however, ask Bill, "what's in their arsenal now?"[112]

Although the barrage of criticism caused them to back away from the term, the Clintons had fashioned a formidable copresidency. In public, both "searched for consensus" and sought to make their power-sharing arrangement appear reasonable. In one year, the Clintons, particularly Hillary Clinton, had seemingly evolved from shape-shifters to integrated, model "human beings" for "this post-modern age," as she put it.[113] Shills for *Vogue* and feminist writers praised her as a total woman "who does it all," a model for modern women in all their complexity as they worked—if they chose to—and as they nurtured—if they pleased.[114] "For women of my generation, it's a relief to have a First Friend in the White House," the yuppie playwright Wendy Wasserstein said.[115] Unfortunately for the Clintons, this moment of triumph was fleeting. By the time their 10 December interview reached the newsstands, his presidency and their marriage was once again mired in muck. Within months, health care reform would be dead, and despite the Cassandras who said first ladies were not accountable, Hillary Rodham Clinton would effectively be fired as copresident.

Hillary Rodham Clinton was the first feminist first lady—the first to come of age during the feminist era and to embrace both the movement and the label unambiguously. Eight years in the White House also made her one of America's leading Democrats and one of the world's most famous women. Yet Mrs. Clinton has faced the modern woman's dilemma: how could she achieve fulfillment as a woman while thriving as an equal in what remains, in so many ways, a man's world? She— along with so many of her female peers—struggled to balance tradition and change, family and career, her head and her heart, her yearnings to be a genderless, equal citizen of the world and her feminine identity. Here, in 1999, finally comfortable with herself and her image, the first lady participates in a photo shoot for the White House Entertaining Book—not the kind of activity the cartoon version of the feminist first lady would partake in, but part of Mrs. Clinton's definition of the role.

Central to Hillary Rodham Clinton's identity confusion was her operatic relationship with her husband, Bill Clinton. The Clinton marriage was remarkably progressive, given Bill Clinton's reverence for his wife's intellect and their synchronicity on so many work projects. Yet in the way Hillary Clinton subordinated so much of her identity to serve her husband's career, and in Bill Clinton's pathological need to stray, their marriage was also tragically sexist and unbalanced. Here in the East Room in July 1996, as so frequently during their White House years, the Clintons demonstrate the easygoing intimacy that made Hillary Clinton one of the administration's most formidable figures.

Courtesy of the William J. Clinton Presidential Library.

After a conventional 1950s upbringing and her stint as a "Goldwater Girl" in 1964, Hillary Rodham plunged into the 1960s maelstrom during her years at Wellesley College and Yale Law School. Still, she remained a product of her puritanical, Methodist roots. She met Bill Clinton at Yale Law School. As this January 1972 photograph from New Haven shows, his bushy beard and Mountain Man look, and her heavy, dark glasses and plain-Jane look were part of the era's uniform—and would feed later criticisms of them as radical "McGoverniks."

To the dismay of many friends and relatives, Hillary Rodham followed her heart—and her boyfriend—to Arkansas after graduating from Yale Law School, then working for the congressional committee investigating Richard Nixon. After marrying in 1975, Hillary Rodham—who kept her last name—found herself frustrated by life in Arkansas and often eclipsed by her husband's career, as in this picture from Bill Clinton's swearing-in as the youngest elected governor of Arkansas—and the nation—on 9 January 1979.

Courtesy of the William J. Clinton Presidential Library.

The Arkansas first lady, who maintained her maiden name, became a partner at the Rose Law Firm, and refused, 1960s style, to adopt the Southern belle look. She proved to be most unconventional and highly controversial. Despite facing mounting political criticism, the Clintons nobly refused to exploit for political gain the birth of their long-awaited daughter, Chelsea Victoria Clinton, in March 1980. By November 1980, Bill Clinton was the youngest ex-governor in the land. For the comeback run two years later, Hillary took her husband's last name and began the first in a series of image makeovers. Somewhat disingenuously, she dismissed the whole last name brouhaha by insisting, "It meant more to them"—Arkansans—"than it did to me."

Courtesy of the William J. Clinton Presidential Library.

The 1992 presidential run was supposed to be a campaign of sweet vindication, an opportunity to leave Arkansas' smothering provincialism, and shine on the national stage that Hillary Clinton preferred. But it turned into a searing campaign as controversies festered over Bill Clinton's Vietnam-era draft finagling, his philandering, and a financial investment in vacation properties known as Whitewater. The egalitarian dreams of the Clintons' "two for one" campaign launch disappeared as Hillary Clinton found herself forced to be her husband's chief defender while also being targeted herself. Characteristically, she described what she was doing as she denied doing it, most famously during the Clintons' post–Super Bowl 60 Minutes *interview. Trying to dismiss Gennifer Flowers's claims of a long-standing affair with Governor Clinton, Mrs. Clinton huffed: "I'm not some little woman standing by her man like Tammy Wynette." Cracks like these about a country singer many working-class women admired made many perceive Hillary Rodham Clinton as a yuppie feminist, representing the worst of the 1960s and the worst of the 1980s. In fact, Mrs. Clinton was struggling to synthesize her traditional background and puritanical Methodism with the Progressive faith and idealism of the 1960s while remaining relevant in the 1980s and 1990s.*

From AP/Worldwide Photos.

While insisting on what they would call a "zone of privacy," the Clintons felt compelled to trot out their daughter Chelsea so voters would not think of them as a childless—and soulless—power couple. Here, at the Democratic National Convention, held in New York, in August 1992, the Clintons began trying to map out the one-way street they desired, wherein they exposed what they wished of their private lives when convenient while discouraging prying reporters from violating their privacy when it was inconvenient.

Courtesy of the William J. Clinton Presidential Library.

Despite the troubles, the Clintons captured the White House. Together with the new vice president and his wife, Al and Tipper Gore—shown here in 2001 at the end of the Clinton administration—the Clintons viewed their ascent as the changing of the generational guard. The baby boomers had arrived.

Courtesy of the William J. Clinton Presidential Library.

Although Democrats delighted in their new, hip young leaders, Hillary Rodham Clinton became a lightning rod for conservative concerns that the Clintons were too liberal and too countercultural. In drawing criticism that otherwise might have singed her husband, Mrs. Clinton unhappily fulfilled a role other predecessors had filled, especially Mary Todd Lincoln, Eleanor Roosevelt, and Nancy Reagan. Even the Jackie Kennedy–style hat Mrs. Clinton wore during the January 1993 inauguration and inaugural parade prompted snickers that a flying saucer had landed on the first lady's head. Hillary Clinton would struggle over the next few years, searching for a look that would suit her—a struggle paralleled by her search to define her role.

The Clintons had joined a most exclusive historical club, and some of Hillary Clinton's dilemmas were rooted in the peculiarities of being first lady, an extraconstitutional, improvised, extraordinarily public, and challenging position. Ever the good student, the new first lady devoured books about her predecessors, especially Eleanor Roosevelt. Mrs. Clinton parroted the conventional wisdom that the role of first lady is what you make of it, ignoring the unspoken but relatively clear protocols constraining first ladies—a lesson many of the women shown above at the 1997 dedication of the George H. W. Bush Presidential Library had eventually learned, but rarely admitted. Shown above, from left to right are Lady Bird Johnson, Jimmy and Rosalynn Carter, George and Barbara Bush, the Clintons, Gerald and Betty Ford, and Nancy Reagan.

Courtesy of the William J. Clinton Presidential Library.

Fueled by conventional wisdom, feminist aspirations, liberal ideology, the working protocols of their lifelong partnership, a sweeping, idealistic ambition, and a heavy dose of hubris, the Clintons set out to establish a copresidency. In the White House, a relatively old, relatively small, office building wherein real estate represented real access to power, the first lady had an office in the West Wing, close to the president's Oval Office. Back in the East Wing, the traditional headquarters of the first lady, a dedicated team of loyal aides established "Hillaryland." Many of these staffers were ideologues from Hillary Rodham's volunteer world of child advocacy and legal aid. In a tempestuous administration that would be infamous for its staff sloppiness, infighting, instability, and leaks, Hillaryland would be an island of calm, loyalty, and steadiness, although if pushed, many of these aides seemed far more loyal to the first lady than to the president.

Courtesy of the William J. Clinton Presidential Library.

The effort to reform health care tested the Clinton copresidency. Mrs. Clinton headed this initiative, which could have affected one-seventh of the American economy and every single American. Forgotten now is that both Democrats and Republicans assumed that there would be some health care reform and spent most of 1993 debating just how revolutionary the transformation would be. Ecstatic Democrats echoed the legendary "Give 'em hell Harry" slogan from President Truman's 1948 underdog win, cheering the first lady: "Give 'em health Hillary."

Courtesy of the William J. Clinton Presidential Library.

Despite the hype—and to an extent, because of the hype that may have made the Clintons too arrogant and thus too rigid at a time when Reaganized Americans mistrusted big government—the health care reform failed. Opposition to the program, discomfort with Mrs. Clinton's outsized role, and outrage at the growing Whitewater mess in an increasingly scandal-plagued White House fed a backlash against the Clintons, particularly against the first lady. As this January 1996 Thomas Oliphant cartoon of Hillary Clinton as Lady Macbeth scowling at Socks, the family cat, demonstrates, traditional sexist stereotypes further damaged the first lady's image. Mrs. Clinton's resentment of the chauvinism blinded her to the traditional gossamer shackles limiting most first ladies, which had to do with this unelected, seemingly unaccountable individual's proximity to power.

Inured by years of scandalmongering, the Clintons responded aggressively to accusations of wrongdoing. In retrospect, Mrs. Clinton and many key aides would regret their stubborn refusal to release more Whitewater-related records; this refusal led to the appointment of an independent counsel. With these decisions, rather than any health care innovations, Hillary Clinton had her greatest impact on her husband's first term. When missing Whitewater-related billing records from the Rose Law Firm mysteriously appeared in the Clintons' well-guarded private residence, Hillary Clinton was saddled with an unhappy first lady first: she became the first first lady called to testify before a grand jury. Determined not to show weakness and trying to woo the citizens doing their duty, Hillary Clinton swept into the courthouse, dressed extravagantly, smiling flamboyantly, and waving confidently at the photographers. On the basis of this divalike performance, the acerbic postfeminist writer Camille Paglia deemed Mrs. Clinton "The First Drag Queen" as the first lady learned how to embrace and exploit her celebrity status.

From Getty Images.

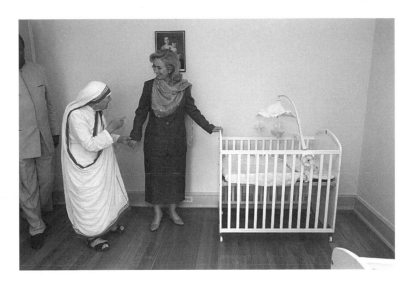

Hounded by the failure of health care reform, constant controversies, legal troubles, and the fear of losing in 1996, Mrs. Clinton retreated from the copresidency—proving that there was accountability, even for activist first ladies. Plunging into more traditional first lady–like roles, Mrs. Clinton became the nation's leading volunteer and do-gooder in chief. Here, seeking an infusion of virtue, Mrs. Clinton tours a home for infant children with Mother Teresa in June 1995.

Courtesy of the William J. Clinton Presidential Library.

Increasingly comfortable demonstrating her more stereotypically feminine side, Mrs. Clinton, pictured here with the White House pastry chef Roland Mesnier, became involved in more traditional activities. Although critics claimed that the nation's first feminist was hiding behind a new, safe Suzy Homemaker pose, Mrs. Clinton was continuing to do what she had been doing for years. Rather than making a series of false choices, she—and millions like her—were attempting to synthesize, reconcile, and harmonize their more traditional and family-oriented values with modern demands and ambitions.

Courtesy of the William J. Clinton Presidential Library.

Burned by the health care criticism, Mrs. Clinton now tended to travel only to select crowds. On such trips, her core constituents cheered wildly as if she were a rock star. In speeches before groups such as this Hermantown, Minnesota, school in 1996, Mrs. Clinton articulated a philosophy that was more traditional, more rooted, and more moderate than the "McGovernik" philosophy critics attributed to her. Still a Midwestern Methodist, Mrs. Clinton wanted to define a modern, Progressive, family-friendly morality that maintained standards while eschewing intolerance. She refused to cede to conservatives on "family values," calling for policies that "value families." Seeking a crucial middle ground on the difficult abortion issue, Mrs. Clinton echoed her husband's request that abortion should be "safe, legal, and rare."

Courtesy of the William J. Clinton Presidential Library.

In 1996, Bill Clinton enjoyed a relatively smooth reelection campaign, becoming only the third twentieth-century Democrat, along with Franklin D. Roosevelt and Woodrow Wilson, elected to a second term. When Chelsea graduated from high school in June 1997 and began preparing for a cross-country move to Stanford University, the Clintons seemed to be beginning a calmer phase of their lives and his presidency. The nation was enjoying a period of peace and prosperity. The Clinton marriage also seemed stronger, on its way to becoming yet another presidential marriage that healed during the White House years as the two became increasingly reliant on each other.

Courtesy of the William J. Clinton Presidential Library.

This illusion of marital bliss, maintained both publicly and privately despite what may have gone on in Arkansas, made the revelations of Bill Clinton's affair with a White House intern that much more unnerving—and perhaps that much easier for supporters and his spouse to dismiss. Shortly after word about her husband's friendship with Monica Lewinsky leaked in January 1998, Mrs. Clinton appeared on the Today Show *with Matt Lauer. Squelching or hiding whatever private misgivings she had, Mrs. Clinton counterattacked, blaming the Clintons' troubles on a "vast right wing conspiracy." Not since a newly widowed Jackie Kennedy retroactively labeled John Kennedy's administration in November 1963 "Camelot," had a first lady uttered a more potent—and ultimately history-shaping—phrase. Hillary Clinton's charge became a rallying cry that saved Bill Clinton's presidency.*

Courtesy of the William J. Clinton Presidential Library.

Through the winter and spring of 1998, Bill Clinton's denials continued, reinforced by Hillary Clinton's counterattacks. When physical evidence of the president's betrayal forced a presidential confession in August 1998, to maintain her own credibility, Hillary Clinton had to insist that she had believed her husband, furthering the public humiliation. For both Clintons, the crisis was simultaneously excruciatingly public and intensely private. Amid calls to resign, the president scrambled to keep his job and make amends, both publicly and privately with his wife. Meanwhile, the first lady struggled to manage her and Chelsea's emotions while also mourning her failure to jump-start the conversation about morality and family from the left, which the Clinton scandals undermined.

From Reuters/Corbis.

Ultimately, Hillary Clinton saved Bill Clinton's presidency by deciding she had no qualms about defending "my President" from the Kenneth Starr and Republican assault, even as she needed to sort out her private emotions. Plunging into the November 1998 midterm election campaign, then rallying the Democrats during the congressional fight over impeachment that December, Mrs. Clinton seemed to relish her renewed relevance and power, even while reeling from the personal blow. On 19 December 1998, after a badly divided Congress voted to impeach the president, both Clintons seemed downright giddy as congressional Democrats paraded to the White House from the Capitol. Here, the president and first lady, followed by Vice President Al Gore, House Majority Leader Richard Gephardt, and Chief of Staff John Podesta, meet with Democrats outside the White House, secure in the knowledge that, if nothing else was clear in their relationship, their enemies were wrong and had to be defeated.

From Brooks Kraft/Corbis.

The entire lamentable episode of the Monika Lewinsky scandal proved oddly liberating for Hillary Clinton. After decades of serving her husband's career, she found her own voice. After years of searching for just the right plane on which to meet the American public, and often missing it, she found a surprising popularity in the role of victimized wife and impassioned Democrat. Mastering the celebrity game, seemingly more secure in her identity, even more comfortable with her increasingly glamorous look, Hillary Rodham Clinton thrived as the Clinton presidency ended. But in addressing adoring crowds such as the one at the September 1998 Vital Voices Conference in Belfast, Northern Ireland, the one-time "copresident" was staying within the first lady's more conventional parameters. Like many of her more publicly oriented predecessors, Hillary Clinton had finally figured out how to use what Nancy Reagan called the "white glove pulpit" effectively.

Courtesy of the William J. Clinton Presidential Library.

Surprisingly, even the Clintons' relationship seemed to recover. After weeks during which they barely spoke, both reported they were talking and working together with renewed intensity and intimacy. During this June 1999 visit to a Kosovar refugee camp in Macedonia, the president and first lady hugged and squeezed and held hands with as many victims of the Balkan conflict as they could touch. In bringing joy to these people and in challenging the world not to abandon them, the Clintons were doing what they did best and living up to their highest expectations for themselves.

Courtesy of the William J. Clinton Presidential Library.

In announcing her candidacy for U.S. senator from New York, on 6 February 2000, surrounded by New York's Democratic leadership including the retiring Senator Daniel Patrick Moynihan, Hillary Rodham Clinton wrote her own happy ending to her tumultuous tenure as first lady. By ending on this bold, substantive note, Mrs. Clinton guaranteed historical comparisons with her heroine, Eleanor Roosevelt. Her compromises shrank to deviations from a master plan to be a pioneering, independent first lady. Mrs. Clinton's rocky road had a mixed impact on the office itself. Like the streak of a meteor in the sky, her ambitions, and the aspirations of the millions of women whom she inspired, illuminated the role's potential and the hopes that a high-profile, visionary, ambitious, politicized first lady can generate. But these dreams were spectacular and fleeting. If anything, the first feminist first lady legitimized the low-profile, apolitical traditionalism of her immediate predecessor and successor, Barbara Bush and Laura Bush. By highlighting the position's constraints and by causing too much tumult, Hillary Clinton's exhausting, polarizing turn as first lady blazed the trail for the calmer and more calming Laura Bush. As senator, Hillary Clinton still had critics, but her actions now had a legitimacy that they had previously lacked. She was not barraged by accusations of power hunger and Lady Macbeth–like tendencies, further proof of the peculiarities of the first lady's unelected, and still undefined, position.

Courtesy of the William J. Clinton Presidential Library.

CHAPTER 4

BACKLASH: HARRY AND LOUISE VERSUS HILLARY AND BILL

Bill Clinton and Hillary Rodham Clinton entered the White House in 1993 presuming to represent "our generation" of baby boomers. They immediately established a copresidency based on their egalitarian partnership and characterized by power sharing. Yet a year later, their copresidency was a dud, their health care scheme a dead letter, and his presidency in shambles. She would endure the lowest public approval ratings of any modern first lady until she transformed herself into a more traditional—and seemingly less formidable—public figure. And only in 1998, when she endured the humiliating revelations of her husband's frolic with a White House intern half her age, would Hillary Rodham Clinton achieve the mass popularity she craved. The failure of the Clintons' power copresidency revealed their own faults, the citizenry's rejection of their elite values, the post-Reagan backlash against big government, the national confusion about gender roles, marriage, and morality, and most Americans' peculiar but clear demands for a first lady who helps her husband with image making but avoids any suggestion of power sharing.

On Monday, 20 December 1993, Clinton's presidency unraveled. The evening before, CNN broadcast interviews with two Arkansas state troopers describing Governor Clinton's sexual escapades, charging that the president tried to silence one of their colleagues with a job offer. That day, the *American Spectator* published a lurid exposé describing a libertine governor with countless conquests, including one named "Paula," and his profane, neglected wife, who yelled during one of their many shouting matches, "I need to be f—ed more than twice a year."[1] The Clintons had "more a business relationship than a marriage," the right-wing journalist David Brock charged in a rambling article he later regretted but did not disprove.[2] Meanwhile, the *Washington Times* alleged that Clinton aides removed Whitewater files from Vince Foster's office after he committed suicide in July—ostensibly because criticism of the travel office purge depressed him. Troopergate, Travelgate, Foster-gate, and Whitewatergate merged together. As pundits merrily searched for a new scandal-connoting suffix, Clinton aides scrambled to defend their boss. Political consultant Paul Begala told George Stephanopoulos, "I think I'm going to throw up."[3]

Both Clintons were devastated. The president found it particularly hard to endure such accusations with his mother and mother-in-law visiting for the holidays. Still, he had spent his life coping with emotional messes. It was Hillary the goody-goody who was unequipped. She first tried directing her rage toward the press. On Tuesday, she reprised her campaign paranoia that "the Establishment" was after them. She charged: "I find it not an accident that every time he is on the verge of fulfilling his commitment to the American people, and they are responding—whether its forging ahead in the polls in New Hampshire or now with very high popularity—out comes yet a new round of these outrageous, terrible stories that people plant for political and financial reasons."[4] This statement did not refute the charges, but it did anticipate the first lady's aggressive counterattack during the Monica Lewinsky scandal in 1998.

The first lady's conspiratorial fears were fueled because, by an accident of fate, just as the Clintons were entering the most delicate phase of the health care reform effort, the "bimbo eruptions," the White House travel office firings, Vince Foster's suicide, and Whitewater blurred together to distract and undermine the president and first lady. The cumulative effect was devastating as each doubt or accusation reinforced the other. The mighty American media's magnifying glass—which the Clintons' ideological foes in both Little Rock and Washington positioned brilliantly, if manipulatively—ignited personal debris that in earlier times or a different context would have been irrelevant or ignored.

Even with the "Eleanor Roosevelt" buzz in September, by the fall of 1993, the health care effort had lost some momentum. Bill Clinton's first instincts were right. Just as Franklin D. Roosevelt had done with the first phase of the New Deal, just as Ronald Reagan had done with his blitzkrieg against the budget and taxes, those first hundred days in office offered a singular opportunity. But rather than pitching a visionary idea for Congress to implement quickly, Bill Clinton and his wife, months later, were offering an unreadable policy tome that had already been picked apart and become mired in controversy.

As the task force meetings dragged on, the questions proliferated and the dilemmas became more complex. The Clintons had released a number of trial balloons regarding how to pay for such an ambitious plan. Operating in a Reaganized America, well aware that George Bush's presidency imploded when Bush broke his "read my lips, no new taxes" pledge, Bill Clinton recoiled at the thought of being labeled a tax-and-spend Democrat. Talk of a European-style VAT (value-added tax) did not mollify. Suggestions about increasing "sin taxes"—sales taxes on alcohol or tobacco, usually accompanied by a puritanical Hillary Clinton sermon about the high cost of indulging—infuriated tobacco farmers, beer drinkers, and smokers, who were already feeling harassed. More broadly, to the extent that the government became intimately involved in every health care decision, conservatives feared both that individuals would lose autonomy and that government financing meant government sanction for behavior they abhorred. Funding abortion threatened to become an issue, as did difficult questions, in an era of universal health care, regarding funding "illegal aliens," mental health treatment, substance abuse programs, or medically controversial practitioners from chiropractic to acupuncture.

Like valedictorians from small Arkansas high schools who assumed they would ace their Harvard classes, both Hillary and Bill Clinton were surprised by how hard everything had become. Observers during that first year simply feared that the president had lost his confidence—that indomitable self-assurance that had repeatedly pulled him through in 1992. The first lady, who temperamentally was more brittle and less gregarious than her husband, expressed her frustration by becoming more hostile to opponents and more unyielding in negotiations. Even from the start, when the situation was less tense, Hillary Clinton had vacillated between diplomacy and demagoguery. Sometimes, playing coalition builder, she peddled sentimental stories about women endangered because they could not afford biopsies. Other times, she lambasted the drug companies and insurance industry for "price gouging, cost shifting and unconscionable profiteering."[5]

Similarly, Mrs. Clinton could be exceedingly charming with the players in the medical industry, winning fifteen rousing ovations, say, from doctors at an American Medical Association meeting by promising to free them from mountains of paperwork and the clutches of faceless HMO bureaucrats. But she was also capable of ripping into health care executives, as if their recalcitrance was the only obstacle between the flawed system of today and the Valhalla of tomorrow. "I'd say she's taken the gloves off," Gary E. Fendler, a government affairs specialist with Aetna Life & Casualty Co., said after Mrs. Clinton visited Hartford, the nation's insurance capital. "There's just no need for such a confrontational tone."[6]

Hillary Clinton's growing anger also intensified her stubbornness. In January 1994, the first lady would urge the president to wave a fountain pen during the State of the Union address, promising to veto any bill that did not guarantee universal coverage. Old Washington hands and congressional leaders knew that such a pledge would infuriate Republicans. White House adviser David Gergen begged Mrs. Clinton to drop the idea. At Gergen's urging, the Speaker of the House, Tom Foley, also implored her. Mrs. Clinton refused, and only later did Gergen realize that "it never occurred to me that I might appeal to the President." Part of the problem, of course, was that as a result of the Troopergate controversy still raging, the president of the United States was "deep in the doghouse." As Gergen recalled, "Like a bouncy golden retriever who has pooped on the living room rug,"[7] Bill Clinton was trying to mollify, not challenge, his wife. As they had in the campaign, both Clintons barked at reporters to focus on the people's business, but as the president became more sheepish and the first lady more withdrawn, reporters only became more emboldened.

The Clinton controversies proved irresistible to a "media industry" that knew "that emotional pornography is where the money is," as Professor Stephen Carter of Yale Law School complained.[8] By 1996, there would be 36 books and 1,264 articles written about Hillary Clinton and over 16,000 articles about her husband—most of them negative. In all, there had been 13 books and 149 articles about Barbara Bush and 8,771 articles about George Bush. Bill Clinton and Hillary Rodham Clinton, the king and queen of the "sixties kids,"[9] were particularly vulnerable to attack from the dyspeptic extremists who filled airtime in America's booming "political talk industry."[10] The shameless populists of talk radio and of desktop broadsides lacked the advertising pressures, nonpartisan poses, and professional scruples that tempered network shows like *60 Minutes*. When his claim that Vince Foster was murdered in an apartment Hillary Clinton owned proved false, the right-wing radio radical Rush Limbaugh shrugged, "That's what it said in the fax."[11] The rumors were overwhelming and conflicting: Hillary the witch was a lesbian, Hillary the lawyer was Foster's lover, Hillary the "feminazi" was frigid. With politics as Roman circus, the pun was the thing: "Heil Hillary," the critics would cry, as they attacked "Shrillary's" attempt to bring on "Big Sister."[12]

The hysteria and the accelerated "news cycle" spinning stories around the clock contaminated all journalism. "To make my story fresh, I have to look for an angle—and an angle, by definition, is subjective," Jack Farrell of the *Boston Globe* confessed. "And since the prevailing ethos of journalism is to be skeptical about sources of power, the angle is almost always critical."[13] Journalists in the 1950s, such as Walter Lippmann and James Reston, had played to the Washington elite; modern reporters played "to the masses" and recycled all kinds of garbage, the *Washington Post*'s media critic, Howard Kurtz, mourned.[14]

Even as she retreated, Hillary Rodham Clinton paid dearly for overstepping her boundaries. Now, she became the great scapegoat of the Clinton administration. As with Nancy Reagan, many preferred to attack the assertive, power-hungry wife who made a career out of protecting her husband than the accommodating, nimble husband who made a career out of being likable. Like Ronald Reagan, Bill Clinton projected a breezy masculinity that appealed to many men and women. Reporters depicted him as a lumbering, bearlike empath with gargantuan appetites. Bill could be soft yet tough, his bad-boy image rounding out his New Age emoting, Bubba balancing out the policy wonk. Hillary Rodham Clinton, however, was an outlaw. Her assault on traditional sex roles saddled her with the worst of the career women stereotypes somehow combined with the worst of the "Stepford wife" caricature.

Wild charges of murder, drug running, and influence peddling mixed with assaults on Hillary Clinton's liberalism. Even those who did not share Rush Limbaugh's conservatism reveled in the jokes that reversed traditional assumptions. Wags hailed the president . . . and her husband, or cited Mrs. Clinton's alleged comment after seeing an ex-boyfriend managing a gas station that, if he had stuck with her, *he* would be running the country and Bill would be pumping gas. More demeaning were the stories about trysts, separate bedrooms, and shouting matches. The opposition was so ugly, so sexist, the Clintons found it easy to dismiss their critics and revert to the aggressive and sanctimonious posture that worked in 1992.

The partisan vitriol was in some ways surprising. Bill Clinton was a moderate who should have emerged as the Republicans' favorite Democrat, balancing the budget, reforming welfare, frustrating many Democratic special interest groups. Moreover, a close look at even Hillary Rodham Clinton's core beliefs would have revealed an unexpected conservative, values-oriented streak. Some in fact theorized that it was precisely that populist centrism partisans found so threatening. From a simple power calculus, the Clintonian potential to make the Democrats dominant terrified and motivated Republicans. But beyond the politics, beyond the untrammeled mainstream media, beyond the enraged conservative media outlets and fiefdoms, beyond the fraying relations on Capitol Hill, the hatred stemmed from something deeper. To some conservatives, the president of the United States was a "queer-mongering, whore-hopping adulterer; a baby-killing, dope-tolerating, lying two-faced treasonous activist,"[15] and the first lady was "angry, bitter, obsessive and even dangerous," a zealot who had "gone to the brink of criminality to amass wealth and power."[16] The intensity of this high-tech witch hunt suggested that in addition to failing to live up to the mythic standards of Camelot, the Clintons' "copresidency" struck some of their fellow citizens as threatening and un-American. Millions still built their assumptions about American morality and destiny on the traditional sex roles.[17] The warnings about Hillary Clinton's "dangerous sexuality,"[18] the attacks on her "feminine credentials,"[19] the trivialization of her motives, the "unnatural" imagery, were classic feminist illustrations of "our gendered concept of governance."[20] John and Jackie Kennedy's Camelot, evoking the Celtic legend of the royal court that originated in the Dark Ages, was more popular than the Clintons' homegrown, egalitarian partnership.

The language reflected people who felt their way of life was under attack, who viewed the 1992 election as nothing less than a "cultural coup d'état." As Michael Joyce, the head of the conservative Lynde and Harry Bradley Foundation in Milwaukee, explained, "We're fighting the dominant liberal culture, the towering institution of an elitist liberalism which despises ordinary Americans' daily life."[21] Such perceptions raised the stakes. And both Clintons' pathological combination of self righteousness and moral sloppiness confirmed their enemies' worst fears.

Hillary Clinton could not translate the generic popularity of *Parade* magazine covers into real political power to transform America. As long as she was the president's generically influential wife—and could dodge bullets such as the Zoë Baird Nannygate fiasco—she remained popular. But once she plunged into the public partisan arena in a substantive manner, and especially because that transition coincided with another season of scandal, Hillary Clinton ran into her position's traditional limitations. Noting polls showing that 67 percent surveyed said "she's a warm person" but 62 percent said "she should not be involved in policy making," one *USA Today* headline summed it up: "HILLARY POPULAR AS FIRST LADY, NOT POLICY MAKER."[22]

Dazzled by her celebrity, charmed by her image, and impressed by her intellect, one Chicago psychiatrist at an American Medical Association meeting described Mrs. Clinton as "an unbelievably effective speaker. It was like she was giving a brilliant closing summation to an unfriendly jury." Yet had he been a juror judging her plan, he would have "voted for a mistrial"—he did not see enough evidence to sway him. Ultimately, many other Americans were charmed, fascinated, but unconvinced.[23]

Unfortunately, historians' and journalists' obsession with power misled Hillary Clinton during her opening tutorials. Having learned that "Hillary's Merely the Latest in a Long Line of Partners who Pitch in," or that "Before Hillary, There was Eleanor," she underestimated the delicacy of her new position.[24] Most modern historians, when they bothered paying attention to first ladies, ended up justifying the importance of the subject by constructing a narrative of ever-expanding powers to match the ever-growing acceptance of women in American society and politics. Edith Wilson's role as "Mrs. President" when Woodrow Wilson suffered a series of strokes in 1919 often served as the great aberration of the premodern presidency and the supposed harbinger of future power. Most modern narratives were rooted in the larger-than-life heroics of Eleanor Roosevelt, who certainly did create all kinds of precedents and revolutionized the role. Thereafter, and especially with the rise of feminism, it was easy to create the march of first lady firsts. Jackie Kennedy became the first first lady to captivate Americans with a prime-time special, her televised tour of the White House. Lady Bird Johnson became the first first lady to lead a focused, substantive, policy-oriented crusade with her beautification campaign. Betty Ford became the first first lady to plunge into the difficult controversies surrounding feminism and the sexual revolution. Rosalynn Carter became the first first lady since Eleanor Roosevelt to testify before Congress for a particular piece of legislation, when she lobbied for a mental health bill. Even a traditionalist like Nancy Reagan played an important role in her husband's administration, be it pushing her conflict-averse husband to fire people she deemed disloyal or encouraging him to make peace overtures to the Soviets.

In fact, the story was more complicated and contradictory. Many of the most popular first ladies, such as Mamie Eisenhower, Jackie Kennedy, and Barbara Bush, avoided policy entanglements as much as possible. The first ladies who plunged into policy matters and political fights encountered criticism and often had to retreat. Betty Ford's candor about sex delighted reporters and liberals but may have helped alienate Gerald Ford's all-important conservative base. In the final year of the Carter administration, as Rosalynn Carter emerged as a power, she seemed to eclipse her hapless husband. And Nancy Reagan had to fight her "dragon lady" image by tackling a safer, more "first lady–like" concern: leading Americans to "Just Say No to Drugs."

Rather than learning about the peculiarities of the first lady's position from the torrent of criticism that activist first ladies attracted, it became an article of faith among first ladies and most of their chroniclers that criticism just came with the job. The historian Blanche Wiesen Cook, promoting her new Eleanor Roosevelt biography, offered encouraging advice to the new first lady, quoting Mrs. Roosevelt's counsel in June 1936 that "every woman in political life needs to develop skin as tough as rhinoceros hide."[25] At a dinner in December 1992, Rosalynn Carter offered similar advice, telling Hillary Clinton, "You're going to be criticized no matter what you do, so be criticized for what you think is best and right for the country."[26] Echoing this dangerous inability to learn from critics, Mrs. Clinton would say, "If you lived your life trying to make sure that nobody ever criticized you, you would probably never get out of bed—and then you'd be criticized for that."[27]

The Clintons united in rage. Theirs was the angriest administration since Richard Nixon's. Both the president and first lady ranted repeatedly against aides, reporters, and each other. "The questions *won't* stop," Clinton bellowed at George Stephanopolous, who suggested releasing some Whitewater information to mollify reporters. "They'll always want more," he mourned. "No president has ever been treated like I've been treated."[28]

Instead of seducing their New Class cohorts, the Clintons froze out reporters. The first lady was particularly hostile. "Hillary Clinton is the first First Lady to have a legitimate policy role in the Administration, and she is the first one I have covered out of five who has totally ignored and avoided the White House press corps,"[29] ABC's Ann Compton complained in February 1994. Mrs. Clinton avoided interviews, often barred reporters from her plane, and bristled if they approached. Naturally, reporters retaliated.

Although first ladies from Mary Todd Lincoln to Nancy Reagan had triggered various controversies over the years, Hillary Rodham Clinton was the first first lady ensnared in her husband's scandals. Traditionally, husbands shielded their wives from the occasional high crime or misdemeanor. The Watergate revelations, for example, shocked Pat Nixon because the vulgar and scheming Richard

Nixon she heard on tape was not the courtly and shy husband she knew; and despite all her brushes with the press, Nancy Reagan was never besmirched by involvement with the Iran-Contra scandal.

By contrast, many of the Clintons' transgressions were cooperative ventures. Hillary Clinton may have been the one eventually hauled before the Whitewater grand jury, but the alleged cover-up first concerned her husband's sins as governor—and needed obscuring because of his 1992 presidential campaign. Private citizens are free to enter into all kinds of business arrangements for all kinds of reasons every day. At bottom, the Whitewater case began with reporters and investigators wondering about possible quid pro quos because Bill Clinton was the governor of Arkansas and his partner, James McDougal, ran an ill-fated, government-regulated savings and loan. Only later was Hillary Clinton's legal work targeted.

By 1994, Whitewater became largely Mrs. Clinton's problem. As a partner in the Rose Law Firm, earning more than her husband, she had been the "boss" of the Clinton money. Moreover, she was the one who represented Jim McDougal's bank and worked on the fishy Castle Grande real estate deal. She knew her position was precarious—and she may have realized just how much embarrassing information could emerge. Deputy Treasury Secretary Roger Altman noted that Mrs. Clinton "doesn't want [an independent counsel] poking into 20 years of public life." As a result, she stonewalled. She opposed creating a special prosecutor and repeatedly misled investigators. Unfortunately for the first lady and her husband, in America's scandal-sensitive culture, and with well-financed and furious conservatives encouraging reporters and prosecutors, her protective lawyerly instincts caused great political damage. "It's not even a scandal—it's not a scandal," she said, revealing a Nixonian tendency to repeat untruths. It was simply "a failed land transaction."[30]

Travelgate, too, fell more heavily on her. Bill Clinton's image as a tough pol and effective administrator could possibly have been enhanced by patronage power plays in the travel office, let alone Clinton's claim that the White House travel office's no-bid contracting and financial mismanagement required fixing. In fact, FBI reports confirmed the accusation, identifying at least $50,000 in mishandled money. But news that the first lady demanded the firings of longtime staffers to get "our people in" would prove she was the

"yuppie wife from hell." For that reason, she had a White House lawyer tell the General Accounting Office that she "had no role in the
decision to terminate the employees"—even though aides would
testify of fearing "there would be hell to pay if" they ignored her
brusque instructions,[31] which to some was the Hillary haiku: "We
need our people in. We need the slots."[32]

Even more embarrassing was the revelation that this daughter of
the 1960s, this aspiring philosopher appalled by Reaganite "greed,"
made $99,537 in speculative cattle futures off a $1,000 investment in
nine months, thanks to well-placed friends in the commodities market. "It is the curse of the '60s generation to be continually judged
by what they said and believed at 19 or 20 years old," the columnist
Ellen Goodman sighed.[33] Still, just as the Clintons, and most especially the first lady, were exhorting Americans to think communally
and act idealistically, the accusations rankled in particular.

At one town meeting in Charlotte, North Carolina, on 5 April
1994, the president became increasingly enraged as the people pum-
meled him with questions. First a questioner asked, "Mr. President,
with recent news reports about the first lady's cattle futures earnings
and with all these Whitewater allegations, many of us Americans are
having a hard time with your credibility. How can you earn back our
trust?" The next question was, "Mr. President, are you one of us middle class people, or are you in with the villainous money-grubbing
Republicans?" That one-two-punch led to the moderator's follow-
up, which also struck at the core of the Clintons' political identity
and public image: "You pledged with your administration an administration that would work hard and play by the rules. There are analysts, however, that feel in terms of Mrs. Clinton's investment in the
commodities, that that investment was not handled by the rules. In
fact, it appears to them it was given preferential treatment to protect
her from any potential loss."[34] Sputtering "it's just not true" five times
when giving the final answer, Clinton fumed: "So it's just not true
that she did anything wrong or that I did anything wrong. And if we
did, that's what we've got a Special Counsel for. And we've given him
all the information. And everybody that's reviewed it said we haven't
behaved like previous Presidents, we haven't stonewalled, we haven't
backed up, haven't done anything. We've just given him the information. Everybody that's looked at this has said we've been very open

with this Special Counsel. So let him do his job and let me be President. That's what I think we ought to do."[35]

By the year 2000, such interactions would be perceived through the color-coded prism of red versus blue America. Coming from Arkansas, a quintessentially red (traditionalist) state, but the hero of yuppie, cosmopolitan, blue America, Bill Clinton may have been the late twentieth century's most effective purple politician, appealing to Americans across the divide. Hillary Clinton was much more of a blue icon, despite her Arkansas voting address. But the questioners revealed that much of this color coding was reductionist and simplistic. Middle-class anxieties and fears that the superrich and the yuppies played by different rules transcended regional variations. Many of the values clashes were class driven, as was the opposition against the Clintons in general. Critics of Hillary Clinton and the health care plan in particular were most effective when exploiting America's often-unspoken but omnipresent class divides.

Hillary Clinton's refusal to come clean, due partly to her sanctimony and partly to her legal training, undermined her moral, political, and legal standing. Just as Iran-Contra was a peculiarly conservative scandal, with legal niceties sacrificed on the altar of excessive patriotism, Whitewater was peculiarly liberal, with legal niceties sacrificed for the sake of reform. Hillary Clinton and her aides set off the classic post-Watergate tripwires. The possible crimes of the cover-up—suborning prejudice and obstructing justice—would overshadow the original sins. In the media's "gotcha" culture, where reporters did not distinguish between high crimes and misdemeanors, most especially among veterans of the Nixon administration, the irony of Hillary Clinton's role investigating Watergate delighted them and erased any sense of proportion. One cartoon showed a blonde woman in a suit with jowly cheeks, flashing a "V for Victory" sign—"Hillary Rodham Nixon."[36]

There was something terribly romantic about the Clinton scandals. Whitewater and Travelgate offered an ironic tribute to the Clintons' teamwork. The more Americans learned about their lives—and their sins—the clearer it became that the Clintons shared a vital and loving, if complicated and unconventional, marriage.

Sadly, rather than health care reform, Hillary Clinton's determination to stonewall on Whitewater may have been her most significant contribution to the first Clinton administration. "If a genie offered me the chance to turn back time and undo a single decision from my White House tenure, I'd head straight to the Oval Office dining room on Saturday morning, December 11, 1993," George Stephanopolous would write. The night before, White House counsel Bernard Nussbaum, the Clintons' private attorney David Kendall, and Mrs. Clinton decided to reject the *Washington Post*'s request to review Whitewater-related documents. Looking back, Stephanopolous saw this as the moment when the appointment of an independent counsel, and thus the eventual injection of Kenneth Starr into the Clintons' lives, became inevitable. The media suspicion grew out of control, as would the ever-expanding mandate of the special prosecutor, which eventually encompassed non-Whitewater questions such as Clinton's behavior during the Paula Jones sexual harassment suit and his actions hiding the Monica Lewinsky affair. Alas, the loyal underling mourned, "on this issue, Clinton wasn't commander in chief, just a husband beholden to his wife. Hillary was always the first to defend him on bimbo eruptions; now he had to do the same for her."[37]

Throughout the winter of 1994, the revelations oozed out, the Clintons' popularity softened, and their health care initiative died. Hillary took out her fury on conservative Democrats and members of the medical establishment who dared to differ with her. Compromise became impossible. Both Clintons' political fumbles and a shrewd, multimillion-dollar lobbying effort turned the great health care debate into a political lynching. When Bill Clinton spoke about "managed competition" in 1992, it was a deliciously ambiguous phrase. Few people knew what he meant, and as one Heritage Foundation policy analyst explained, liberals could get excited about a national management project, while conservatives were reassured by talk of competition.[38] But four months after the great health care program debut, when Hillary Clinton promised health care "for all," or "insuring the uninsured," more and more Americans wondered "how much?" When she talked about "purchasing cooperatives," "managed care," and "health care alliances," Americans started thinking "rationing." When she talked about "a health security card" and "gatekeepers," more and more Americans feared huge, unwieldy Big Brother bureaucracies.

As the Clintons lost control of the health care debate, the two powerful streams in modern American ideology that defeated the copresidency merged. Cartoons of the "Evil Queen" offering up a Pandora's box of "Socialized Medicine" linked ancient and modern obsessions about government power and powerful women. Partisan Republicans and jilted reporters described an out-of-control, crusading radical feminist and her henpecked, secretly liberal husband imposing another arrogant, expensive Great Society failure on the American people. "NATIONAL HEALTH CARE: THE COMPASSION OF THE IRS! THE EFFICIENCY OF THE POST OFFICE! ALL AT PENTAGON PRICES!" one bumper sticker seen in 1994 proclaimed.[39] This crude caricature encapsulated many of the antigovernment themes developed in the 1980s and demonstrated just how successful the Clintons' opponents had been in transforming the public debate.

In fact, the turnaround was stunning. Throughout the fall of 1993, Republicans were still offering alternative programs, thanking the Clintons for raising the issue, and insisting that the debate did not center about whether to reform health care, only how.[40] But the Clinton controversies, congressional counterattacks, and media carping gradually undermined the effort as well as both Clintons' popularity. Emboldened, Republicans began following the ideologues rather than the moderates. "There has been almost total surrender amidst the largest power grab in U.S. history," former education secretary William Bennett had complained in October 1993.[41] On *Meet the Press,* the Republican Congressional leader Newt Gingrich denounced the plan as "the most destructively big-government plan ever proposed."[42] Gingrich, Bennett, and others led a sustained counterattack, spurred on by conservative activist William Kristol's clever, deflating slogan: "There is no health care crisis."[43]

Most dramatically, health insurance industry executives hired advertisers who created a fictional couple to balance out the presidential couple. In a $20 million advertising campaign, compounded by all the free media coverage it generated, the American people met Harry and Louise, two middle-class Americans struggling with their bills, celebrating Thanksgiving, going to the office—all the while debating the health care reform. In one commercial, the announcer warned: "Things are going to change, and not all for the better. The government may force us to pick from a few health care plans designed by government bureaucrats." "They choose," Harry then says, and his wife chimes in, "We lose." In another, Louise tells Harry: "There's gotta be a better way." Furious—and reflecting just how effectively the Harry and Louise message had penetrated—Mrs. Clinton snapped in November that the insurance companies "have the gall to run TV ads that there is a better way, the very industry that has brought us to the brink of bankruptcy because of the way that they have financed health care."[44] Speaking of Harry and Louise, Ben Goddard, the president of the agency that invented them, noted, "These are people" whom average Americans "feel comfortable with; they might invite them to a Christmas party."[45]

Liberals and Democrats tried to mobilize, but no reply was as effective as the "Harry and Louise" onslaught. One wave of full-page advertisements in the *New York Times* and elsewhere tried to reverse polarities, claiming that all the "attacks on Hillary Clinton have less to do with Whitewater . . . and more to do with her effective advocacy of an issue this country cares about—health care." Boldly proclaiming: "WE INTERRUPT THIS NEWSPAPER TO GIVE YOU THE FACTS!" the ad refuted Whitewater-related charges, endorsed the health care initiative by begging "NOW LET'S GET BACK TO BUSINESS" and confirmed that the whole issue was exceedingly personal by declaring: "WE ARE PROUD OF HILLARY RODHAM CLINTON." The ad highlighted the historian Blanche Wiesen Cook's assessment: "I DON'T THINK THERE IS A FIRST LADY WHO HAS BEEN TREATED AS RUDELY AND MEANLY, EXCEPT FOR ELEANOR ROOSEVELT."[46] An ad hoc group of "Hillary People" funded the initiative, including Professor Cook, Franklin D. Roosevelt III, Mrs. Clinton's old friend Sara Ehrman, feminist political operatives such as the Democratic activist Ann F. Lewis and EMILY's List founder Ellen Malcolm, celebrities such as Tony Randall and Joanne Woodward, and wealthy supporters such as Mr. and Mrs. Walter Kaye, of New York, who would be instrumental in getting the first lady's office to endorse one Monica Lewinsky's application to become a White House intern.

As the Clintons and their allies seethed, the ground gave way. The November 1993 off-year elections defeated some leading liberals such as New York City's mayor, David Dinkins, and New Jersey's tax-raising governor, Jim Florio. Extensive exit polling showed concern about crime soaring and concern about health care plummeting—as was confidence in the Clintons. For the first time in some polls, a majority, 52 percent, agreed that Mrs. Clinton "has too much influence over her husband. More ominous, when asked to choose between two conclusions for a sentence beginning, "The more I hear about Clinton's health care plan . . . ," 53 percent said, "the less I like it," whereas only 41 percent said, "the more I like it."[47] The *Washington Post* noted that approval from the plan was shrinking "from 56 percent at the time Clinton introduced it in September, to 51 percent last month and 46 percent now. Disapproval has climbed from 24 percent to 39 percent and now to 43 percent." A large majority feared paying more for health insurance, and the margin of those who believed the quality would improve was dwindling, "from 31 points in a September poll to 12 points" in November.[48]

By February 1994, Mrs. Clinton was playing "tough cop," targeting insurance companies, drug firms, and private hospitals with puritanical fury. "We're confusing the fact that we have the finest physicians and hospitals in the world with the fact that we have the stupidest financing system for health care in the world," she charged. "You know, the vast majority [of waste] comes from the private sector. . . . It's also rife with fraud, waste and abuse." Still, she recognized the post-1980s zeitgeist to insist, after bashing it: "What we're really trying to do is build on the private sector. This is not a government run health care plan."[49]

As the failure loomed larger, the rhetoric became tougher and more focused on that vague, easily bashed bugaboo of modern American politics, the special interests. "They want to turn back the clock to a time when the rich were taken care of, the poor were subsidized, but everybody in this country who works hard for a living, plays by the rules, makes a contribution, [was] being forgotten in Washington," the first lady would fume in July.[50] "It's unclear what the White House strategy is, to cast blame and identify villains or to forge a bipartisan consensus," said Pamela G. Bailey, president of the Healthcare Leadership Council. "We have very much seen mixed signals over the last few weeks."[51] In March, a Wall Street Journal/ NBC News poll found that "almost half of those questioned said they don't like the Clinton health care plan, but when told of its details—without identifying it by name—three-quarters said it had appeal." The Clintons used the survey to encourage Democrats on

Capitol Hill to communicate the details of the plan more effectively. What the Clintons missed was that now, their embrace of the plan harmed it rather than boosting its chances for success.[52] Showing just how personal the opposition could get, the *Washington Post*'s Jodie Allen, noting the decision to send Chelsea Clinton to the exclusive Sidwell Friends private school, asked, "Does anyone seriously believe this will work? Are the president and his wife, who declined to entrust the education of their child to their local government, really willing to let it take over the major role in deciding their health care options? Are you?"[53]

By April, the postmortems had begun. One consultant who worked on the health care task force initially declared the entire exercise "a waste of time." Arthur Caplan, a bioethics professor at the University of Minnesota, called it "too big, too secret, too bureaucratic, too isolated, too rushed, too eggheady." Robert Moffit of the conservative Heritage Foundation sneered, "It was the '60s kids doing their research project."[54]

Hillary Rodham Clinton became the rare first lady who was less popular than her husband. From February to March 1994, his approval rating dropped 11 points, to 47 percent approving, 45 percent disapproving.[55] Hillary Clinton's unfavorability rating soared from 29 percent in February to a plurality of 42 percent in March. Even when Bill Clinton's numbers would rise slightly beginning in January 1995, hers would continue to plunge.

Mourning the loss of her health care program and her tarnished reputation, Mrs. Clinton did what any self-respecting yuppie would do: she blamed others. In March 1994, Mrs. Clinton reflected on "the learning process you go through when you've never been accused of doing anything wrong before." Wrapping three excuses in one when answering a question about the mishandled Vince Foster papers, she said, "I think that mistakes were made along the way in handling this. I have learned a lot about the needs of the media and how they kind of make stories important. I suppose that in today's atmosphere any unanswered questions are going to be grist for the mill." And as for the critics of her policy role, she ever so delicately accused them of sexism, saying, "People have been doing that to women in this position since Martha Washington. . . . I look at what was said about Eleanor Roosevelt. There's always the possibility that no matter what you do you're going to be criticized. I do think that the fact that I am involved in an issue [health care] of such magnitude with so many interests at stake has raised the visibility of my role and has caused some to question it for their own purposes."[56]

Republicans assembled the modern politician's torture chamber of overlapping congressional and criminal investigations. Being an FOB, and especially a Friend of Hillary, seemed more a curse than a blessing. Vince Foster was dead. Webster Hubbell was on his way to jail. Bernie Nussbaum resigned in disgrace in March. Margaret Williams and other loyalists would be saddled with six-figure legal bills and threatened with indictment for their roles in handling the Foster papers, misleading investigators, or simply having too close a view of the legal train wreck. Given the prosecutors' aggressiveness, even innocents hired lawyers before testifying. The journalist Joe Klein, recalling the destructive couple from *The Great Gatsby*, would call Bill and Hillary Clinton "the Tom and Daisy Buchanan of the Baby Boom Political Elite": "They smashed up lives and didn't notice," Klein wrote.[57] The Clintonistas took up the plaintive post-acquittal cry of Ronald Reagan's first secretary of labor, Raymond Donovan, "Where do I go to get my reputation back?"[58] Still, Hillary Clinton's people did not abandon her. They circled their wagons around their boss, muttering about the barbarians outside and Bill's "white boys" down the hall. They were so committed to Hillary Clinton that Bill Clinton's aides often had to remind them that the main goal was to serve the president, not his wife.

Surprisingly, from all indications—and it was an incredibly porous White House, with staffers as garrulous as their commander in chief—Bill and Hillary Clinton pulled together during the crisis. They still had their eruptions and tensions, especially when Paula Corbin Jones filed a sexual harassment suit against the president in May 1994, prompted by the Troopergate article's vague allusion to a May 1991 incident alleging that Governor Clinton crudely propositioned a government worker named Paula. Nevertheless, the Clinton marriage strengthened during those first difficult years in office. They took refuge in Chelsea and in each other. To the extent that both suffered from some of Hillary Clinton's sins, their mutual accounts were better balanced. "I do not believe for a moment that she has done anything wrong," Bill Clinton would say about his wife. "I have . . . I . . . I . . . just

. . . ," he faltered and chose to speak generally rather than specifically: "if the rest of the people in this country . . . had a character as strong as hers, we wouldn't have half the problems we've got here."[59]

On 24 March, the president convened a prime-time news conference to stop the hemorrhaging. He offered a slippery New Age apology. He had learned "that there may or may not be a different standard than I had seen in the past, not of right and wrong; that doesn't change, but of what may appear to be right or wrong. And I think, that you'll see that, like everything else, this administration learns and goes on." As for his controversial wife—it was time for another makeover. One month later, on 22 April 1994, Hillary Rodham Clinton donned a sensible pink suit and met reporters in the cozy confines of the State Dining Room. She wanted to put this "embarrassing" money-losing affair that "keeps being beaten like the deadest horse there is . . . into a proper perspective." She echoed Bill Clinton's postmodernist apology by explaining that her commitment to "measuring up to the standards you set for yourself" and her "sense of privacy . . . led me to perhaps be less understanding than I need to of both the press and the public's interest as well as right to know." The problem was one of appearances and access. She painted a homey picture of her father teaching her "the stock tables" and, like all members of her elite, defined her money-making ploys as attempts to "create some financial security for our family." Republicans speculated for greed; Hillary Clinton and her pals did it for their children's college educations. Always keen, she said people misunderstood her conflicting statements, because "I've been traveling, and I'm more committed to health care than anything else I do."

At one point, the crisp yet warm first lady joked that her "zone of privacy" was being "rezoned." The change was more dramatic than that. As she abandoned the copresidency, she played shamelessly to working women, especially the women reporters paid to cover her. "It's a little difficult for us as a country maybe to make the transition of having a woman like many of the women in this room, sitting in this house," she said. "So I think the standards or to some extent, the expectations of the demands have changed."[60]

Mrs. Clinton had to know that this Friday afternoon press conference, held as Richard Nixon lay dying, would not galvanize the public. What NBC's Andrea Mitchell called an "unprecedented extraordinary performance" was directed at reporters.[61] Hillary Rodham Clinton was ready to take on the job as first lady. The new image would mollify the 49 percent who thought she had too much power and the 62 percent who thought she should not make policy. Back in 1982 at the Gridiron Press Club, Mrs. Reagan sang a satirical song, "Second Hand Rose," proving she was hip by making fun of her penchant for borrowing designers' clothes; twelve years later, Mrs. Clinton had to prove to reporters she was an old-fashioned Midwestern girl in a mixed-up, modern world.

Hillary Clinton's public sangfroid amazed White House staffers. "Whenever I go out and fight I get vilified, so I have just learned to smile and take it," she sighed. "I go out there and say, 'please, please kick me again, insult me some more.' You have to be much craftier behind the scenes, but just smile." She had learned this technique from her husband, who, aides noted, was "the master of the public smile that masks private rage."[62] Still, in the privacy of the Executive Mansion, both Clintons had to fight off self-pity. Mrs. Clinton simply stopped watching television news or reading most newspapers. The news summaries her staff prepared offered a sanitized roundup of media reports concentrated on the issues.

On 26 September 1994, the Senate majority leader, George Mitchell of Maine, announced to reporters, "Under the rules of the Senate, a minority can obstruct the majority. This is what happened to comprehensive health insurance reform." Republicans in the House and the Senate had made it clear that "they will oppose any health care bill this year, modest or not, bipartisan or not." The system had worked if you were a Newt Gingrich Republican and had failed miserably if you were a Clinton Democrat. Ultimately, Mitchell's assessment was that "the combination of the insurance industry on the outside and a majority of Republicans on the inside proved to be too much to overcome."[63] In truth, the divided Democratic party, with as many as 100 House representatives demanding an even bolder reform than the Clintons' plan, did not help. And as the Harvard sociologist Theda Skocpol would argue, the Clinton plan itself had boomeranged. By incorporating a heavy layer of regulation—trying to cut costs and avoid raising taxes—the Clinton plan offered an easy target to conservatives, who had as much fun combating regulations—meaning big government—as taxes.[64]

CNN's Bill Schneider, demonstrating what Professor Skocpol called his willingness "to articulate the conventional opinions of the day, even if they are 180 degrees opposite to what they earlier were," blamed the presidential couple. "The Clinton administration displayed awesome political stupidity," he insisted. "It turned health-care reform over to a 500-person task force of self-anointed experts, meeting for months in secret, chaired by a sinister liberal activist and a driven First Lady. Who elected them? They came up with a 1,300-page document that could not have been better designed to scare the wits out of Americans. It was the living embodiment of Big Government—or Big Brother."[65]

In November 1994, the Democrats experienced a loss even more devastating than the loss of health care: they lost the House of Representatives for the first time in forty years. Representative Newt Gingrich's Contract for America, calling for smaller government, succeeded, in many ways, as a contract on the Clintons and their health care system. Shortly before the election, beginning to anticipate the scale of defeat—and revealing the elitist condescension that helped explain the defeat, the Massachusetts congressional Democrat Barney Frank would shake his head and sigh: "The voters are no bargain."[66]

When Hillary Rodham Clinton offered her own mea culpa for the health care fiasco, blaming a "demonization of the Health Security Act," she missed an essential point. The failure of national health insurance legislation was also a judgment on her role as first lady. She, too, had been demonized. Contrary to popular belief, the position of first lady is politically treacherous. Even when popular, first ladies rarely win votes. The common wisdom tends to focus on first ladies' successes, celebrating Eleanor Roosevelt's Progressivism, Lady Bird Johnson's beautification campaign, and Betty Ford's candor. This bipartisan trinity offers palatable heroines to American women, feminists and traditionalists alike. Furthermore in our media-saturated modern polity, we tend to confuse fame with popularity, and first ladies certainly are famous. First ladies consistently top lists of America's most admired women, and they often score higher in popularity polls than their husbands, be they as outspoken as Betty Ford or as seemingly deferential as Barbara Bush.

And yet a closer look at first ladies in the twentieth century reveals that they often lost more votes than they won. We tend to forget the curses hurled at Eleanor Roosevelt, the tomatoes pelted at Lady Bird Johnson. Few Americans will vote for a president because they like his wife—but many more refuse to vote for him if they dislike her, as Gerald Ford discovered after Betty Ford's controversial candor about the Ford family's sexual mores. Similarly, few Republicans, even if they liked Mrs. Clinton, said they were willing to vote for her husband, but millions of Americans refused to vote for him because of her. During the course of the health care debate, Hillary Rodham Clinton came to personify Americans' fears that the president had a more liberal agenda than the one he initially revealed. The *New Republic* analyzed the documents released by Mrs. Clinton's health care task force and deemed the plan creeping "Rodhamism"[67]; Rush Limbaugh and his ilk pounded "Hillary" day after day. Mrs. Clinton was demonized, and the health care bill stalled.

The health care debate also tapped a wellspring of public anger at Mrs. Clinton's own duplicity. First ladies have always had to tread carefully because of their proximity to power without an electoral mandate or a constitutional limit. By the 1992 Democratic National Convention, Hillary Clinton—as she was known at the time—had pulled back from her early promises that voters would be getting two leaders for the price of one. Barbara Bush addressed the Republican National Convention, but Hillary Clinton stayed quiet, having traded in her power suit for an apron, her scarves for a chocolate-chip cookie recipe. Only after her husband's victory did she reemerge with her maiden name and her corporate look intact.

The 1994 Clinton collapse was as dramatic as Richard Nixon's Watergate-driven fall in 1973, Lyndon Johnson's Vietnam stumble in 1968, and Harry Truman's Korea, communism, and corruption troubles in 1950. In November, when the Republicans recaptured Congress, the rout was complete. Congressman Newt Gingrich had cleverly nationalized the elections with his Contract for America, so that even when voters repudiated individual Congress members by slim margins, Republicans could claim an anti-Clinton mandate. "I just don't know what to do. I just don't know what works anymore," Hillary Clinton sighed. "I don't trust my own judgment.

Everything I do seems not to work."[68] The president of the United States would soon whine that he was still relevant, while his wife retreated into the land of safe projects, foreign travel, and soothing nostrums. "A good wife isn't always advising," a humbled Margaret Williams confessed.[69]

CHAPTER 5

A STRATEGIC RETREAT?

It was a very public, very personal failure for a woman used to achieving great success. Although she shrugged it off in public, the venom shocked Hillary Rodham Clinton. On a trip to Seattle, protesters shouted "Go Home, Hillary" and waved signs saying "Heil Hillary." "It was one of the most hate-filled crowds I've ever seen," said Neel Lattimore, Mrs. Clinton's deputy press secretary.[1] "I seem to be portrayed in one extreme or another. I don't understand why I have such problems with my image," the first lady sighed.[2]

As the postmortems for the health reform initiative proliferated, the conventional wisdom blamed the first lady's failures as part of the explanation. Her strategy and her rhetoric had been too rigid, too demagogic, too harsh, too unforgiving. Her task force had been too detailed, too wonkish, too secretive, too statist. One columnist, Elizabeth Auster, refused to frame the failure as a feminist issue or as a first lady issue. Rather, Auster argued, Hillary Clinton's failures were personal, reflecting an inability "to transcend her inexperience." Portraying the first lady as an incompetent and unelected leader, Auster noted, "From the obsessive secrecy of the task force she gathered to write the plan, to her periodic moralistic volleys about the rightness of her approach and the bankruptcy of her opponents, she has shown a blindness to the importance of building consensus, of including rather than excluding, of listening respectfully rather than shooting off impatiently. These are forgivable failings in a social reformer who hopes to stir up debate at any cost. But they are fatal flaws in a leader who hopes to unify and deliver."[3] Years later, in thinking about the defeat, Mrs. Clinton herself would admit—framed in her characteristic self-improvement mode—"I learned some valuable lessons about the legislative process, the importance of bipartisan cooperation and the wisdom of taking small steps to get a big job done."[4]

As in so many dimensions of White House life, the institutional and the personal blurred. The program had been far too grandiose and complex, given the growing American disillusionment with Lyndon Johnson's grandiose, complex Great Society programs. The Clintons did not acknowledge that they were defying the prevailing political winds, given a Reaganized America's mistrust of big government. The Clintons' rhetoric about the intense and ever-growing health care crisis also never recognized the anomaly of American health care: it worked beautifully for millions of blue-collar workers protected by unions or effective corporate insurance plans. As a result, it was not clear just who needed what, and millions of citizens from across the political and class spectrums were committed to keeping benefits they enjoyed and the status quo, if it suited them. In such an environment, the Clintons' refusal to compromise only made things worse. Looking back on that time, presidential adviser David Gergen would blame both Clintons, asking of the president, "Might he have passed a bipartisan reform plan if the shadow of his past had not hung over his relationship with his wife?"[5]

Close friends acknowledged that the first lady was disappointed, but not, they insisted, despairing. Repeatedly saying she "learned a lot," she admitted to some regrets that the way the task force "functioned was so misunderstood and that we did not do a better job of either explaining how it functioned or making some revisions in how it functioned." Still, she insisted, "There has never been a process of drafting any piece of legislation that included more people. And those people were not only from the public sector, they were also from the private sector and they included members of Congress's staff."[6] Asked if she would abandon health care, the first lady risked being accused of being a yuppie as she rededicated herself to her Methodist mission, admitting, "I am the result of privilege. I am the result of good health. I am the result of a great education. Why would I not want to do what I could in any small way to make it possible for others to have the same opportunities that I have had over my lifetime?"[7]

Once again redefining herself without admitting it, she continued to insist that the role of first lady was undefined and malleable. "You know we all try to do what we can to support our husbands and our families, to make the contributions that we can to improving the country in whatever way we think is appropriate for us, and to fulfill the traditional duties that come with being in the first lady position." In a dramatic inversion, however, she stopped posing as a trailblazer and tried to blend into the historical woodwork. "I was not the first first lady to testify before Congress," she reminded reporters. "I was not the first first lady to hold a press conference. I was not the first first lady even to have a job in the government. All of that was done in the past, but each of us has tried to do what is right for our husbands and ourselves and that's what I have tried to do. So I will continue to play many different roles, which I think is appropriate given the great opportunities that come with being in this position."[8]

By 1995, the Clintons needed to regroup personally and politically, individually and as a team. Hillary Clinton no longer positioned herself next to the president in meetings. She avoided many strategy sessions for nearly two years. Still, she had Bill Clinton's ear. Even while struggling to maintain a liberal foothold in the White House, she encouraged his move to the center, as he had done after his 1980 defeat. At her urging, he hired the mastermind of that comeback, the New York–based political consultant Dick Morris. Morris had complicated relations with both Clintons, each of whom loathed different aspects of his personality or ideology while respecting his insights into what swayed American voters. Morris soon had the president "triangulating" positions, balancing tax-and-spend liberals against heartless conservatives.[9] In public, Bill Clinton would win reelection by flying solo and navigating toward the center.

Similarly, Hillary Rodham Clinton would also fly solo, orienting toward the center. Although assuming a more traditional first lady–like posture, Mrs. Clinton continued to try to reconcile Park Ridge and New Haven, her upbringing with her awakening, her Methodist mission with her liberal vision, Puritanism with Progressivism, a decidedly centrist, even conservative cultural orientation with a more typically left-wing political agenda. The result, in many ways, was that while the public and the media focused on Hillary Clinton's eclipse, her ideas shined through more clearly than ever. In hundreds of speeches, news conferences, public appearances, and conferences, the first lady embraced a muscular, thoughtful, thought-provoking social agenda that just may have shown Hillary Rodham Clinton at her best.

Ever since Eleanor Roosevelt's legendary tenure, first ladies felt compelled, at the very least, to adopt a project. Bess Truman and Mamie Eisenhower had headed various charity drives. Jackie Kennedy had beautified the White House, and Lady Bird Johnson sought to beautify America, bringing an important message to middle-class Americans that today would be seen as environmentalist. Pat Nixon endorsed volunteerism; the more politicized and outspoken Betty Ford crusaded for the Equal Rights Amendment and breast cancer awareness. Rosalynn Carter built on the Johnson and Roosevelt policy-oriented precedents and championed mental health. Nancy Reagan embraced foster grandparenting, then spearheaded the "Just Say No to Drugs" campaign. Barbara Bush focused on literacy.

Hillary Rodham Clinton would adopt a number of safer, first lady–like projects while integrating them into a broader social vision for a more ethical America. Just as Lady Bird Johnson's beautification program elaborated on her husband's Great Society agenda, Hillary Clinton's values talk elaborated on her husband's third way agenda. Implementing the Dick Morris plan, compelled, as always, to seduce, Bill Clinton apologized to businessmen for raising their taxes and endorsed columnist Ben Wattenberg's lacerating critique of the Clinton administration for forgetting that "Values Matter Most."[10] The president decided he wanted to be a good father, not a bad boy.[11] During his 1996 State of the Union speech, he preached about the importance of "restoring our fundamental values," of the centrality of family, of the needs for parents to assert control by turning off the television and inculcating some "character education" along with teachers. Moreover, the first president to be born into an American social welfare state, the draft-dodging, noninhaling poster boy of 1960s liberalism, the architect of the most ambitious presidential stab at social engineering in American history, declared that "the era of big government is over."[12]

Curiously, at a time when the national conversation turned more and more to the problem of America's "character-starved culture," when George Gallup Jr. found Americans "more concerned about the state of morality and ethics in their nation than at any other time in the six decades of scientific polling," most tolerated a president whose integrity they doubted.[13] Clinton and his minions continued to play politics cleverly. They lambasted flawed exposés such as *Unlimited Access,* written by former FBI agent Gary Aldrich, hoping to break the chain of evidence at its weakest point. And the president continued to play the role of the nation's moral leader. Just as they deviated in their daily lives from the moral standards they swore by, many Americans distinguished between this president's private life and his public calls for morality, sobriety, discipline, and respect for women. Clinton benefited from a renewed appreciation of the culture of appearances in which public morality obscured private indiscretions, and a weariness with a culture of exposure that mixed private libertinism with a lurid, cynical public Victorianism. The mixed messages, both public and private, were overwhelming. The media would bombard America's teens and adults with top ten hits of 1995 such as "This Is How We Do It," "Take Your Time (Do It Right)," "Sexual Healing," and "Fantasy." At the same time, Nancy Reagan's "Just Say No" message was being extended from drugs to all kinds of indulgences, and reporters loved to whip Americans into moralistic frenzies over politicians' personal sins.

Like the president, the first lady also triangulated, although this time she left her name and hair color alone. "My first responsibility," she now said, "is to do whatever my husband would want me to do that he thinks would be helpful to him . . . whatever it takes to kind of be there for him."[14] The retreat was stunning, even as her supporters rejected the notion of a "new Hillary."[15] "No, she's not running health care, but we're not doing health care," Representative Pat Schroeder said in March 1995. "She's remaining active in the things she really cares about, like spending time with her adolescent daughter."[16]

Just as Nancy Reagan had done in the 1980s, Mrs. Clinton navigated between gender feminism and tradition to celebrate what she called "family feminism."[17] The broad-based prejudices against feminists and feminism in an America transformed by that very movement led many women to experiment with moderating their tone, softening their message, emphasizing their openness to different life journeys. "We need to understand that there is no one formula for how women should lead their lives," she preached.[18] A feminist, she said, is a person who supports "equal political, social and economic rights for women," not the "rejection of maternal values, nurturing children, caring about the men in your life."[19] As the first first lady to speak at the Pentagon, she emphasized the importance of respecting women's "choices" and their freedom "not to be stereotyped." In celebrating women's contributions, she singled out "not only those done by generals, but those done by mothers, sisters, daughters, all of us."[20]

Sensitive to the popular stereotype of feminists as harsh, judgmental, and unforgiving, and still gun-shy after being caricatured in that way during the 1992 campaign, the first lady tried to give feminism a more welcoming, open-minded visage. Preaching about "respect" for all the different choices women can make while participating in New York City's Women in Policing awards ceremony, Hillary Clinton insisted, "There should no longer be any room for anyone undermining or criticizing a women's choice, if that woman is choosing what is best for her. And all women ought to support each other so that all of us are able to fulfill our own potential and achieve the level of personal security that comes from knowing we are doing what we want to do as well as we are capable of doing it."[21] Showing her range, and emphasizing the breadth of choices women enjoyed in the 1990s, in April 1995 she attended a ceremony her critics would have expected her to disdain: the Mother of the Year awards. There, Mrs. Clinton complained, "Too often we fall into the trap of blaming many of society's problems on the fact that now 70 percent of American mothers work outside the home, and at the same time, when mothers stay at home to care for their children full-time, they are often criticized or disrespected for wasting their education and their potential. It's another one of those classic female binds—You get it whichever decision you make."[22]

Even more than Mrs. Reagan had done, Mrs. Clinton defined the attacks on her as an assault on all strong women. Kenneth Walsh of *U.S. News & World Report* noted that this first lady "talked mostly to idolizing groups of working women, liberals, social activists, feminists and earnest achievers," ignoring "working-class folks . . . homemakers . . . conservatives." The "a lot of people don't like a strong woman" defense resonated with these professional women, who stood by their champion.[23] Yet the rebuttal undercut Hillary's—and her sisters'—demands to be treated equally, overlooked the idiosyncrasies of the unelected first lady's position, and ignored the mounting charges of misconduct.

The repackaged first lady shifted from trying to be copresident to being the social worker in chief, like so many first ladies before her. Retreating into the women's sphere, Mrs. Clinton helped establish the Mother Teresa Home for Children in Washington, D.C., and became honorary chair of the president's Committee on the Arts and Humanities. She also denounced the Republican Speaker of the House Newt Gingrich's call for more orphanages as "big government interference," battled for soldiers suffering from gulf war syndrome, promoted mammograms to fight breast cancer, redecorated the Blue Room, and followed in Jackie Kennedy's footsteps with a well-publicized pilgrimage to India and Pakistan.[24] Unlike Mrs. Kennedy, Hillary took her daughter along—posing for family travelogue scenes—and visited the poor.

By using the magic of the White House, Mrs. Clinton spotlighted policy challenges that concerned her, both large and small. Her Web site in 2000 would list the following issues, each with a series of subheadings as well: Helping Parents Balance Work and Family; Addressing the Needs of America's Children and Youth; Strengthening America's Public Schools; Improving Health Care for All Americans; Advancing Women's Economic Security and Empowerment; Advancing Democracy, Civil Society, and Women's Full Participation around the World; Supporting the Arts; Celebrating the Millennium.[25]

In fairness, while tackling more traditional first lady issues, Hillary Rodham Clinton remained the brainy, socially conscious, liberal activist with a tinge of culturally conservative values she had

long been. Echoing Lady Bird Johnson's intellectually oriented social critiques rather than Jackie Kennedy's girlish cooing about fine
White House furniture, Mrs. Clinton effectively used what Nancy
Reagan called the first lady's "white glove pulpit." Like all of her predecessors, Mrs. Clinton found herself on a seemingly endless
merry-go-round of speeches, conferences, award ceremonies, and
trips, both foreign and domestic. But demonstrating her Progressive
faith in attending conferences, performing research, and finding the
right programmatic solution, many of the initiatives were specific
and substantive. She would speak at the Long Term Care Event at the
White House and the White House Event Concerning the Diagnosis
and Treatment of Children with Emotional and Behavioral Conditions. In 1997, she would host the White House Conference on Early
Childhood Development and Learning: What New Research on the
Brain Tells Us about Our Youngest Children. In 1998 it would be the
White House Conference on School Safety: Causes and Prevention
of Youth Violence and the White House Strategy Meeting on Children, Violence and Responsibility. In 1999 there would be the White
House Conference on Philanthropy: Gifts to the Future, and in
2000, the White House Event Concerning the Diagnosis and Treatment of Children with Emotional and Behavioral Conditions.

Typical was a speech she gave via satellite to a Children Now Conference in March 1994. Student journalists ranging from ten to
twenty years old were in the crowd, with some selected to question
the first lady after her talk. Any politician, let alone a first lady,
would have been tempted to dispense nostrums—but not Hillary
Clinton. "American children are immersed in a culture of violence,"
Mrs. Clinton complained, tackling a difficult question—and for
Democrats dependent on Hollywood donors, a politically volatile
issue. Her speech struggled with the complexities. She discussed the
accumulating research linking television violence and the crime
rate, the balance between fulfilling a journalistic obligation to report
about crime versus feeding a voyeuristic and desensitizing obsession
with violence, and the tension between press freedom and journalistic responsibility. "After all, good judgment and caution, or prudence, do not violate the journalist's First Amendment rights," Mrs.
Clinton concluded, calling for "the sort of balance that we know is

difficult but imperative if we expect our children to be given a fair shot at a childhood that allows them to develop emotionally and psychologically into adults [who] can be productive and deal with the world in all of its good and bad, in a constructive way."[26]

Mrs. Clinton remembered the media beating the vice president's wife, Tipper Gore, endured in 1987 and 1988 by questioning the vulgarity of rock lyrics. The Clintons could not afford to alienate Hollywood, which pumped millions of dollars into the Democratic campaign coffers. Nor could they lose California, with its treasure trove of electoral votes. Entertainers, as well as many journalists, hysterically yelled "censorship" any time anyone dared to question the coarsening of American culture. Moreover, after Ronald Reagan's presidency and the outbreak of the culture wars, moralistic cultural critiques were too often considered conservative territory. Media depictions of the culture wars caricatured America as torn between conservative fundamentalists eager to bring government control into the bedroom while limiting government social programs versus liberal libertines trusting big government bureaucracies to micromanage the economy and society while staying out of individuals' private lives. Steering clear of any discussion of government limitations, refusing to cede this important area of moral leadership to fundamentalists, Mrs. Clinton, trying to bridge the divide valiantly insisted, "This is a debate that is long overdue."[27]

Hillary Clinton's speech did not solve the problem, but her audience responded with equal seriousness. Lydia Chang, the student body president of Leland High School in California, challenged Mrs. Clinton's generalizations about children growing up with "cynicism, anxiety and fear," asking whether "adults watching the news [are] also garnering images that are false of young people." Before addressing the question substantively, Mrs. Clinton, making her first reference that day to the president, quipped, "My husband and I never watch the news. We consider that part of our mental health routine." Luis Cruz, an eighteen-year-old college freshman, asked the first lady whether the Clintons' decision to send Chelsea to private school didn't also contribute to the lack of "good stories in the media about public education." And one ten-year-old journalist asked about the many "kids of color" portrayed on the media as wanting "to shoot up somebody," while an eleven-year-old reported that "my dad doesn't like me watching the news because . . . he doesn't want me to go to sleep with bad nightmares."[28]

Children remained at the center of Hillary Clinton's efforts. In talking about children, she articulated her criticism of the culture, her vision for the future, and her fusion of activist government with traditional family values, her Progressivism with her Puritanism. This approach synthesized her experiences as a social activist with the Children's Defense Fund and as a working mom in Little Rock. "The American dream is an intergenerational compact," she would say, or she would quote some unidentified sage: "Our generation is supposed to leave the key under the mat for the next."[29] But dismayed by "consumer capitalism," which she distinguished from the more constructive "free market," Mrs. Clinton feared "there is a sense that nothing is really permanent in our society anymore, not family, not neighborhood, not jobs, not even our values."[30] Mrs. Clinton repeatedly blasted negative role modeling, cynicism, alienated families, and violence distorting young Americans' perspectives: "We are fed through the media, a daily diet of sex and violence and social dysfunction and unrealizable fantasies. We live too often in a disposable, throw-away society, where the yearning for profits and instant gratification, overshadows the need for moderation, and restraint and investing for the long-term." The challenge she posed, then, was, "Do we define ourselves by style or by substance? By the logo on our sneakers or the generosity in our hearts? By the celebrity we crave or the reputation we earn?"[31]

In emphasizing this cultural dimension, Mrs. Clinton was reinforcing her message that government was not the answer to every problem. She recoiled at the stereotype of 1960s types as antifamily, anticapitalism, or antifaith, or hopelessly addicted to Big Brother. She rejected the "false debate" between blaming "the economy, stupid" or "family values" for the problems, which naturally led either to calls for government intervention to change economic structures or demands for a conservative resurgence to improve values. "I do not believe it is an either/or choice. It is both/and," she insisted in one of many calls for synthesis and balance.[32] "Now, there is no way for anyone to write a prescription or pass a law that tells people, be good parents, be loving grandparents, be caring teachers, be sensitive employers, be thoughtful public leaders, and always consider first and foremost what children need to develop and grow," Mrs. Clinton would observe.[33] "As the Catholic conference has noted," she said, saluting an important constituency, " 'no government can love a child and no policy can substitute for a family's care.' But there is much that we can do to help parents do their duty to their children." What was most needed, she believed, offering a mix of maternalism and paternalism, was "a different attitude and a set of expectations, about our children and about ourselves."

Despite all the media attempts to depict a polarized society torn by culture wars, Hillary Clinton was not the only liberal seeking to resurrect a sense of community, a commitment to morality, and an appreciation for tradition. In the 1990s, leading political philosophers such as Harvard's Michael Sandel would warn that modern rights-based liberalism's obsession with individual prerogatives threatened democratic citizenship's communal and reciprocal basis. This critique echoed Professor Amitai Etzioni's long-standing call for a new democratic "communitarianism" and resonated with Professor Robert Putnam's well-publicized 1995 lament that Americans were "Bowling Alone" rather than in leagues. These thinkers were trying to restore what Putnam called the "social capital" democracies needed to function, to rebuild a sense of "civil society," one of the items Mrs. Clinton listed in her agenda.[34]

In blazing her middle path, Mrs. Clinton identified a "three-legged stool" propping up individuals and communities. There was, she preached at the World Economic Forum in Davos, Switzerland, the "free market system," which offers "the greatest capacity to create employment, income, wealth and investment." Simply making that statement in Europe to so many intellectuals who benefited from capitalism but detested it was bold. At the same time, she called for "effective, functioning, competent governments . . . that are neither . . . too strong and authoritarian" on one hand, "nor on the other hand, so weak" that they cannot balance out the market when necessary. This affirmation repudiated the Reagan assault on big government. But the third, oft-overlooked, endangered, yet critical dimension offering ballast was "civil society," which she defined as "the stuff of life. It is the family, it is the religious belief and spirituality that guide us. It is the voluntary associations of which we are a member. It is the art and culture that makes our spirit soar."[35]

Distancing herself from conservatives' mindless mantra of "family values" by calling for policies and attitudes that "value families," she sewed together governmental initiatives associated with the left and traditionalist rhetoric associated with the right. Incorporating the 1960s' countercultural critique of American society into her vision, she denounced the rampant materialism, selfishness, violence, and hedonism coarsening American culture and politics. Celebrating the 150th anniversary of the First Women's Rights Convention at Seneca Falls, New York, Mrs. Clinton called on the enthusiastic hometown crowd to "finish the work begun here" by advocating "policies like a universal system of health care insurance that guarantees every American's access to affordable, quality health care. Policies like taking all steps necessary to keep guns out of the hands of children and criminals. Policies like doing all that is necessary at all levels of our society to ensure high quality public education for every boy or girl no matter where that child lives. If we are to finish the work begun here—we must ensure that women and men who work full-time earn a wage that lifts them out of poverty and all workers who retire have financial security in their later years through guaranteed Social Security and pensions." But she ended her liberal litany offering a more traditionalist flourish tinged with a 1960s touch, saying, "If we are to finish the work begun here—we must be vigilant against the message of a media-driven consumer culture that convinces our sons and daughters that what brand of sneakers they wear or cosmetics they use is more important than what they think, feel, know, or do."[36]

In the 1980s, Ronald Reagan's gilded age offered Americans guilt-free prosperity. Reagan never connected the dots between some of the social pathologies undermining tradition that he lamented and the impact of the mass consumerism he celebrated on those traditions. The Clintons, as good yuppies, offered money-making with angst. And as products of the college campuses of the 1960s and 1970s, they were more used to articulating deeper social criticisms. Hillary Clinton especially was willing to address the fallout from a hyperindividualistic, leisure-obsessed, shopping-crazy society and understand that prosperity came with attendant costs. But she, too, was not willing to pursue the line of inquiry too far and really question the fundamentals of modern American capitalist consumerism or Clintonite boom time boosterism. Instead, many of her criticisms served as useful safety valves, offering thoughtful guilt-o-grams meeting the post-1960s baby boomers' need to contemplate, criticize, and agonize, while continuing to earn and spend at prodigious rates, if they could.

Well practiced in the art of political deflection, Mrs. Clinton also demonstrated an impressive ability to wrap a controversial institution such as the Legal Services Corporation in benign and socially visionary rhetoric. Mrs. Clinton had headed the LSC, which conservatives had targeted for years as the radical left's legal strike force. Although it was one of the institutions responsible for expanding America's "rights consciousness,"[37] the LSC often sued the very government that funded it. Mrs. Clinton said the LSC "shines as a beacon of hope and a last line of defense for millions of poor Americans—mothers seeking child support, and children without access to health care; families facing homelessness or living in intolerable housing conditions; welfare recipients seeking training, and nursing home residents deprived of basic care and dignity; farmers losing their livelihoods and women seeking protection from abuse."[38]

Mrs. Clinton's concerns about children, schools, and school violence grew as American communities endured a spate of widely publicized school shootings, culminating in the Columbine High School massacre of twelve students and a teacher on 20 April 1999. Shortly after the murders, the first lady wrote a column about a nine-year-old who came across an ad promising, "More fun than shooting your neighbor's cat. Bang! Meow! Bang! Meow! Come on already. It's time you move up the food chain and take aim at something that sounds better when it explodes." Other advertisements in the magazine the student picked up in the video store invited players to "get in touch with your gun-toting, cold-blooded side," and "Kill your friends guilt-free."[39] Mrs. Clinton had long warned of the often deadly combination resulting from the volatile emotions and occasional bad judgment of childhood or adolescence in a world awash with violent images and easy access to guns. Columbine reinforced her commitment to her more benign mixture of traditional values and liberal policies—in this case, gun control.

For six years, Hillary Rodham Clinton peddled this vision to adoring crowds on the road and at home, in Africa, Asia, Europe, and Australia, as well as in the American north, south, east, and west. Rhetorically, she was not addicted to government; she recognized its limits while appreciating its strengths. Despite her reputation as America's harshest feminist and the administration's angriest ideologue, she even applied her synthesizing centrism to the hot-button issue of abortion. At the thirtieth anniversary of NARAL, the National Abortion and Reproductive Rights Action League, she hewed to her middle path, mourning that this difficult issue had become what Harvard Law Professor Laurence Tribe called a "Clash of Absolutes." "Unintended pregnancies are down," she said. "Abortions are down by a full 12 percent. And all of this happened under a pro-choice president who has refused to back down in his support of a woman's right to choice. . . . And who has worked to make good on the promise he made seven years ago to work to make abortion safe, legal and rare."[40]

Taking potshots at partisanship, as she would with increasing frequency, Mrs. Clinton blamed "the loudest voices" who prevented "the American people" from hearing about those who worked "to find common ground to meet our goals of giving human rights and dignity to all people." Seeking that golden path on one of the most polarizing issues, she said, "I have met thousands and thousands of pro-choice men and women. I have never met anyone who is pro-abortion. Being pro-choice is not being pro-abortion. Being pro-choice is trusting the individual to make the right decision for herself and her family, and not entrusting that decision to anyone wearing the authority of government in any regard."[41]

In the same spirit, the Clintons tried to offer a model of marriage that triangulated between the 1950s' lifeless perfectionism and the 1990s' dysfunctional cynicism. "Bill and I have always loved each other," Hillary Clinton insisted. "No marriage is perfect, but just because it isn't perfect doesn't mean the only solution is to walk off and leave it. A marriage is always growing and changing." Rejecting radical feminists who denounced marriage, and traditionalists who disregarded alternative lifestyles, she said, "This is my choice. This is how I define my personhood—it's Bill and Chelsea."[42]

As her heroine Eleanor Roosevelt had done, Hillary Rodham Clinton began writing a syndicated column about "the human dimension of our lives."[43] In "Talking It Over," a chatty and sensible woman familiar with the concerns of working women emerged. "I wake up every morning trying to figure out how to mesh my responsibilities to my family, my public duties and the friend who might be stopping by for dinner," she said. The incongruous image of the savvy lawyer blathering about her "corny" devotion to her husband repelled Maureen Dowd. The *New York Times'* resident cynic quipped that Mrs. Clinton "has a talent for taking on the aspects of those she once scorned," proving to be as secretive as Richard Nixon, as greedy as Ronald Reagan, as domestic as "the women who bake cookies."[44]

Now, when the first lady's actions edged toward the controversial, the White House shuddered. Her plans to go to China for the United Nations Fourth World Conference on Women in September 1995 enraged conservatives. Senator Bob Dole said she was condoning oppression out of loyalty to "this misguided conference and its left-wing ideological agenda." Once there, her pointed denunciation of human rights abuses—clearly directed at her Chinese hosts—proved that Mrs. Clinton was not a patsy. "Let me be clear," she thundered, in a speech emphasizing the linkage between human rights and women's rights and detailing violations of both. "Freedom means the right of people to assemble, organize, and debate openly. It means respecting the views of those who may disagree with the views of their governments."[45] A *New York Times* editorial said the speech "may have been her finest moment in public life." Yet her husband undermined her heroism by claiming that "there was no attempt to single any country out"—even though Mrs. Clinton responded "yes" to a series of pointed questions on CNN about whether she was thinking about China when she specified certain violations.

Throughout 1994 and 1995, Bill Clinton kept a certain public distance from his wife, even as they spent more time together in the private quarters. He felt guilty about the suffering his ambitions had caused her. "Insofar as there's been any misunderstanding" about desiring a copresidency, he said, "it's probably my fault, because I asked her to do a job that probably nobody should ever have been asked to do." He insisted, however, that "she didn't advocate a position or push an issue that I didn't agree with."[46] Despite the distance, after the Oklahoma City bombing in April 1995, Hillary and Bill

Clinton acquitted themselves in their Reaganesque star turns as America's chief mourners.

At the same time, Bill Clinton struggled to control his libido. He insisted that he was "retired"[47] and allegedly admitted that while he had had "hundreds of women" in his youth, he had tried to be faithful since turning forty.[48] Both Mrs. Clinton and his staffers wanted to believe him. "I was certain that Clinton was too smart and too ambitious to be so self-destructive," George Stephanopolous would ruefully recall.[49] For her part, it appears that Mrs. Clinton trusted that the intimacy, intensity, and round-the-clock scrutiny of White House life kept her husband in check.

Alas, even as the president of the United States of America, Bill Clinton could not resist temptation. Rumors about extramarital affairs kept inside-the-Beltway gossips buzzing throughout his tenure. He clearly had a penchant for pretty girls. Aides would confirm that, on any given workday, some of the president's boys would try to make sure that a provocatively dressed woman crossed paths with the president; Hillary's people were often on the lookout for "clutches" who were dressed inappropriately and in the wrong place at the wrong time.[50]

If Monica Lewinsky's testimony is to be believed—and Bill Clinton eventually staked his presidency on her credibility because she swore he did not tell her to lie or to obstruct justice—she and the president began their "intense flirting"[51] within weeks of her arrival in the White House in July 1995. Their now far too famous first kiss occurred at approximately 8 P.M. on 15 November 1995, when the federal government budget shutdown furloughed paid employees and gave unpaid interns like her unprecedented access to the Oval Office. Ironically, just hours before Ms. Lewinsky flashed her thong underwear at him, the president had signed a proclamation for National Family Week. That proclamation celebrated a "shared commitment to the importance of family life" in which Americans "first learn important lessons about responsibility."[52]

Two hours after that first stolen kiss, the two had their first "sexual encounter," as the Starr report called it when trying to remain somewhat decent. "I'm usually around on weekends, no one else is around, and you can come and see me,"[53] the president told Ms. Lewinsky. Six weeks later, Monica Lewinsky still wondered whether the president knew her name—which he did. Two and a half months and half a dozen "encounters" into the relationship, they had their first "lengthy" conversation. Two weeks after that, on President's Day, 19 February 1996, the president tried to break off the intimate contact. But after a five-week hiatus, the contact resumed on 31 March, while Mrs. Clinton was visiting Ireland.

Bill Clinton's eighteen-month on-and-off relationship with Monica Lewinsky began during a particularly low point for Hillary Clinton—during the buildup to her appearance before the independent counsel's grand jury. If the Lewinsky-Clinton liaison was a singular lapse, as President Clinton wanted Americans to believe—and as his love-struck girlfriend herself wanted to believe—that would justify speculation about what was going on in the Clinton marriage at that time. But this romance seems to have been more routine than exceptional. In a rare moment of restraint, the Starr report mentioned, without editorializing, the "Northwest Gate Incident" of Saturday, 6 December 1997, when Monica Lewinsky discovered that the president was meeting with Eleanor Mondale, the former vice president's stunning daughter. "Livid," Lewinsky stormed off. As a result, the infidelities simply offered further proof of Bill Clinton's now-legendary capacity to compartmentalize. Clinton boxed off his compulsive flirtations and his many assignations from his love for his wife and his professed belief in family. In his memoirs, the ex-president would blame this on the "parallel lives" his troubled childhood had him leading.

Eventually, in January 1996, Bill rallied around his wife. At the time, Hillary Clinton's book tour was marred by new evidence of her role in Travelgate and the surprise reappearance of her firm's Whitewater billing records in her office in the heart of the executive mansion, with her fingerprints. Echoing Harry Truman, who threatened a music critic after he panned Margaret Truman's singing, Clinton regretted he could not punch William Safire of the *New York Times* for calling Hillary a "congenital liar."[54] Clinton enjoyed defending his wife against her foibles—and saw his popularity surge as hers declined.

Unfortunate timing aside, a secretary's discovery of these billing records on the third floor of the White House undermined the first lady's credibility in two ways. Mrs. Clinton had denied doing much legal work for Jim McDougal's Madison Guaranty Trust, and she claimed ignorance of a particularly shady Madison deal called Castle Grande. Moreover, she had denied knowledge of the billing records' whereabouts. Yet, there they were, in her private, well-guarded garrison, with her fingerprints on computer printouts detailing sixty hours of work for the bank and eight-nine tasks completed, including thirty-three discussions with bank officials and a dozen calls to Seth Ward, the manipulator behind Castle Grande.

According to investigative reporter Bob Woodward, as the first lady's aides suffered crushing legal fees and the stress of subpoenas, as reporters mocked the Clintons' insensitivity to that suffering, Mrs. Clinton had become more willing to testify before a grand jury—if only to restore her self-image as a caring person. "That is not who I am!" Hillary Clinton had said, crying to the White House lawyer managing the scandals, Jane Shelburne, after Joe Klein called the Clintons the Tom and Daisy Buchanan of American politics. "I take care of people." Then, while promoting her new book on the *Diane Rehm Show* in January 1996, Mrs. Clinton, typically, had overstated, claiming that the Clintons had disclosed everything the *New York Times* wanted to see in 1992, saying, "We took every document we had—which, again, I have to say, were not many—we laid them all out." The statement was particularly outrageous given the recent reemergence of the elusive billing records. George Stephanopolous called Shelburne, who called Hillary's protector, Susan Thomases. "Oh, my God, we didn't," Thomases exclaimed, and helped draft a retraction in the first lady's name. Informed that same day that the special prosecutor, Kenneth Starr, was subpoenaing her to testify in front of the grand jury about the mysterious billing records, Mrs. Clinton sputtered, "I can't take this anymore. How can I go on?" she asked. "How can I?"[55]

Hillary Clinton was worried. As a lawyer, she knew that the threat of a perjury indictment compounded the risks of testifying about the various Whitewater-related episodes. Doubting the special prosecutor's discretion, enraged that Kenneth Starr kept on expanding his mandate far beyond the Arkansas land deal, Mrs. Clinton feared a trap. "I couldn't eat or sleep for a week before my appearance, and I lost ten pounds—not a diet I would recommend," she joked weakly in her memoirs. Her biggest challenge, she later admitted, was working "on how to control my anger at the whole process." She focused on the grand jurors who "were performing their duty as citizens. They deserved my respect, even if the lawyers working for Starr did not."[56]

Taking a page from her mother-in-law's approach to life, and demonstrating that she had learned something in the three years of living in the White House fishbowl, Hillary Clinton complied with the subpoena—and grandly swept into the federal courthouse. "I was determined not to let him break my spirit. I might be the first wife of a President to testify before a grand jury," she would write, "but I'd hold it on my own terms." Downplaying the humiliation, Mrs. Clinton dressed for her part. Wearing a trendy flowing black cloaklike winter coat with an embroidered design on the back that reporters decided looked like a dragon, Mrs. Clinton beamed at the reporters camped outside in the crisp January air. After her testimony, and after signing a copy of her book for a juror who had asked for her autograph (and who would later be dismissed for that inappropriate request), Mrs. Clinton spoke briefly to the reporters. "I, like everyone else, would like to know the answer about how those documents showed up after all these years. I tried to be as helpful as I could in their investigative efforts." "Would you rather have been somewhere else today?" a reporter asked. "Oh," Mrs. Clinton deadpanned, "about a million other places."[57]

Hillary Clinton's performance worked. The acerbic postfeminist writer Camille Paglia deemed the first lady "the First Drag Queen" in the online magazine *Salon,* claiming that after years of squelching her sexuality as "Sister Frigidaire," Hillary Clinton had learned to tap her feminine power—and her star power. Lapsing into that peculiarly self-referential analytic mode that their generation pioneered and in which the Clintons often indulged, Professor Paglia proclaimed that she, too, shared Hilllary Clinton's baby boomer angst and struggle to mature: "In her combination of grand idealism and coercive, ends-justify-the-means tactics, Hillary encapsulates the arrogance and self-delusion of my generation, with its evangelical sense of social mission. I identify strongly with her and recognize in her present difficulties an echo of my own career disasters."[58]

Hillary Clinton's 1996 book, *It Takes a Village,* was the most dramatic mark of the first lady's makeover as both celebrity and as traditionalist. In her now-infamous *New York Times Magazine* portrait, the saintly philosopher had mused, "I hope one day to be able to stop long enough actually to try to write down what I do mean."[59] This bucketful of bromides, suggesting "Security Takes More than a Blanket," "Child Care Is Not a Spectator Sport," was a pale reflection of those ideas and lacked the zing of many of her speeches.[60] The power player and thinker of 1993 had become the mom and aphorist of 1996. She was still trying to synthesize liberalism and conservatism, Progressivism and Puritanism. She regretted that children suffered "from violence and neglect, from the breakup of families, from the temptations of alcohol, tobacco, sex, and drug abuse, from greed, materialism, and spiritual emptiness." This was Hillary the good, the devout Methodist, the faithful wife, the authoritative mom, and the crusader for children—the safest of all first lady projects. In this oddly denatured book, even some of her signature stories over the years were gussied up or diluted. Here was where she first made her legendary confrontation with a neighborhood bully at four years old nonviolent. Rather than admitting that when forced to stay outside by her mother, she walloped the bully, Hillary reported vaguely, "I stood up for myself and finally won some friends." Such trimming gave the book a forced, saccharine quality.

Although this best-seller fit alongside Nancy Reagan's soporific *To Love a Child,* about grandparenthood, and Barbara Bush's best-selling tome *Millie's Book,* supposedly written by the first couple's dog, Hillary Clinton's book was a milestone in American cultural history. Equal parts Martha Stewart, Nancy Reagan, and Jane Addams, it reflected the odyssey of an elite that rejected traditional mores, only to rediscover them. Hillary Clinton publicized studies showing—to much surprise—that divorce harms kids, drugs are destructive, promiscuity is degrading, and that "every child" needs an "intact, dependable family." Even while prescribing a government program for every problem and validating alternative families, she proclaimed, "every society requires a critical mass of families that fit the traditional ideal."[61]

This makeover had to be painful for Hillary Clinton as she embraced what feminists scorned as the "acceptable face of femininity."[62] One Arkansan recalled that back in 1980, Hillary Clinton found it particularly depressing "to have made all those sacrifices for him and then to be blamed for his defeat." She often advised other political wives, "Don't ever lose your own identity in this process. Don't lose yourself to your husband's career."[63] Yet in the White House, Hillary Clinton was sacrificing her dreams of a copresidency and still shouldering the blame as she became the first first lady to testify before a grand jury, and, with 54 percent disapproving at the start of the 1996 election year, the most unpopular first lady in history.[64]

Fortunately for the first lady, on most road trips and in public meetings, crowds enveloped her in warmth and thrilled to her message. At the podium, rather than on camera or before reporters, Mrs. Clinton let loose. Her speeches and her vision were more pointed and more substantive, and in the insane dynamics of modern American political culture, more overlooked. Thus most of the public watching her through the media saw a first lady cowed, but Hillary Clinton's aides and fans, as well as the first lady herself, experienced a more three-dimensional, provocative, maturing power and intellect.

It all seemed familiar. The poised first lady sat across from Larry King during May, one of TV's critical sweeps months. Both she and Larry were too savvy to waste her appearance on an ordinary night. Her heavy gold jewelry gleaming, her blonde hair perfectly coifed, she answered questions thoughtfully, smoothly, effectively. This was not the tigress who had spawned countless stories about her influence, but a pussycat. This was not the provocative intellectual heard at Davos or at a battered woman's center, but a purveyor of soothing nostrums. This was not a modern powerful first lady for a feminist age, but the embodiment of mainstream middle-class values—loyal, deferential, community-oriented, empathetic. She spoke about how nasty the attacks on her had been and called for civility in public discourse. She sounded hurt and surprised that her critics were so mean. She had no interest, no angle, beyond helping "my husband"—whom she now mentioned repeatedly—and representing the United States of America.

Experienced pro that she was, she pooh-poohed claims that she wielded power or that she represented the liberal faction in the White House. Accusations against her were all misunderstandings that her silly critics exaggerated. All she wanted to talk about was her benign yet surprisingly popular crusade for America's kids. As often as she could, she mentioned "my husband" and defended his presidency. Her appeal was gracious and directed to her core constituency: women. Even though her body language and the crook of her neck occasionally betrayed her bitterness and her determination, it was hard not to be charmed by this warm, poised woman. When Larry King asked her a personal question, her smiling refusal to "answer any questions" like that seemed just about right.[65]

Surprisingly, by the spring of 1996, Hillary Rodham Clinton, Wellesley '69, Yale Law '72, feminist, activist, and leading liberal, had morphed—while in the public eye—into one of the great antifeminists of her age: Nancy Reagan. In keeping with the protocols of the exclusive sorority to which she belonged, Mrs. Clinton refused to offer any advice to her successors. She said, as her predecessors had, that her job was an idiosyncratic one, that she "would not pre-judge how somebody would fulfill their responsibilities," even as she took solace in the fact that all, "starting with Martha Washington," had been abused.[66] That statement was as disingenuous as her performance with Larry King, and in the White House overall.

Hillary Rodham Clinton betrayed many of her longtime political allies as she tried to fulfill her duty to her husband. Her discomfort was palpable as she avoided saying that she was not a liberal, but would not admit that she was; as she avoided admitting she was a scapegoat for feminism, but would not deny that she was not. Yet even as she steered the conversation away from policy, she revealed her true self. She told "Larry" that her best preparation for what she endured in Washington "was playing sports with boys in my neighborhood growing up. She got "used" to their "razzing" and "that's why I urge girls to play competitive sports with boys at an early age."[67] This feminist critique of Washington's ugly "gotcha" culture masquerading as an innocuous childhood reminiscence betrayed a contempt toward men—an anger she learned to repress but could not suppress.

As their predecessors had for decades, presidential couples continued opening their private selves to public view. And for the fourth time in a row, a bold, idiosyncratic, headstrong first lady had regressed toward the mean. The converging public images of these very different women—Betty Ford, Rosalynn Carter, Nancy Reagan, and Hillary Clinton—underline the unspoken yet quite definitive job description for first lady of the United States. Those who violated the protocols risked the kind of witch hunts Nancy Reagan and Hillary Rodham Clinton endured. In the second and final half of her husband's presidential saga, Hillary Clinton would find a vindication of sorts by playing the perfect wife. She would see her popularity soar and would save his presidency, ultimately being the one person most responsible for his acquittal in his impeachment trial. But the public acceptance and historic impact would result from searing private pain and unimaginable public humiliation. As they had wished, the Clintons would indeed succeed in establishing the most substantive political partnership since the Roosevelts. But, sadly, characteristically, in seizing the brass ring they coveted, they tarnished it too. Theirs would also appear to be the most dysfunctional White House marriage since the Nixons. And all of Hillary Clinton's preaching about responsibility, sobriety, and balance would founder on the rocks of her husband's irresponsibility, immaturity, and immorality.

Hillary Clinton's vindication began with her calculated campaign to retreat in public into a traditional role without abdicating her precedent-setting behind-the-scenes power. It received a great boost in early 1996 from the great success of *It Takes a Village,* which became a best-seller. Its audio version made Mrs. Clinton the first first lady in American history to win a Grammy award. The Grammy—like Jackie Kennedy's Emmy award for the first televised White House tour thirty years earlier—symbolized the first lady's acceptance of her celebrity. Margaret Williams noted that "One of the things she's learned about being First Lady, [is] it's not just about doing, it's about being a symbol."[68] On television, Hillary Clinton would emphasize her role as a traditional icon rather than as a White House powerhouse. Instead of facing the nation on the Sunday talk-show circuit, the new Mrs. Clinton reincarnated herself as a warm and fuzzy soccer mom who giggled, squealed, and happily smooched with Oscar the Grouch on the *Rosie O'Donnell Show.* Mrs. Clinton would gush about dressing up like a 1950s bobbysoxer and dancing in the arms of "my handsome husband"[69]—charming viewers by seeming to open a window into the Clintons' private life and illustrating the strength and joy of their marital bond.

The *New York Times* would find it incongruous that "on the same day that she made her confectionary appearance on Ms. O'Donnell's syndicated show . . . she delivered a speech at a development conference . . . declaring: 'Microcredit is an invaluable tool in alleviating poverty, promoting self-sufficiency and stimulating economic activity.' "[70] But herein was Mrs. Clinton's great contribution and great challenge. While her husband triangulated, she wanted to synthesize. She rejected the simple media polarities whereby traditionalists were happy homemakers and feminists were humorless careerists. Hillary Rodham Clinton set out to prove to feminists and antifeminists alike that modern career women could also be good old-fashioned moms: they could serve tea and make policy, too.

Mrs. Clinton learned to relish her role as the hostess, art maven, and fashion plate of the East Wing without relinquishing her influence in the West Wing. During her husband's second term, her White House home page would highlight "Life in the White House: Special Events, Arts, Holidays and Food," just below "At Work on Issues." True, the issues she developed in 1996 and tried to focus on throughout the second term were traditionally feminine, such as children, health care, education, and women's rights. But her approaches were substantive, technical, and occasionally even controversial, such as extended family and medical leave, a continuing push for health reform, charter schools, and microcredit. In the United States and abroad, Mrs. Clinton bristled when these "women's issues" were "dismissed as marginal to the large challenges our nation is facing or derided as the 'feminization of politics.' What an unfortunate term," she exclaimed. "Instead of the 'feminization of politics' I prefer to think of this phenomenon as the humanization of politics in America. . . . That represents a maturing of politics. . . . Will democracies come to understand that issues affecting women are not soft or marginal but are central to the progress and prosperity of every nation?"[71]

The first lady was not the only adaptable Clinton. Bill Clinton was also tailoring his image and his agenda to boost his poll ratings. Determined to win reelection, Clinton hijacked the Republicans' agenda. With the Machiavellian consultant Dick Morris whispering sweet poll numbers in his ear, Clinton tacked right. Policy stances, broad themes, tactical moves, even the Clintons' summer vacation plans were poll tested. The 1995 budget showdown, wherein Clinton refused to yield even as he appropriated the traditional Republican mantra demanding a balanced budget, reflected Morris's recommended mix of strategic resolve and philosophical fluidity.

Prodded by Morris, President Clinton made his "values agenda" a central part of his reelection campaign. For the first time in a generation, a Democratic president parried the Republican counterattack on the counterculture. The 1996 State of the Union speech inaugurated Clinton's appeal to the 65 percent of Morris's respondents who "thought values issues such as crime, school discipline, TV violence and curbs on tobacco advertising were the most important" issues.[72] Tackling these safe, mainstream concerns reinforced Mrs. Clinton's message in *It Takes a Village*. Thus, throughout the 1996 campaign, Clinton not only continued to market his wife and daughter aggressively, he also followed author Naomi Wolf's advice and continued playing the role of the good father to the American people.[73] His appeal to the soccer moms, his paternalistic, small-scale policy initiatives aimed at improving middle-class Americans' quality of life, blurred his role as good father and great leader—with great success.

As usual, for the sake of the campaign, the Clintons endured an invasion of their privacy—but on their terms.[74] In September 1996, the Clintons granted Barbara Walters a rare joint interview. Both looked ebullient as they held hands, exchanged warm glances, and cuddled for the American people. Blissfully unaware of what had gone on in the Oval Office with Monica Lewinsky on slow Saturday afternoons, during their anniversary, after church on Easter Sunday, Mrs. Clinton celebrated the positive impact White House life had had on the Clinton marriage. "I think it's been a great time for us, personally, for little reasons, like the fact that he works 'above the store,' so to speak, and so, he's able to come home in the middle of the afternoon, if I'm there, if Chelsea's there. We eat dinner together most nights, so it's, so it's for me been a really great four years." Bill Clinton agreed. "Since I've been here we do have more time together and some of it's quite romantic in spite of all the pressures of the moment," he said. "This may sound hokey, but my happiest times here are when we go down alone to the movie theatre with two bags of popcorn. . . . or we'll get up in the bed and watch whatever's on television—or we'll play games together, we play a lot of games.

These things, you know, they sort of keep your life human, they remind yuh that you're still a, still a person, which is pretty easy to forget around here sometimes."[75]

In blurring his private and public roles, in marketing his family commitments to demonstrate his love for the American people, Bill Clinton was giving Americans what they wanted. Ever since its founding, and despite its many imperfections, the American republican experiment has been obsessed with virtue. The Founding Fathers believed that a virtuous citizenry and a virtuous nation needed virtuous leaders. The unique institution of the American presidency, combining the head of state and the head of government, invested a great deal of symbolic significance in one individual.

President Clinton's reorientation of the Democratic party frustrated many liberals. But with his public approval ratings bumped up to 60 percent and holding steady, the president would not yield. He squelched internal White House debate about his signing a Republican bill allowing states not to recognize gay marriages sanctioned in other states—an affront to the Democrats' nationalist orientation and human rights commitments as well as their gay constituency. "If there are people here who don't like it," he snapped, "well, I've created seven and a half million new jobs and maybe it's time for them to go out and take some of them."[76] The rise of Dick Morris, the mad triangulator, derailed Hillary Clinton's agenda without marginalizing the first lady. Morris's rivals considered her "still the most powerful liberal in the White House" and desperately lobbied her as "the president's other late night adviser."[77] At the same time, Morris respected her as "always pragmatic and shrewd," with an unusual ability to help her husband "see the larger picture." Having endured her wrath in the past—and owing her for his return to the president's good graces—Morris "made it a point to meet with Hillary at least every other week throughout 1996."[78]

Although both Clintons desperately wanted to stick with Morris's poll-driven, centrist program and win reelection, both struggled over the welfare reform bill. The Republicans had seized on candidate Clinton's 1992 promise to end welfare "as we know it" and fashioned a "workfare" bill. Hillary's comrades in the Children's Defense Fund estimated it would fling a million children into poverty. The president had vetoed the first two versions, but the Republicans returned with a third, more palatable bill. With Morris screaming "if he vetoes, he'll lose,"[79] Hillary Clinton shrank from the whole passionate debate. In a dramatic departure from her typically more inclusive vocabulary, she spoke of "the president's decision." That such a phrase marked a deviation from standard operating procedure revealed just how involved this first lady was in most presidential decision making. The first lady consoled herself that "we have to do what we have to do, and I hope our friends understand it."[80] Still, allies attributed her uncharacteristic passivity to the fallout from the health care crusade and Whitewater. "Political prudence and the balance of power in their marriage weighed against a decisive Hillary intervention," George Stephanopolous noted. "She couldn't be positioned—publicly or privately—to take the fall if he vetoed the bill and the race went south."[81]

Compromise came more easily to Bill Clinton: "What good will you do if you lose?" Morris insisted, sounding the Clintonites' characteristic the-ends-justify-the-means trumpet blast. "If you veto that bill and lose, what will the Republicans do then to the very people you want to help?" Secure in the knowledge that he amassed power to do good, President Clinton asked, "You think I'll carry Congress if I sign the bill?" and proceeded to end welfare as three decades of Americans had known it.[82]

Even with the Barbara Walters interview, playing the "good father" role was risky for a man who launched a thousand late-night TV jokes about his propinquity. In his book on the 1996 election, *Show Time,* the journalist Roger Simon cataloged many of the quips. "Clinton has this race sewed up unless there is a big scandal by November," David Letterman joked. "Like if he's caught in bed with his wife."[83] Americans were well aware of their president's shortcomings. When one survey in June 1996 asked respondents to name the best aspect of Bill Clinton's character, the top response was that he did not have one. A Pew Research Center poll found that people used these words to describe the president's personal image: "good, wishy-washy, okay, dishonest, liar, fair, trying, intelligent, slick, great, honest, crooked, leader, two-faced."[84] Bill Clinton's roguishness was so legendary even the president himself could not resist going for cheap laughs at his own expense now and then, as he joked that only the vice president could get away with comments about being too "stiff."[85]

It was hard to fathom how a president elected as part of the backlash against the Anita Hill–Clarence Thomas sexual harassment scandal could pull it off. "It used to drive me crazy," said Karen Hinton, a Democratic activist whom Governor Clinton had propositioned. "I used to say to people, 'Why doesn't it matter that we have a president who walks into a room and sees an attractive woman and proceeds to hit on her without any concern how that woman might feel about it?' "[86] Some critics linked the president's private and public behaviors, saying that Bill Clinton, the great seducer, lacked fidelity to his principles *and* his wife. *Newsweek* columnist Joe Klein chided the president for being "indiscriminate, casual and irregular" in foreign policy, domestic policy, and his personal affairs. "The character flaw Bill Clinton's enemies have fixed upon—promiscuity—is a defining characteristic of his *public* life as well."[87]

Part of the answer stemmed from the fact that Bill Clinton built his reputation amid the debris of pols before him. As Simon would note in *Show Time,* many Americans "felt that *all* politicians were immoral and Bill Clinton was no worse than the rest of them."[88] White House aides exploited Americans' characteristic mix of resigned cynicism and unrequited idealism—even as Americans dismissed politicians they yearned for salvation. As they had done in 1992, Bill Clinton's consultants urged their boss to change the subject. "Inspire. Preach. Soar. Lift People. Do what you do at a rally, when you become the voice of a million frustrated, desperate, decent, middle-class voters," one memo had urged in 1992.[89] As in 1992, the campaign deployed Mrs. Clinton to vouch for her husband. When a caller on one radio talk show asked Mrs. Clinton to identify her husband's character flaws, the first lady chirped, "Hogging the remote control. And chewing ice."[90]

Bill Clinton and his aides exploited the media's weakness for false polarities, guiding the national conversation to choose between effective leadership and virtue. The staffers' "internal mantra" was "public values trump private character."[91] Thus the president's people felt vindicated when one poll showed that 77 percent of the voters thought it was more important to have a president "who understands the problems of people like you," while just 22 percent said it was more important to have a president of "the highest moral character."[92] Both in 1992 and 1996 Bill Clinton was blessed with opponents who could not free their campaigns from that either/or, so in 1992, the choice appeared to be for character or for a change from the policies that created recession; and in 1996, it was character or the booming stock market.

Yet even as they developed this idea of a virtual presidency distinguishing the man from the office, staffers remained edgy. Their campaign always seemed half a misstep away from scandal. Surprisingly, in the middle of the 1996 Democratic convention, the broad net tabloid journalists used to troll for scandal caught Dick Morris, the architect of the values agenda himself. When the deputy chief of staff, Erskine Bowles, asked Morris to resign after the *Star* photographed him cavorting with a prostitute, Morris asked "Why? What the hell did I do that he [the president] wasn't accused of doing in the exact same magazine four years ago?" Unintentionally offering a poignant commentary on integrity in the age of Clinton, Bowles replied, "You've admitted it's true."[93]

White House staffers, most of whom detested Clinton's shadowy adviser, were furious at Morris. Hillary Clinton stepped in and forbade public attacks on the disgraced consultant. Although Vice President Al Gore and President Clinton also called Morris to offer support, Morris would remember that "Hillary was the most understanding and sympathetic."[94] Hillary's generosity paralleled that of Lady Bird Johnson when Lyndon Johnson's aide, Walter Jenkins, was caught propositioning someone in a men's room during the 1964 presidential campaign. These two first ladies, both married to raw, impulsive, wandering men, understood more than most about man's basest impulses, about the human struggle with weakness and sin, about the Christian teaching to forgive.

The press played Morris's peccadilloes as the sick behaviors of an egomaniac; Bill Clinton's unconfirmed escapades, by contrast, seemed more harmless, more reflective of a frat boy than a pervert. In general, Bill Clinton's roguishness was a central part of his rugged appeal—to both men and women. In the 1990s, women were not the only ones bewildered by mixed messages and confusing sex roles. Both presidents and first ladies were bombarded with conflicting messages: he was supposed to be strong but sensitive, she was supposed to be independent but deferential. Most Americans still preferred to have John Wayne than Jerry Seinfeld in the

Oval Office. There was no room for self-doubt or indecision when navigating the ship of state—or vying to be its captain. Jimmy Carter the farmer and George Bush the oil wildcatter learned that for all their macho achievements in the military and in rugged outdoor professions, occasional incertitude in office defined them as wimps. Despite being a genuine war hero, Bob Dole too often appeared weak, tired, and old. By contrast, Ronald Reagan, the faux warrior, career actor, and oldest president in history, appeared tough because he never questioned himself or his actions. Gradually, throughout his first term, Bill Clinton, draft evader and policy wonk, learned that Americans prefer tough talk, nostalgic moralizing, resolute action, and even bad-boy charm, to New Age psychobabble, tidbits about underwear preference, and reasoned moderation that might seem wishy-washy.

Like Hillary Clinton, Bob Dole's wife, Elizabeth Dole, had an impressive Ivy League résumé. A Cabinet secretary in both the Reagan and Bush administrations, Mrs. Dole left her job as executive director of the American Red Cross to campaign for her husband. One mischievous feminist, reporting "from behind enemy lines at the Republican National Convention" in San Diego, noted the contrast. Vicious buttons and signs denounced the first lady for being a strong woman—"Get the wicked witch out of the White House," "Impeach the President and her husband, too," "Hillary wears the pants; Bill does the dance." Yet Mrs. Dole was clearly a strong woman as well. She was a Harvard Law graduate, not a Yalie; she had lightened her hair rather than darkening it; and she had started as a Democrat and turned Republican, rather than following Hillary's opposite trajectory.[95] Yet Hillary Clinton was keeping a low profile during the campaign and struggling with a disapproval rating greater than her approval rating, 39 to 35 percent, while Mrs. Dole was deemed an asset to her husband's campaign.

Dole's prominence and popularity suggested that Hillary Clinton was wrong. The American people did not object to an accomplished woman campaigning with and for her husband. The discomfort centered around Mrs. Clinton's apparent hunger for power, her disingenuousness, and her active assault on the gender roles millions of Americans still wanted reinforced in the White House, even as change threatened the mores of Main Street.

Raising the stakes, Mrs. Dole used a portable microphone and, Oprah-style, talked about her husband in a stagey conversation with delegates in the San Diego Republican Convention pit. Mrs. Clinton knew better than to compete, despite initial pressure to match her rival. Sticking to the standard speaking format, Hillary Clinton's Democratic Convention address responded to Senator Dole's claim that *It Takes a Village* begged for "a collective, and thus the state, to raise a child" instead of a "family." In a substantive speech calling for health care reform and endorsing family leave, the first lady invoked the Clintons' experience raising Chelsea and said that "to raise a happy, healthy, and hopeful child, it takes a family. It takes teachers. It takes clergy. It takes businesspeople. It takes community leaders. It takes those who protect our health and safety. It takes all of us." Pausing dramatically, she said, "Yes, it takes a village," as the delegates cheered. And, she concluded, "It takes a president. It takes a president who believes not only in the potential of his own child, but of all children; who believes not only in the strength of his own family, but of the American family. . . . It takes Bill Clinton."[96]

CNN described the "reinvented first lady," meaning the less controversial, less policy-oriented first lady who had emerged after the health care debacle. But the first lady had also been reinvented as a more effective public figure. Here was an emerging political force learning to tap one of the greatest power sources of modern America: her celebrity.[97]

Both Clintons felt vindicated by the reelection victory over Bob Dole, even though Bill Clinton once again failed to capture more than 50 percent of the popular vote. Each looked forward to starting afresh, to crafting a bold historic legacy, and to leaving behind the first term's frustrations, false steps, and failures. Relishing the prospect of only the third Democratic reelection to a second term in the twentieth century, the Clintons overlooked the continuing fallout from the Whitewater investigations, the growing fury against the president's prodigious fund-raising, and the continuing demand from an angry young Arkansan woman for an apology from the president of the United States.

CHAPTER 6

MRS. CLINTON, MR. PRESIDENT, AND MS. LEWINSKY

Hillary Clinton was particularly proud of the AmeriCorps. A domestically oriented, 1990s update of the Peace Corps, the program reflected the Clintons' ambitions at their most noble—and grandiose. Using the ideal version of John F. Kennedy's administration as their standard, the Clintons hoped that they too could motivate members of a new generation to ask what they could do for their country.

Addressing potential recruits at the 1995 Brooklyn College commencement, Mrs. Clinton gushed, "National service is an idea that the President made into a program. It is built on very old-fashioned values of hard work, discipline, sacrifice and community service. It is about rewarding people for being good citizens." Mrs. Clinton preached that "education and service" are "noble goals" because "they are about building character. Character is one of the anchors of society. And when we talk about character we don't just mean talk, we mean action." Character was one of the essential building blocks of Mrs. Clinton's cherished "civil society that actually lives up to its ideals." Distancing herself from her husband's relativistic "character is a journey" rhetoric in 1992, Mrs. Clinton feared that modern American culture threatened this noble pursuit of character building, by mocking rather than idealizing, by indulging rather than sacrificing. "Consumerism and materialism go unchecked, run rampant through our culture dictating our tastes and desires, our values and dreams," she warned.[1]

In charging the graduates, Mrs. Clinton brought together many of her favorite themes, emphasizing the need for an updated vision that preserves the best of tradition while adapting to modern realities. Character was central to her vision—character meaning strong, resolute, moral action, wherein humans seek transcendence and the common good by being the best they can be, rather than succumbing to their most base impulses. This vision of character was rooted in her Methodism, shaped her liberalism, and inspired her opposition to what she considered to be Reaganite selfishness and materialism. Given her own ideology, given the terms on which she wished to be judged, her husband's betrayal of her, their marriage, and the very ideals of loyalty, discipline, and integrity she cherished was all the more profound. Bill Clinton's scandalous behavior mocked Hillary Rodham Clinton's Puritanism while dooming any far-reaching Progressive goals they shared. That in supporting him she also had to undermine the moral values, traditional structures, and character-oriented rhetoric she revered and championed must have been all the more humiliating—and devastating.

Mountains of ink have been spilled about the personal betrayal and public humiliation Hillary Rodham Clinton suffered during the Monica Lewinsky scandal. Few, however, have paid attention to the ideological, political, and policy double-crosses. For a couple so invested in their public mission, living in the White House fishbowl, which so blurs the personal and the political, the fallout from Bill Clinton's adulterous liaison with Monica Lewinsky was multidimensional and deeply unnerving.

Amid the dozens of books, thousands of articles, and millions of words printed about the Lewinsky episode, four relevant questions for this query emerge. First, what did Hillary Clinton know, and when did she know it? Second, how did her actions affect Bill Clinton's full court press to survive the scandal and remain in office? Third, how did these actions shape Hillary Clinton's tenure as first lady—and her political future? And, finally, what does Hillary Clinton's role in this sordid episode teach us about the modern dilemmas of the American first lady? Ironically, in the long run, amid this most degrading of scandals, Hillary Rodham Clinton probably made her most significant historical contribution to her husband's administration—while also setting the stage for her emergence as a political power in her own right.

The Clintons began the second term hoping to return to substance, yet perennially overshadowed by scandal. Governor Bill Clinton's boorish behavior with a young state worker in a Little Rock hotel continued to haunt his presidency. While the legal clash between Paula Jones and Bill Clinton dragged on in the courts, journalists took a second look. A week before Election Day, 1996, Stuart Taylor reexamined the Jones case in Steve Brill's journal, *American Lawyer*. Taylor chided reporters for dismissing Jones as "some sleazy woman with big hair coming out of the trailer parks," in the words of *Newsweek*'s Evan Thomas. Taylor concluded that Jones's claim of "predatory, if not depraved, behavior by Bill Clinton is far stronger than the evidence supporting Professor Anita Hill's allegations of far less serious conduct by Clarence Thomas," the Supreme Court nominee pilloried by feminists in 1991. Taylor attributed the contrasting responses to Professor Anita Hill and Paula Jones to the "hypocrisy (or ignorance) and class bias of feminists and liberals."[2]

As a result of Taylor's analysis, Paula Jones appeared on *Newsweek*'s cover just two weeks before Clinton's second inauguration.[3] The week that Bill Clinton was inaugurated, the Supreme Court heard the case of *Jones v. Clinton*. Clinton's attorneys, who had postponed the case until after the election, argued that the president of the United States should not be subject to a civil lawsuit until after he leaves office. In May, the Court would reject that argument unanimously—although in April 1998 Judge Susan Webber Wright would dismiss the case, and that November, after the Paula Jones case elevated the Monica Lewinsky affair from a private indiscretion into a possible obstruction of justice and perjury case, the president would settle the case for $850,000 but no apology.

Hillary Clinton's values-laden rhetoric helped shape Bill Clinton's second inaugural address, which called for "a nation that balances its budget, but never loses the balance of its values." Fusing liberal dreams of social justice with conservative commitments to "responsible citizenship" and enduring values, the president proclaimed: "There is work to do, work that government alone cannot do: teaching children to read; hiring people off welfare rolls; coming out from behind locked doors and shuttered windows to help re-claim our streets from drugs and gangs and crime; taking time out of our own lives to serve others. . . . With a new vision of govern-ment, a new sense of responsibility, a new spirit of community, we will sustain America's journey."[4] Surrounded by his wife and daugh-ter, the president sought to build his bridge to the twentieth-first century on the enduring foundations of community, responsibility, citizenship, and social justice.

Now, amid the headline-driven dramas of White House life, the first lady often offered some ballast—a reality check, as the psycho-babblers liked to say. This first lady's staid, sober idealism propped up the president, both legitimizing him personally and reinforcing his message politically. Interestingly, when things soured, for some, his sins undermined her; for others, her forgiveness redeemed him. Regardless, it came at a great personal and political price.

Even as the whispers about Paula Jones grew louder, critics were screaming about the campaign finance scandal. Politicians' push to raise money had become all-consuming. Congressmen and senators complained about the hours burned dialing for dollars, which began almost as soon as a winning campaign ended. Facing similar pres-sures, and desperate to raise funds, the Clintons imported the sleazy tactics they perfected in Arkansas state politics to the White House. Bill Clinton's failure to distinguish between the state house and the White House undermined the majesty of the presidency and trig-gered traditional republican fears of decline. His aide, Harold Ickes, had made it clear in a memorandum that an unprecedented effort was underway for 1996, noting, "The fund-raising needs for the D.N.C. will require a *very substantial* commitment of time from the President, the Vice President, the First Lady and Mrs. Gore."[5] Thou-sands of subpoenaed documents like this one, conveying deference for the office while orchestrating tawdry activities, underlined and undermined the powerful commodity peddled at "Motel 1600."

In an ironic tribute to the first lady's central role in this age of the copresidency, Hillary Rodham Clinton helped sell off access to sa-cred parts of the White House. Ninety-eight coffees averaging $50,000 per schmoozer—which works out to $16,666.66 per Danish served—and Lincoln Bedroom sleepovers at over $100,000 a pop gave wealthy Americans a chance to write mom a letter on White

House stationery, or to attend a state dinner hosted by America's chief celebrity couples: the Clintons and the Gores.

Clinton had exploited the nature of the modern celebrity presidency, auctioning off opportunities to bathe in his afterglow. "Ready to start overnights right away," the enthusiastic president scribbled on one fund-raising memo. "Give me the top ten list back, along with the 100, 50,000" dollar donors.[6] As the first president born into the television age, Clinton understood that celebrity begat celebrity. Clinton mined Hollywood for its mother lode of fame and glamour as well as money. Democrats hoped that hobnobbing with Barbra Streisand and Steven Spielberg delivered more votes in the late twentieth century than even Boss Tweed and Mark Hanna did in their day.

The fund-raising scandal had a man-bites-dog appeal. Republicans were supposed to kowtow to corporate bigwigs and sell their souls to the highest bidders, yet it was the Democratic Vice President Al Gore who stiffly said, "I am proud to have done everything I possibly could to help support the reelection of this president and to help move his agenda forward."[7] This Clinton-Gore rationale that the ends justify the means showed how the baby boomers applied their 1960s guerilla tactics and self-righteousness to serve money and power. Just as they enjoyed catching Hillary Clinton profiteering like a good Reaganite on the 1980s commodities market, reporters loved watching "McGoverniks" who cut their teeth during the Watergate era indulging in Nixon-style fund-raising. With a media invested in showing that all gods have clay feet, the Clintons simply elaborated on the story line and added to the cynicism.

The Clintons' sins here were more moral than legal. The Clintons vetted their activities with lawyers well versed in contemporary ethics and campaign law. Al Gore was probably correct when he said, robotically, seven times in one press conference, some variation on the legalistic defense that "My counsel advises me that there is no controlling legal authority or case that says there was any violation of law whatsoever."[8]

Situating the president's office in his home blurred the boundary between politics and government. What kind of law could demand that the president and first lady show more respect as custodians of the "people's home"? How could a law compel a president and vice president to have tact, dignity, class? Much of the scandal stemmed from the lowest-common-denominator moral evasiveness captured in Gore's claim that "Everything that I did I understood to be lawful."[9] "I've never believed in legislating morality or forcing members of Congress to be honorable through codes of official conduct," Senator Barry Goldwater often said. "Our integrity must shine like a light from ourselves. It's that simple."[10] In the modern era, Americans turned to law as the consensus about morality shattered, but convicting some donors and politicians would not give the president of the United States—or his closest allies—the moral gyroscope he and they obviously lacked.

The Clintons responded characteristically. Just after Election Day in 1996, Bill Clinton said that the fund-raising scandals swirling about him had "shown us once again that our campaigns cost too much, they take too much time, they raise too many questions, and now is the time for bipartisan campaign finance reform legislation." Typically, few Americans were more eloquent in attacking money in politics; few politicians were more shameless in collecting funds. As questions multiplied in 1997, the president offered long-winded explanations that clouded the issues while dispatching shock troops to offer what one of them, Lanny J. Davis, would call "a credible counterpoint message."[11]

If nothing else, the scandal over the Democrats' fund-raising excesses righted the balance within the Clinton couple. This time, public outrage focused mostly on the president's actions. Mrs. Clinton was just as willing to peddle her office as he was, but access to the "FLOTUS" cost less than access to the "POTUS." Her involvement in fund-raising reflected her role as the brightest star in the galaxy of luminaries orbiting around the president.

By now, the cat-and-mouse squabbling over scandal had become ritualized. In Congress, the Republicans hauled presidential aides before committees and subpoenaed truckloads of documents, while the Democrats condemned the partisan witch-hunt and tried to block the appointment of another special prosecutor. In the White House, the damage control unit tried first to suppress damaging information, then leaked it at the last minute to put the information in "context." In the newspapers, bold headlines gradually faded into short summaries as the public stifled yawns. As for Bill and Hillary

Clinton, they kept on doing their jobs, outfoxing Republicans, staying above the fray, and shepherding a booming economy.

Most reporters said they preferred poring over campaign minute books to peering into the president's sex life. Even many of the most aggressive journalists "felt ambivalent," as *Newsweek's* Michael Isikoff claimed he did, about tracking down rumors of "a consensual sexual relationship." But Isikoff and others came to believe that Bill Clinton "was far more psychologically disturbed than the public ever imagined." The "scale" of Bill Clinton's "private misbehavior . . . required routine, repetitive and reflexive lies to conceal itself." Bill Clinton's instinctive tendency to parry, evade, and lie to avoid even minor embarrassments—then shift the cover story if caught—forced loyal aides to mimic, corroborate, and spread the lies. This "culture of concealment" had "infected his entire presidency," Isikoff believed, with "corrosive effects" on the administration and the body politic.[12] Such a widespread epidemic justified the most aggressive reporting, especially in the wake of Watergate.

By Christmas 1997, depositions in the Paula Jones case were pending. Isikoff was already pursuing leads about the president's affair with an intern named Monica Lewinsky fed him by a former White House employee, Linda Tripp, and her literary agent, Lucianne Goldberg. President Clinton had already enlisted the help of his secretary, Betty Currie, and his fixer, Vernon Jordan, in neutralizing the threat that the Jones attorneys would discover his affair with Ms. Lewinsky. Yet calm prevailed within the Clinton White House. During the Clintons' getaway to St. Thomas, a photographer caught the first couple dancing on the beach in their bathing suits. Some—by now inured to the Clintons' never-ending spin—were sure the picture was staged; others—well aware of both Clintons' reluctance to bare the excess poundage of middle age—were equally sure that the picture caught the Clintons in a natural and loving moment. Back home, at one of the first couple's endless Christmas parties, the Clintons' battle-weary scandal fighter, Lanny Davis, had told his boss, "I think it's Okay for me to return to my law practice, Mr. President, because all the worst scandal stories are behind us."[13]

Within weeks, Lanny Davis and others were fully engaged in the great Lewinsky scandal of 1998 and 1999, which would lead to the only impeachment of a president in the twentieth century, and only the second impeachment in American history. On Saturday, 17 January 1998, the presidential limousine took Bill Clinton, flanked by his lawyer and bodyguards, to the Washington offices of Skadden, Arps. The day before, unbeknownst to the president, Kenneth Starr's prosecutors had taped, then detained, Monica Lewinsky after her ill-fated lunch with the friend who betrayed her, Linda Tripp, in the Pentagon City Mall. Now, nearly seven years after the alleged encounter, four years after Paula Jones first filed suit, the president of the United States endured a wide-ranging six-hour interrogation. Ironically, the interrogation in a sexual harassment suit could be that broad thanks to the efforts of Hillary Clinton and many of her peers to shift the burden of proof in such matters from the alleged victim to the suspected predator. Much of the indignation the Clintons and their supporters expressed ended up being situation-specific as they dodged the broader implications of what happened when one of their own was ensnared in this ever-stickier legal web.

Again and again, the Clintons mocked the seemingly tenuous connection between a failed land deal that began in 1978—Whitewater—with a middle-aged president's White House affair nearly twenty years later. Here the Democrats were combating another largely Democratic invention, the special prosecutor. Thanks to the PR savvy of Hillary Clinton and her buddies, the independent counsel, Kenneth Starr, appeared to be a fundamentalist Frankenstein, an insatiable Republican monster obsessively hounding the Democratic president. But Starr was following the inexorable logic of the independent counsel statute, which was rooted in the Democratic investigation of the Richard Nixon White House, in which young Hillary Rodham had played a supporting role. In Watergate, disparate break-ins, campaign dirty tricks, and payoffs led to a unifying cover-up that revealed a president and his men who considered themselves above the law. To Starr and his people, what linked Whitewater, Travelgate, the Billingsgate with the Paula Jones sexual harassment case and the Monica Lewinsky affair was a repeated pattern of violating the rules—and often the law—then covering up the lapses with a combination of perjury, obstruction of justice, and intimidation.

Those who considered the Clintons guilty in one of those realms usually saw the connection and understood that the special prosecutor was justified in expanding his scope as he targeted this pattern of behavior. Others might even condemn both Clintons for moral laxity in different contexts, but they simply could not fathom how the sloppiness became felonious and why the special prosecutor did not use some prosecutorial discretion and stop making a federal case out of moral foibles. Moreover, the relentless, often unreasoning, and well-financed opposition further undermined the accusers' credibility, encouraging Democrats to rally around their leaders.[14]

As he and his lawyers had planned, once under oath, Bill Clinton did admit to one sexual encounter with Gennifer Flowers. To his surprise, much of the deposition concentrated on the more recent relationship with a government employee, "Jane Doe Number 6," which he denied categorically. "I have never had sexual relations with Monica Lewinsky," he said. "I've never had an affair with her."[15]

To Bill Clinton's good friend and ardent defender, Harvard Law Professor Alan Dershowitz, submitting to this deposition was "the most disastrous decision of his presidency."[16] Lewinsky's affidavit denying the relationship emboldened the president. But affirming these lies under oath catapulted Bill Clinton's sexual cover-up from the political to the legal, from a potential embarrassment to a possible felony. Dershowitz and others had advocated a settlement or a default, simply refusing to contest the suit to avoid the deposition. Bill Clinton's superlawyer, Robert Bennett, feared that retreating would draw other women "out of the woodwork." Monica Lewinsky would report that the president simply seemed to be "in denial" about the potential damage the suit could cause, while others insisted that Hillary Clinton vetoed any settlement. Dershowitz would claim that when he finally asked Bill Clinton eight months—and multiple humiliations—later, on Martha's Vineyard, why he had not defaulted, the not-always-honest president and graduate of Yale Law School told the often-self-promoting advocate that "until just now," "nobody ever told me I could default instead of testifying. I thought I had to testify."[17] Mrs. Clinton later regretted opposing earlier "opportunities to settle with Jones out of court."[18]

Typically, rather than admitting the emotional baggage clouding her judgment, the rationalist first lady claimed she "opposed the idea in principle, believing that it would set a terrible precedent for a president to pay money to rid himself of a nuisance suit. . . . With the wisdom of hindsight, of course, not settling the Jones suit early on was the second biggest tactical mistake made in handling the barrage of investigations and lawsuits. The first was requesting an independent counsel at all."[19] These two miscalculations did incredible damage to the Clintons' missions. They highlighted Hillary Clinton's incendiary part in the Clinton psychodramas as she juggled the roles of wronged wife, chief defender, coconspirator, trained lawyer, and independent target.

When Bill Clinton returned to the White House after testifying, he and Mrs. Clinton canceled plans to go out for dinner that night with Erskine Bowles and his wife. That same evening, across town, *Newsweek*'s editors decided to delay publishing Michael Isikoff's tale of the president, the intern, and the confidant who exposed them. But early Sunday morning, scandal-monger Matt Drudge posted a report on the Internet: "NEWSWEEK KILLS STORY ON WHITE HOUSE INTERN."[20] That day, the president called in his secretary, Betty Currie, and asked her a series of leading questions along the lines of, "I was never alone with Monica, right?"[21] That Wednesday, 21 January 1998, the *Washington Post* broke the story, leading to the first wave of scandal that winter, which, after a few weeks, the president seemed to be weathering. A second wave followed that summer when physical evidence on a Gap dress linked the president to Monica Lewinsky and disproved all of his denials. That admission set the stage for the salacious Starr report, released in September, culminating with the president's impeachment in December 1998. Finally, the Senate refused to convict the president and remove him from office in February 1999.

Underneath the torrent of tawdry trivialities, an historic, multilayered, and quintessentially American debate ensued. The ancient quest for virtuous leaders, the traditional emphasis on marital monogamy and civic propriety, the three-centuries-old sense of American exceptionalism, and the unique character of the American presidency clashed with the moral and sexual confusion of the 1960s, the political cynicism and scandal hunting emanating from the 1970s, the celebrity politics of the 1980s, and the "all news, all the time" media invasion of the 1990s. The very meaning of marriage, along with the fundamental rules of sexual behavior, had changed, giving even the president of the United States more room to roam. At the center of this debate stood the charming, talented, intelligent, idealistic, wonkish, magnetic, tough, ambitious, duplicitous, arrogant, amoral, scheming, defiant, tragic, priapic, roguish, trashy, chauvinistic, self-centered president of the United States and his equally baroque wife, who skillfully maneuvered through a difficult emotional and political thicket playing the wronged wife, the avenging angel, the partisan politician, the cherubic cheerleader, and the substance seeker.

Ironically, even as Americans tolerated the president's escapades—either generously or cynically, the historian Nancy Cott notes—the first lady remained ensconced in a more traditionalist shell. Hillary Clinton's tone was crucial here. Although Cott is correct that the "debacle of the impeachment forced public cognizance of marital conduct as private and of marital infidelity as too common a failing to promote civic excommunication," the first lady had to play the injured party for both their sakes.[22] A more modern, relativistic, boys-will-be-boys attitude would have backfired. In this, as in so many other ways, the role of the first lady remained rooted in old-fashioned models and values; even if a president was allowed to trailblaze, first ladies were supposed to reassure.

Overall, the Clinton-Lewinsky scandal was an ugly moment in American history. Unlike during the Watergate era, no heroes emerged, and few ideals triumphed. Reputations shattered. Public language coarsened. Truth became pliable. Partisanship raged. Deathbed conversions were the order of the day as Republicans who, in the Reagan-Bush years, had championed executive privilege, denounced special prosecutors, and denigrated sexual harassment law, now condemned Bill Clinton's evasive strategy built on presidential prerogatives, defended Kenneth Starr's ever-broadening inquiry, and worried about Monica Lewinsky's hostile work environment. Conservative moralists who bemoaned the deterioration of standards flooded the airwaves with far too detailed and vivid accounts of Bill Clinton's most intimate acts.

For their part, Democrats zealously defended their president's right to privacy while gleefully spreading stories about Republicans' affairs. The Democrats replaced their instinctively expansive reading of law with a strict construction of the independent counsel statutes, grand jury rules, perjury standards, and the Constitution's impeachment clauses. Forgetting all they had done to construct a rather invasive and restrictive legal regime giving women the benefit of the doubt in sexual harassment cases, the Democrats also decided that women did not always tell the truth about male sexual predators, especially if the accused was a pro-choice president. Democrats who had skewered Richard Nixon gave Bill Clinton the benefit of the doubt for the sake of the presidency; those who had aggressively published Republican Senator Bob Packwood's diary when he was accused of sexual harassment now worried about Bill Clinton's privacy; those who had uncritically believed Anita Hill's claims of sexual harassment doubted Paula Jones; many who understood why Professor Hill kept in touch with Clarence Thomas for a decade dismissed Kathleen Willey, whom Clinton pawed, for writing a few obsequious notes to the president. All the while, the media and the electorate played both sides of the fence—as usual—condemning the spectacle while feeding it, as ratings and newsstand sales spiked despite the distaste those surveys expressed to the pollsters.

When it was all over, too many people had learned too many bad lessons from the president of the United States. Schoolchildren had learned more than they needed to know about lying and sex. Sexually precocious teenagers and preteens had a new, presidentially sanctioned rationale for engaging in certain sexual behaviors while still considering themselves pure. Feminists had boasted to the *New York Observer* that they would happily do for the president what Monica had done for him. Criminals had learned that when in doubt, skewer the prosecutor. Predatory bosses had learned that sex with their juniors could be excused as "consensual." Perjurers had new ways to slither past direct questions. Meanwhile, a young woman had been hounded by reporters for a year; her mother had been hauled into court; her friends' intimate e-mails had been broadcast; a president had been impeached and a first lady humiliated; a special prosecutor was demonized, two Republican Speakers of the House deposed, and various affairs and love children, some dating back to the 1970s, had been exposed. In the notorious pornographer Larry Flynt's America, the most frequently invoked presidential pantheon was not the foursome of Washington, Jefferson, Lincoln, and Theodore Roosevelt, whose lasting virtues seemed as enduring as the granite of Mount Rushmore. Instead it was the adulterous trio of FDR, JFK, and LBJ, whose peccadilloes confirmed the Clintonites' "everybody does it" defense.

It was easy to dismiss the whole sordid scandal as an aberration. Those like Alan Dershowitz and George Stephanopolous who saw "disastrous" junctures on the way to impeachment, implied that it was indeed preventable. Those who contrasted the ugly political and cultural war with the happy-go-lucky ethos of the 1990s boom considered it anomalous. And those who emphasized the compulsive amorality of a Bill Clinton, the tenacity of a Kenneth Starr, the ferocity of Clinton's defenders, the zeal of his conservative tormentors, treated it as idiosyncratic. Yet in many ways, Bill Clinton's impeachment marked the logical culmination of the Watergate and Iran-Contra scandals, the Judge Robert Bork, Senator John Tower, Justice Clarence Thomas, and Senator Bob Packwood inquisitions. Although many bizarre twists—from Bill Clinton's promiscuity to Linda Tripp's anger to Lucianne Goldberg's mischievousness to Monica Lewinsky's obsessive love—shaped the scandal, it was also the result of the many cultural, social, and political forces that made the presidential couple the stars of the national show, for better and for worse. With the president and the first lady cast as America's king and queen, their marital highs and lows necessarily became a centerpiece of the political culture. In 1998, many Americans realized that the health of American political culture was far too dependent on the health of the presidential marriage.

At the heart of the scandal was the dilemma of the president and first lady in the celebrity age: how do you maintain your privacy while peddling your life story? Over the years, the Clintons had danced, smooched, and horsed around on camera, for all the world to see. Mrs. Clinton's book *It Takes a Village* boasted that she and the president had weathered difficulties but were teaching the country that marriage was and should be a resilient institution, especially when children are involved. The Clintons also flamboyantly demonstrated how protective they were of their daughter, Chelsea—living proof of the Clintons' loving and warm marriage. At the end of the day, the Clintons treated privacy as a one-way street. The presidential couple had the right to invite the public in for glimpses of their happy marriage as they watched old movies in bed, of their warm family life as they reveled in Chelsea's achievements. However, prosecutors, reporters, and the American people did not have the right to verify those images, or peer in when the couple put up a "Do Not

Disturb" sign. To the Clintons, then, privacy meant the right to hide embarrassing details even as they marketed benign, attractive ones.

If, at their darkest moments, even Bill Clinton's most loyal foot soldiers wondered how could he do this to them—how could he risk his and their dreams for some cheap thrills with a young intern—even Hillary Clinton's fans wondered, "What did she know and when did she know it?"[23] This question would be critical for the first lady's credibility. If she knew her husband was lying when she defended him and attacked his attackers, that made her a liar; but if she had no idea what was going on—after, by his own admission, "hundreds" of instances of marital infidelity over the years, did that make her a fool?

In both their memoirs, Bill and Hillary Clinton would tell similar stories about two critical moments in the scandal that would consume them for over a year. On Wednesday morning, 21 January 1998, Mrs. Clinton would recall, "Bill woke me up early. He sat on the edge of the bed and said, 'There's something in today's papers you should know about.'" Mrs. Clinton replied: "What are you talking about?" Her husband, Mrs. Clinton recalled, said "there were news reports he'd had an affair with a former White House intern and that he had asked her to lie about it to Paula Jones's lawyers." At the time, the president denied the report and suggested that Ms. Lewinsky was a needy young woman, Hillary Clinton would recall, "who had misinterpreted his attention, which was something I had seen happen dozens of times before. It was such a familiar scenario that I had little trouble believing the accusations were groundless."[24]

Nearly eight months later, in Bill Clinton's words, "On Saturday morning, August 15, with the grand jury testimony looming and after a miserable, sleepless night, I woke up Hillary and told her the truth about what had happened between me and Monica Lewinsky."[25] "I could hardly breathe," she would recall. "Gulping for air, I started crying and yelling at him, 'What do you mean? What are you saying? Why did you lie to me?'"[26] For his part, Bill Clinton remembered that his wife "looked at me as if I had punched her in the gut, almost as angry at me for lying to her in January as for what I had done." The president of the United States thus experienced one of the most perilous days of his tenure: testifying to Kenneth Starr's grand jury, then describing his about-face to the American people in a nationally televised speech—all while in the marital doghouse.

Giving new meaning to the hip psychological term *enabler,* Mrs. Clinton was the primary victim of Bill Clinton's adulteries and yet also his defender in chief. The need to defend her husband precisely when he most betrayed her most publicly must have been particularly difficult—and it fed the stereotypes of Mrs. Clinton as soulless, power hungry, and simply committed to preserving her arrangement with the president so she could be first lady.

In fact, the Clintons' anger at their opponents was both bonding and blinding. Fighting against Kenneth Starr, the Republicans, and the "right-wing conspiracy" united the couple even when the president was exiled to the couch and when, as Mrs. Clinton would write, "I could barely speak to Bill, and when I did, it was a tirade." Hillary Clinton's confidence in the unreason of the special prosecutor and what she would call "the culture of investigation" primed her to believe her husband's lies. "After all," she would note in her memoirs, "since he had started running for public office, Bill had been accused of everything from drug-running to fathering a child with a Little Rock prostitute, and I had been called a thief and a murderer." Mrs. Clinton was confident that "Bill had been blindsided . . . the unfairness of it all made me more determined to stand with him to combat the charges."[27] Of course, in this case especially, it was far easier for Mrs. Clinton to think the worst of her opponents than to confront the truth about her marriage.

The gap between Bill Clinton's compulsive, promiscuous philandering and Hillary Clinton's professed shock suggests just how deep her own denial may have been. Going considerably beyond the cognitive dissonance all relationships require at some levels, for Hillary Clinton, both the personal and professional threats may have been too great to acknowledge. On top of the political risks Bill Clinton's adultery wrought, such repeated betrayals struck at the core of Hillary Clinton's feminine and feminist dilemmas. The baby christened with the unisex name, the brainiac girl who refused to hide her smarts from potential suitors, the feminist activist who shielded her sexuality behind mannish glasses and drab clothes, indeed had been taught by her parents and others that success in a man's world demanded such masquerading and squelching. But to become the superlawyer repeatedly abandoned for riper sexual beings was devastating. Didn't she deserve a husband who would liberate her from that Hobson's choice, rather than imprisoning her in this false dichotomy again and again?

It seems that the frustrations of six years of scandal dodging reinforced over twenty-five years of enabling. It was easier to believe her husband's denials, easier to override her feminist instincts and demonize the accuser, easier to trust the sense that the relationship had improved, easier to rely on watchdogs like Hillary Clinton's ally on Bill Clinton's staff, Evelyn Lieberman, who had, albeit belatedly, banished Monica Lewinsky to the Pentagon. Master manipulator that he was, the president reinforced his deception by feeding his cover story to one of the first lady's most loyal allies, the journalist turned Clinton apologist, Sidney Blumenthal. The president told his aide that Monica Lewinsky was known among other interns as "The Stalker," that she had pursued him, and that he felt like a character in the Arthur Koestler novel about the smothering web of lies in communist purge trials, *Darkness at Noon*. Looking back on it, realizing that "this was the most detailed story the president had given to anyone, including his lawyers," even the faithful Blumenthal would realize that "he probably had told this elaborate story only to me because of my relationship with Hillary. He knew we would share information and develop our politics together."[28]

Still, Hillary Clinton seemed quite subdued that first week of the scandal in January 1998 for a woman whose husband had simply been "ministering" to a troubled youngster. To anyone who could get close to her, including some reporters, she clearly was struggling with her emotions, trying to transform creeping feelings of shame and growing waves of anger at her husband into rage against the Republicans. One friend would report that when word leaked out that one of the many gifts President Clinton had bestowed on Ms. Lewinsky was Walt Whitman's poetry classic *Leaves of Grass*, Mrs. Clinton winced, remembering that her husband-to-be had given her the same book when they were courting.

Encouraged by devoted aides like Blumenthal, who would make a flow chart mapping out the "right wing conspiracy," the Clintons settled into their battle stations. The two never seemed happier with each other, more in synch, and more in love than when they were fighting a common enemy. Bill Clinton was notoriously self-absorbed. After the odd role reversal entailed by Filegate, Travelgate, and Whitewater, when it was Hillary, not Bill Clinton, who messed up—when Hillary, not Bill Clinton, needed defending—both Clintons seemed reassured to revert to their usual roles.

Mrs. Clinton would not just vouch for her husband. She spearheaded the counterattack. She applied the essential Clintonesque jujitsu honed from years of scandal busting: change the subject, dominate the story line, demonize others, attack the attacker. After Dick Morris warned the president that an abject apology to the American people would not work ("You can't tell them about it—they'll kill you"), Bill Clinton knew what to do. "Well, we'll just have to win, then," he said.[29]

Six days after the charges first emerged, taking advantage of a previously planned interview on NBC's *Today* Show to promote her child-care campaign, Hillary Clinton all but single-handedly saved Clinton's presidency. The first lady airily mocked all the "rumor and innuendo." Recycling the Blumenthal information—just as her husband planned—Mrs. Clinton responded to Matt Lauer's questions about the gifts Monica Lewinsky received by saying, "I've seen him take his tie off and hand it to somebody. . . . He is kind, he is friendly, he tries to help people who need help."[30]

Having humanized her husband, ever so subtly criticized his girlfriend, and rhapsodized about their marriage, Mrs. Clinton then demonized Kenneth Starr, directing all of her partisans' ire against the Republicans and the independent counsel. Betraying a concern with journalistic narrative that in other circumstances would have been deemed manipulative, Mrs. Clinton announced what the Reagan administration called "the line of the day" and what media theorists would call the "metanarrative": "This is the great story here, for anybody who is willing to find and write about it and explain it, it is this vast right wing conspiracy that has been conspiring against my husband since the day he announced for president."[31]

Hillary Clinton's "vast right wing conspiracy" hyperbole gave dispirited supporters a rallying cry. Not since Jackie Kennedy waxed emotional about "Camelot" after John Kennedy's assassination had a first lady uttered a more potent phrase. Feeling jazzed by her TV antics, Mrs. Clinton returned to the White House, sauntered into the White House solarium, and boasted to her friends, TV producers

Harry Thomason and Linda Bloodworth-Thomason, "I guess that will teach them to f—k with us."[32]

That January night, Bill Clinton did his job, which was to illustrate the choice between the scourge of scandalmongering and his focus on governance. The day before, on his fourth try, he categorically denied having "sexual relations with that woman, Miss Lewinsky. I never told anybody to lie, not a single time—never," he insisted. "These allegations are false. And I need to go back to work for the American People." The president then rolled up his sleeves and delivered a masterful performance in his 1998 State of the Union address. True, all the riffs originally planned about responsibility and character had to be excised. True, aides sanitized the text, cutting anything that might be ripe for innuendo or that would trigger a wave of knowing guffaws from the Republicans. True, he did not dare to speak directly to or about his wife, but he did mention her in a working context twice, once about a Christmas trip with the Doles to Sarajevo, and a second time when discussing their plans for "the White House Millennium Program to promote America's creativity and innovation, and to preserve our heritage and culture into the 21st century." But in his detailed policy proposals, his celebration of the economic boom, his promise of "balanced budgets as far as the eye can see,"[33] and his disciplined refusal to acknowledge the scandal, Bill Clinton made it clear that he had no intention of letting Kenneth Starr, Monica Lewinsky, or Linda Tripp prevent him from functioning as president of the United States of America.

Eight months later, in August 1998, after the discovery of Monica Lewinsky's stained blue dress, the president risked a perjury conviction if he lied to the grand jury. Mrs. Clinton's anger saved both her marriage and the presidency. Feeling "dumbfounded, heartbroken and outraged that I'd believed him at all," she would write, "I hadn't decided whether to fight for my husband and my marriage but I was resolved to fight for my President."[34] Mrs. Clinton was convinced that Kenneth Starr was more evil and more dangerous than her wayward husband.

Bill Clinton's defenders cleverly paired two mutually exclusive arguments. At the same time that they insisted that the affair never happened and was a shocking accusation to make against the president, they argued that even if it did happen, it did not matter, and it certainly did not affect his ability to do his job. The argument that nothing happened—which dominated from January through June 1998—bought enough time for the "even if it did happen, it did not matter" defense to take hold. As always, in the world of media-stoked partisan politics, truth was a fungible commodity—and the race went to the one with the most compelling story. By the summer, the president's people had developed a dramatic plot line about an overzealous prosecutor spending $40 million to persecute a president he and his other right-wing coconspirators disliked. This argument was politically compelling, but it emphasized Bill Clinton's legal vulnerability if there was any physical evidence to take the argument beyond a "he said–she said" situation wherein the president would win by default.

Unfortunately for Bill Clinton, the soiled dress was his worst nightmare, not a phantom; DNA evidence linked him to Monica Lewinsky. On 28 July, Ms. Lewinsky signed an immunity deal with Starr's office. The next day, the image-conscious president agreed to testify before a grand jury via video in the White House rather than enduring a "perp walk" into the federal courthouse. Speculation grew about what the president might say. A senior Republican senator, Orrin Hatch, begged the president to come clean before the grand jury, assuring him that many leaders from both parties wanted to move beyond a scandal neither party had successfully exploited. Within the White House, aides apparently pushed their reluctant boss to confess to his wife and daughter, as well as to the grand jury. "PRESIDENT WEIGHS ADMITTING HE HAD SEXUAL CONTACTS," the *New York Times* of Friday, 14 August, declared.[35] By this time, the Clintonites' mastery of the art of spin was so legendary, and their reputation for veracity so tattered, no one quite knew what to believe: was the president really reluctant or just appearing that way? Was the leaked headline a trial balloon, a way to force the president's hand, or a warning to the first lady? Did the president actually have to confess to the first lady, or did they need a cover story about a confession so that she, too, would not appear to have been a coconspirator in her husband's eight-month lie to the American people?

On 17 August 1999, Bill Clinton testified before the grand jury. Although he admitted having "inappropriate contact" with Ms. Lewinsky, he adamantly denied having committed perjury in his Paula Jones deposition when he denied having an affair with the intern. That night, in a nationally televised speech, the bitter president lashed out at Starr. America's chief executive continued splitting hairs, as he had done earlier in the day, saying of his deposition in January, "While my answers were legally accurate, I did not volunteer information." In four minutes he used the word "private" seven times, insisting: "Even presidents have private lives. It is time to stop the pursuit of personal destruction and the prying into private lives and get on with our national life." The short speech was, according to *Newsweek*'s "Conventional Wisdom" column, an "utter disaster: Too angry, too lawyerly, and he never apologized."[36] In its vindictiveness, in its self-pitying demand for privacy, in its failure to read what the public wanted, the speech bore all the marks of a Hillary Clinton special.

"No matter what he had done, I did not think any person deserved the abusive treatment he had received," Mrs. Clinton ultimately decided. "I also know his failing was not a betrayal of his country." Mrs. Clinton said, "If men like Starr and his allies could ignore the Constitution and abuse power for ideological and malicious ends to topple a President, I feared for my country."[37] As a result, the Clintons had to reverse the process that they had happily experienced over much of the decade. In the highly personalized office of the American presidency, presidents and first ladies usually spend time trying to blur the office and the individual. As the man becomes the president and his wife becomes the first lady, their tenure becomes stabilized, their popularity increases, their claim on American history and public memory solidifies. Bill Clinton survived politically—and by her own admission Hillary Clinton survived psychologically—by trying to divorce the individuals from the offices they held.

The day after Kenneth Starr delivered his detailed, humiliating report of the entire affair to Congress in September 1998, Mrs. Clinton recalled, the Clintons "attended a Democratic Business Council reception, where I introduced him as 'my husband and our President.' Privately, I was still working on forgiving Bill but my fury at those who had deliberately sabotaged him helped me on that score."[38]

Bill Clinton had often said that "character is a journey." As he stumbled in the wake of his stunning, begrudging admission that he had spent the last eight months lying to his wife, his daughter, his aides, and his lawyers, and squandering their credibility to affirm his lies, it was Hillary Clinton who took the American people along on her own journey of mourning and, eventually, forgiveness. Understandably, she was loath to share her private pain with the public; but she knew that every gesture she made and did not make, everything she said and did not say, would be deciphered. On a trip to China, when reporters speculated about why Hillary did not join Chelsea and Bill for one outing, Mrs. Clinton had archly observed, "I often refer to my life before the White House as when I was a real person. Because when you are in a position like this, people, in particular a lot of these people—with their pencils and cameras—try to record everything you do and then try to put meaning into it, whether you intend meaning or not."[39]

First, to preserve her own public credibility, the first lady had to convey her anger. Four of five Americans surveyed did not believe that Mrs. Clinton had first learned that the affair was sexual over that fateful August weekend. As *Time* magazine would note, "two irreconcilable story lines began seeping out" of the White House, "one so painful it was hard to hear, the other so cynical it was hard to believe." The question came down to "whether it was worse for Hillary to appear as a stupid, duped wife or as a conniving wife who had been covering for her husband all year."[40] The president's men claimed that Mrs. Clinton had known the true story for some time; the first lady's aides disagreed. Under instructions from Mrs. Clinton, her press secretary, Marsha Berry, called one hundred reporters to insist that the president "misled" his wife too. "It was an extraordinary spectacle," Howard Kurtz, the *Washington Post* media critic, would note, "a president and first lady peddling competing accounts of her awareness that he was cheating on her."[41]

The first lady faced a delicate tactical moment. Whatever arrangements the Clintons had in their marriage, Hillary Clinton had repeatedly acted as Bill Clinton's guarantor to the American public that a Clinton White House would not have to witness such shenanigans. She was the one who was always blaming their enemies, prejudice against "our state," meaning Arkansas, or random forces in the air, such as the Hale-Bopp comet, for what she insisted were baseless attacks.[42]

"There can be no question that Hillary Rodham Clinton's longtime defense of her husband aided and abetted the persistence of his outrageous and risky behavior—even after he became president of the United States," Professor Barbara Kellerman observed. "By definition, therefore, she shares responsibility" for this fiasco. Calling Mrs. Clinton the "President's enabler-in-chief," Kellerman said that the scandal was "about a man who became president even though it was clear from the start that he had a character problem. It is about a woman who chose for whatever constellation of personal and political reasons to go along."[43]

Even so, it is easy to believe that her husband's public admission of betrayal had devastated Hillary Clinton. Similarly, it is hard to believe that even the picture showing the three Clintons walking across the South Lawn with Chelsea between her two estranged parents on their way to vacation was not staged. As long as the public discussion focused on sex and the dynamics of the Clinton marriage, rather than the more devastating charges of perjury and obstruction of justice, Bill Clinton had a chance. He—and his wife—were banking on the American people's distaste for invasions of privacy and genuine post–sexual revolution confusion about rights and wrongs.

Word from the White House—from both the East and West Wings—insisted that Mrs. Clinton was furious and the president suitably contrite. The subtext was that Mrs. Clinton—not Kenneth Starr—was meting out the appropriate punishment. *Newsweek*'s editor at large, Kenneth Auchincloss, witnessed the first couple embracing lovingly as they wandered onto a neighboring beach. Howard Kurtz reported that the powers that be at *Newsweek* "decided the incident was ambiguous and didn't fit into their coverage."[44] The Clintons, as usual, were dictating the story line.

Hillary Clinton had time—and public permission—to wallow on Martha's Vineyard during the mid-August vacation, but she also had to start working on acceptance and forgiveness if her husband's presidency was to survive. The media discourse cast it in psychological terms, looking for resolution. By all accounts, Mrs. Clinton was more theologically inclined. She was never one for introspection; even her own mother said, "We don't talk about deeply personal things."[45] Some friends found her emotionally tone-deaf. But as a good Methodist, she understood sin, redemption, and the healing power of faith—and her husband the Baptist was always ready to be redeemed, again and again. The night before her husband's public crucible, Hillary Clinton had invited the Reverend Jesse Jackson to counsel her and Chelsea. In welcoming one of the least discreet ministers in America—who would describe their session in full in *Newsweek*—Mrs. Clinton demonstrated that she understood that the public needed its window into the private drama. But it appears that even in private, much of the dialogue the Clintons engaged in was religious. And friends reported that, at the end of the day, Hillary Clinton felt that it was un-Christian to refuse to forgive her husband.

Over the next few months, reporters scrutinized the couple for signs of anger—and redemption. Not since Prince Charles and Lady Diana were squabbling had so much been made about the wayward glance here, the missed moment there. On Martha's Vineyard, reporters discovered that the Clintons appeared at a party, but split up immediately, with the first lady working the room and the president moping on the sidelines. In early September in Ireland, reporters noted that whenever the president approached the first lady, she repelled him. Finally, in December, when the Clintons were in Israel, paying their respects to their martyred friend, late Israeli Prime Minister Yitzhak Rabin, CNN's cameras captured the first lady yanking her arm away from her husband, in what the *New York Post* called an "icy graveyard brush-off."[46]

Clinton's closest allies were also struggling to balance their loyalty and their fury. White House aides received talking points coaching them to say, "It's been said that he who cannot forgive others breaks the bridge over which he must pass himself. Of course I [forgive him]." Some, including Joe Lockhart in the press office, simply threw the paper in the garbage.[47] One longtime friend from the annual Renaissance Weekends sighed, "We're still quite supportive of his goals. And you want to be supportive of *him*. But let's be frank. What kind of a—hole jeopardizes everything this way?"[48] For all these friends the challenge would be—as with Hillary—to figure out how to stop the condemnation just short of abandoning him.

That August of 1998, support for the president was draining away. "There is a tidal feeling of betrayal and embarrassment running across the country today," a *New York Times* editorial announced.[49] When the president interrupted his vacation to bomb sites in Afghanistan and the Sudan, 40 percent surveyed believed that Bill Clinton was following a "wag the dog" scenario, predicted by a Dustin Hoffman movie of that name, using military action to divert attention from his sex scandal.

More than 140 newspapers demanded the president's resignation, including the pro-Clinton *USA Today.* "Clinton is a cancer on the culture, a cancer of cynicism, narcissism and deceit," Andrew Sullivan thundered in the *New Republic.* "At some point, not even the most stellar of economic records, not even the most prosperous of decades, is worth the price of such a cancer metastasizing even further. It is time to be rid of it. For good and all. Sooner rather than later."[50]

The moral fallout from the affair was considerable. Rather than making the Clintons' second term a moment to repair the breech from the 1960s, to reconnect liberalism and morality, Progressivism and Puritanism, all the moral issues Hillary Clinton had raised over the previous few years now had to be expunged from White House discussions and distanced from the Clinton mandate. Even more distressing for the first lady must have been a steady stream of articles and polls, beginning in January 1998 and continuing long after the president's impeachment saga ended, talking about how Bill Clinton's behavior further coarsened the nation's culture, disillusioned America's children, and legitimized some problematic teenage sexual mores. In America's twelve-step culture, many newspapers felt compelled to print guidelines for parents, with psychologists and self-help gurus explaining to parents what to explain to their kids about Bill Clinton's crimes—depending on the child's age, of course.

A spate of academic studies following John Kennedy's assassination in 1963 confirmed what people had known instinctively for decades: the president loomed large as a moral figure for America's children. In an age of media saturation, widespread cynicism, and teachers desperately seeking relevance, it was difficult for children to avoid learning about the president's lies on television, from the playground and in school. Some students took President Clinton's behavior as a license to lie: "It's normal," Suzanne Tabaro, age fifteen, a sophomore at Benjamin Cardozo High School in Bayside, Queens, said. "It's like, everybody else does it."[51] A Roper Center study in spring 1999 and *USA Today* polls, however, suggested that children judged the president more harshly than adults did. The kids had not yet learned modern adult America's supposedly more "sophisticated" approach to lying, especially when it came to sex. Some of these studies also showed that disappointment in the president undermined young people's faith in government and leaders more generally.[52]

The president taught many teenagers and preteens about sex, not just about integrity. Marking a profane intersection where Hillary Rodham Clinton's abstinence rhetoric and Bill Clinton's reprehensible conduct met, more and more young Americans embraced—and followed through on—the president's distinction between oral sex and what they called "real sex." During the culture wars of the 1980s, a counterweight to the "if it feels good" logic of the sexual revolution peddled abstinence, or at least a more responsible approach to sexuality. The AIDS epidemic fed a concern with "safe sex" and the rediscovery among some young people of what they called "monogamy," with the enthusiasm of Columbus stumbling on America.

Fed into American popular culture's reductionist maw, being a virgin started to become a badge of honor again among some young people, rather than a mark of universal loserdom. Word of President Clinton's denial that his intimacies with Monica Lewinsky constituted sex or having an affair combined with this push for purity led many young people who engaged in oral sex still to consider themselves virgins. A *Washington Post* report in July 1999 triggered a talk-show feeding frenzy when eleven and twelve year old junior high school students attributed their indulgences to the president's sins. Under the headline "UNSETTLING NEW FAD ALARMS PARENTS: MIDDLE SCHOOLS ORAL SEX," one young girl asked, "What's the big deal? President Clinton did it."[53] By the next television season, an *ER* episode would feature a teenage girl who told the doctors she was a virgin, but suffered from gonorrhea in her throat, having engaged in oral sex.

Of course, experts had detected the trend in middle schools and among self-declared virgins before the Lewinsky scandal. And the general abdication of parental limit setting, baby boomer laissez-faire morality, the earlier onset of puberty, especially for girls, and American popular culture's overwhelming obsession with sex also shaped attitudes and behaviors. In a culture that made the movie *American Pie* a blockbuster—partially because, and not at all despite, its scene of a young man defiling an apple pie—President

Clinton was not wholly to blame. Still, the combined effect of the scandal-driven media blitz that brought the discussion of such taboo topics, in graphic detail, to dinner tables across the land, combined with the shameless behavior and rationalizations of the nation's libertine in chief and his enabling wife, also had an impact. "Bill Clinton gave the definition of oral sex, that it is not sex, and to the whole world," "Donna," complained when calling in to CNN's *Talkback Live* after the *Washington Post* exposé. "The Democratic Senate all agreed with him, Hillary Clinton stood by her man, but I think she should have stood by her daughter, who was a teenager at the time; and insisted that, when everything was going to come out on the air about cigars and knee pads, educating her daughter and all the teenagers in this country about things that they probably never even dreamed of. I think she should have stood up to her husband and said it's time for you to step down."[54]

That bleak summer of 1998, with talk of resignation and rumors of divorce raining down on them, the Clintons' public failure and personal pain reinforced one another. The Clintons' manic-depressive presidency had hit rock bottom. Hillary Clinton's dream of transforming American moral discourse was now a mockery, with the specter of becoming the latest Clinton punchline for late night television comics haunting every public utterance or move.

Bill Clinton's behavior precipitated the crisis, but Hillary Clinton's eloquence and idealism exacerbated it. Modern American culture—especially the press corps—reserved particular scorn for the hypocrite. The disconnect between both Clintons' lofty, socially critical rhetoric and their tawdry, individually selfish behavior helps explain their opponents' fury. That both their sermonizing and their rationalizing often touched the volatile issues of sex and money made it worse. The way the Clintons championed family and morality while countenancing adultery, their zeal in preaching against materialistic excess and for integrity while justifying Whitewater real estate, commodities market, or fund-raising shenanigans, infuriated Republicans and embarrassed Democrats. With many Americans fretting about the cultural fallout from 1960s anti-authoritarianism, 1970s libertinism, 1980s materialism, and 1990s high tech hyperindividualism, the calls for moral accountability—and a presidential resignation—mounted.

Yet, remarkably, there were signs of life. Unlike in 1973 and 1974, when the drip-drip-drip of Watergate revelations paralleled a steady dip-dip-dip in American economic fortunes, in 1998 the economy was booming. This presidential drama took place against a backdrop of a happy, wealthy, confident, and thriving America. Moreover, Bill Clinton refused to surrender. He displayed an indomitable will which some Democrats would wish he had demonstrated when fighting for health care or racial harmony, rather than to keep his job. He was blessed with Republican critics who were so angry, so zealous, that they alienated many Americans. And in the end, in many ways, he was saved by the single person most victimized by his "victimless crimes" with Monica Lewinsky, his long-suffering but formidable wife, the first lady Hillary Clinton.

SENATOR HILLARY: "COMPELLING PUBLIC FIGURE" OR "DEGRADED WIFE"?

In August 1998, the devastated first lady had to "go deep inside myself and my faith to discover any remaining belief in our marriage, to find some path to understanding." As she had throughout her life, Mrs. Clinton relied on what she called "John Wesley's invocation. . . . Live every day doing as much good as you can, in every way that you can," and struggled with "what theologians have described as 'the push of duty and the pull of grace.'"[1]

One of Methodism's defining ideas has long been this proactive "Arminian" doctrine of free will rejecting the more passive belief in predestination. Good Methodists believe they are the agents of their own salvation and that redemption comes from their efforts, from their good works. This religious idea—propelled by the more universally Christian notion of forgiveness—helped Hillary Clinton and her husband rise up from the depths to which his sins had brought them. Buttressed by her faith, Hillary Clinton helped save Bill Clinton's presidency and launch her own, independent, epoch-making political career. However, to succeed, she had to jettison her dreams of modernizing her role and fall back on more traditional postures. On the eve of the twenty-first century, mired in a messy, post-modernist sex scandal, both Bill Clinton and Hillary Clinton found personal and political redemption through both religious and secular traditions.

Having survived the summer of 1998, the Clintons took the offensive—albeit gingerly—in the fall. In this epic battle, the president demonstrated dazzling political skills, bamboozling his opponents.

After a direct "intervention" by his chief of staff, Erskine Bowles, Bill Clinton eventually realized he had to stop the hemorrhaging. He started apologizing. Harking back to his Baptist roots and shamelessly exploiting his wife and daughter, the president finally said he was sorry at the annual Religious Leaders' Prayer Breakfast on 11 September 1998. Referring to the fact that he had been on "quite a journey these last few weeks," President Clinton said, "I agree with those who have said that, in my first statement after I testified, I was not contrite enough." He offered a characteristic three-step program. He would "instruct my lawyers to mount a vigorous defense using all available, appropriate arguments"; seek "pastoral support"; and "intensify my efforts to lead our country and the world toward peace and freedom, prosperity and harmony."[2]

Bill Clinton's repeated apologies, always laced with reminders that the country was safe and prosperous, reinforced his six-year message to focus on the program, not the man. President Clinton is a "failed human being but a good President," Senator Tom Harkin of Iowa insisted. Others, like the social commentator Shelby Steele, noted that this baby boomer conceit that "the politically virtuous person is virtuous" produced a black-and-white world wherein "the good guys" were always good, no matter how they behaved, and the bad guys were always evil—an upside-down world wherein "iconography" replaced public policy and serious decision making, and a confused world wherein "a much celebrated male feminist . . . also gropes and harasses women."[3] This ethic, however, was quite widespread.

At the same time, Bill Clinton well understood that he could not begin to remove personality from politics. In fact, more than ever, he needed to deploy his wife, his daughter, and his own considerable charms in this desperate effort to save his administration. Much revolved around what he defined as his "private life." And here Bill Clinton and his defenders could take full advantage of the moral fog that had descended over the country since the 1960s as well as the rights revolution that infused most Americans with an unprecedented tolerance. Privacy meant many different things to many different people. Good people of conscience genuinely believed that certain questions were off-limits, even in an invasive celebrity culture. And especially when it came to sexual matters, Americans granted each other—and themselves—lots of moral latitude. At the same time, more traditional people held to the formula linking personal virtue with national virtue—and success.

A searing national debate ensued over propriety and privacy. Branding the whole affair an episode of "sexual McCarthyism" was doubly effective. By reducing it all to sex, the president's defenders offered built-in justifications for deceit and deviance. Surveying the results of his handiwork over the decades, Hugh Hefner of *Playboy* preached that "sex is the only subject in America that everyone lies about—to their girlfriends, their wives, themselves."[4] The simultaneous "it's only about sex" and "everybody does it" defenses built on nearly a century of Freudianism and thirty years of confusion, confessions, and revelations in the wake of the 1960s revolt. Using the loaded term *McCarthyism* testified to the Clintonites' success in creating moral equivalence between Bill Clinton and Kenneth Starr, the defendant and the prosecutor. In fact, the Clintons and their lawyers were so effective that the hunter became the hunted, as many people agreed with Professor Dershowitz that "the Starr report poses a far greater danger to the American system of governance than anything charged against President Clinton."[5]

Bill Clinton's defenders—and the president himself—once again offered Americans a choice between an effective president and a good man. The argument suggested that the two were mutually exclusive. The litany of strong presidents who betrayed their wives and failed presidents who seemed to have been faithful—Nixon, Ford, Carter—assumed that there were certainly black arts a politician needed to master in order to succeed. At the same time, the "well, at least he's doing a good job" defense blithely assumed that Bill Clinton was indeed doing a good job—a concession many opponents would not have made otherwise.

Clearly, the simplistic, black-and-white, all-or-nothing integrated approach to truth and morality that Americans had worshiped—at least rhetorically—for over two centuries no longer predominated. Hillary Clinton's own Methodism was now passé. Bill Clinton, as usual, was lucky. Rumors about his amatory impulses seeped into popular consciousness during a backlash against the new Puritanism. Historically, Americans have seesawed between collective crusades to purify the body politic and individualistic demands to allow people great freedom and privacy. The libertinism of the 1960s combined with the libertarianism of the 1980s shaped this greater tolerance for moral ambiguity and the accompanying zeal for privacy that emerged as the consensus of the 1990s. Americans now seemed to accept the Protestant theologian Reinhold Niebuhr's notion that "the relevant virtues of an individual differ in accord with the realm in which he or she is acting."[6] As many as 84 percent of those surveyed agreed that someone "can be a good president even if you disapprove of his personal life," and two-thirds consistently defined moral leadership as "understanding the problems of people like you." By contrast, less than a third defined it as having "high personal moral and ethical standards."[7] Sociologist Alan Wolfe explained that there was a new "eleventh commandment" in modern America that seemed to have upstaged the original ten: "Thou Shalt Not Judge" thy neighbor.[8]

Whether people called the new approach "Niebuhrian," "sophisticated," "European," "nuanced," "multidimensional," "relativistic," "decadent," or "amoral" reflected differing philosophies labeling a similar historical interpretation. In a *Psychology Today* issue about adultery, with Hillary Clinton's grim visage gracing the cover, "a leading expert" on adultery, Dr. Shirley Glass, articulated the new ethos. Americans could "separate the way the President is performing in office and the way he appears to be performing in his marriage," precisely because many Americans compartmentalized their own sexual affairs from their otherwise "happy" marriages. Having an affair is not necessarily proof of a "terrible marriage," Glass claimed, saying a husband "might still stray" from the most "wonderful" wife, "if that's in his value system, his family background, or his psychodynamic structure." In keeping with that approach, "the Editors" advised Hillary Clinton that "it's a boundary problem, not a love problem," and "despite the hurt and anger, love can still survive. . . . Some woman or other is going to give him a second chance to prove that he can be faithful," the editors suggested. "Decide if that woman can be you."[9]

While Bill Clinton played to modern Americans' ambivalence about morality, obsession with sexuality, fierce sense of privacy, and genuine capacity for forgiveness, his critics overplayed their hand. In September, Kenneth Starr's report fell into the trap the Clintons' lawyers had set, obsessively focusing on sex to prove Bill Clinton had lied about sex while arguing that the case, fundamentally, was not about sex. In the meantime, House Republicans demanded public access to the Starr report, followed by the videotape of the president's grand jury testimony. Both releases, while humiliating the president, made the House Republicans look vicious. This apparent partisanship kept Democrats from abandoning their president and fed a backlash that the president, the first lady, and their supporters had been nurturing since January.

With the midterm congressional elections of 1998 heating up, the president had to avoid uncontrolled situations, and he spent much of his time jetting from one fund-raiser to another. The first lady still refused to talk about her marriage, but she plunged into the campaign with abandon. Six years into the Clinton revolution, thirty-five years after Betty Friedan's *Feminine Mystique,* sixty-five years after Eleanor Roosevelt moved into the White House, no one questioned the propriety of a first lady fund-raising or campaigning. Dignified enough to use the white glove pulpit, famous enough to generate star power, and furious enough to motivate partisans, the first lady had a powerful impact on the 1998 elections. "We have to send a very clear signal to the Republican leadership in Congress that Americans care about the real issues," the first lady thundered on the campaign trail. "They care about education, health care, and Social Security. And they want a Congress that cares about what they care about."[10] Democrats credited Hillary Clinton for helping Charles Schumer unseat the three-term Republican senator in New York and Clinton foe, Alfonse D'Amato. They thanked her for saving Barbara Boxer's Senate seat in California. In the aftermath, Mrs. Clinton would regret that she did not mobilize enough resources early enough to save Senator Carol Moseley Braun in Illinois.

With her marriage in crisis, and amid all the humiliating revelations, Hillary Clinton achieved a symbiosis with the American public she had never before enjoyed. All of a sudden, she was the Democrats' most popular speaker, their most prolific fund-raiser, and their sexiest star, with a 65 percent approval. "She's come to realize that the symbolism of her office can be very effective as a tool," her press secretary, Melanne Verveer, observed. Publisher Peter Osnos gushed, "She's the most compelling public figure of her time who's not an entertainer."[11]

Alas, the popular Hillary Clinton was more Lady Di than Lady Godiva; it was her Jackie Kennedy poise, not her Eleanor Roosevelt politicking, that did the trick. Mrs. Clinton's core supporters, feminists and working women, continued to love her; her newfound support came from older women, noneducated women, Republican women — all of whom identified themselves as "nonfeminists." "Before, these women regarded her as a challenge to their values, looking down her nose at them," the Democratic pollster Celinda Lake explained. As a victim, as a woman who like them could not control her husband or her destiny, "they now see her as a woman demonstrating their values." Sadly, it was pity, not respect, and appreciation for her dignity, not her depth, that redeemed Hillary Clinton. "He screws up, she covers up. Then they bond over it. I don't see what's so great about that," feminist author Barbara Ehrenreich complained.[12] Columnist Maureen Dowd called Hillary Clinton the "single most degraded wife in the history of the world."[13]

In November, thanks partially to Mrs. Clinton, Republicans nearly lost their majority in the House of Representatives. After a year of all scandal, all the time, the Republicans expected to win big. Instead, the Senate remained unchanged and the Democrats gained five seats in the House of Representatives. The Clintons interpreted the Democrats' strong showing as a message to stop focusing on the scandal and to return to the nation's business. This time, Republicans had enjoyed remarkable progress on the legal front, only to be stymied on the political front.

In the final phase of what had become a wrenching power struggle, despite the Democratic advances, and despite the resignation of Republican Speaker Newt Gingrich, Bill Clinton ended up impeached. As with the dismissal of the Paula Jones case back in April, the president had celebrated victory prematurely. Republicans remained furious—and the president's dishonesty in the January deposition and the August grand jury appearance had provided a legal and thus constitutional dimension to his sins. All hopes of compromise faded when, once again in late November 1998, Bill Clinton overreached and gave dismissive, lawyerly, and slippery responses to eighty-one questions the House Judiciary Committee posed to him. "He mooned the Congress," said an aide to one GOP moderate.[14] Bill Clinton, a politician enslaved to public opinion polls, could not fathom that his opponents would damn him despite the polls. The fact that, as with all presidents, few aides dared to say what they really thought led to his great failure—a bitter impeachment on two counts only six weeks after the midterm election triumph.

Republican conservatives may have ignored the polls, but with many journalists afraid of a reader backlash, the mainstream media emphasized the themes of the Clinton camp: that the president's genius for compartmentalization kept him buoyant, that the first lady had never been happier. True, the first lady often glowed in public, exuding almost a perverse pleasure as her stardom eclipsed his. Amid the humiliation, Mrs. Clinton seemed oddly liberated, freed from serving her husband even as the whole world saw her simply standing by her man.

The signs of marital discord, however, mounted. Mrs. Clinton traveled to Bulgaria to avoid being in Washington on their wedding anniversary. Observers noted the first lady giving the president a cold shoulder in their private compartment on *Air Force One.* "She is still angry. She hasn't forgiven him," one friend observed. Another friend would suggest that "the withdrawal of Hillary's approval . . . brought the president to an inner collapse in mid-December."[15]

The gap between the many glowing press reports and the sad, tense reality was reminiscent of the movie *Men in Black,* wherein only the tabloids told the truth about the aliens inhabiting earth. In this version, *Vogue* might feature an "Extraordinary" Mrs. Clinton as its Christmas cover girl, looking chipper and glamorous in her red velvet Oscar de la Renta dress and Cartier pearl-drop earrings,[16] leaving it to the *Star* to describe her anger and humiliation; the *New York Times* would emphasize how President Clinton was merrily going about his business, leaving it to the *National Enquirer* to describe a despair so bleak and so crippling that the first lady's pity for her husband had eclipsed her anger.

Misled by the election results, the polls, and the changed media tone, the Clintons mobilized too late to stop the impeachment. With the Christmas season approaching, they began to realize just how desperate the situation was. The first lady lobbied furiously, articulating legal arguments while embodying a more emotional argument: if she forgave him, why shouldn't we? At one point, before the election, Mrs. Clinton cornered the chief of staff of Congressman Jim Moran, a Virginia Democrat who was lambasting the president. "Why is Jim doing this to us?" Mrs. Clinton asked. "Because of what the president did to *you*," the aide replied. "Ask Jim to call me," the first lady said, whereupon Moran attacked the president as a philanderer. The congressman added that had he been the first lady's older brother, he would have taken her errant husband behind the house and broken his nose. Mrs. Clinton calmly responded with a legalistic attack on the Republican effort.[17]

Mrs. Clinton's efforts culminated in her charge to the Democratic caucus just hours before the House of Representatives impeached "President William Jefferson Clinton" on two counts: for lying to the grand jury on 17 August and obstructing justice in the Paula Jones case. "You all may be mad at Bill Clinton," Hillary Clinton told the Democrats. "Certainly I'm not happy about what my husband did. But impeachment is not the answer. Too much is at stake here for us to be distracted from what really matters." Fearing "an attempted congressional coup d'état," Hillary Clinton accused the Republicans of risking the Constitution in a crass partisan attempt to "sabotage the President's agenda."[18] Marveling at her performance, Democratic Congressman Dennis Kucinich of Ohio said, "It's lucky for America we have a woman with the strength to lead the nation right now. . . . Everybody understands that she is one of the leaders of the nation right now. As much as the president."[19] With her marriage and their presidency in a shambles, Hillary Clinton finally returned to her copresidency.

Ultimately, once the salacious affair ended up in the constitutional realm, Americans' and the Senate's constitutional conservatism carried the day—as it had for Andrew Johnson 130 years earlier. The many ambiguities the Clinton people had successfully introduced and the vicious attack they had launched against the overzealous and often bumbling special prosecutor made many moderates hesitant to remove the president. The conservatives' plaintive insistence that "it's not about sex" at once suggested that it *was* about sex and conceded to Bill Clinton that lying about sex was somehow okay. Here too, the deep distaste for what President Clinton and the

Democrats called "the politics of personal destruction" united millions of Americans and restrained dozens of senators. Americans remained fascinated and appalled by their own invasiveness. Whether or not it was about sex, it certainly was about the presidential couple. Mrs. Clinton kept an appropriate distance from the impeachment trial in early 1999. Nevertheless, her presence was palpable throughout the proceedings. In this "split-screen presidency," President Clinton delivered his State of the Union speech in the House chamber only hours after his White House counsel, Charles F. C. Ruff, began defending the president in the Senate chamber. President Clinton interrupted his typically substantive speech crafted to emphasize his remarkable ability to focus on his job to hail the first lady, mouthing a very public "I love you" in a tableau of public reconciliation with his private partner.

Two days later, in the emotional high point of the trial, the Clintons' old friend, Dale Bumpers, defended the president to his former Senate colleagues. Once again violating the Clintons' privacy while ostensibly protecting it, Bumpers played the personal card. Conceding that the president's conduct was "indefensible, outrageous, unforgivable, shameless," Bumpers admonished the House managers for showing no compassion for the president or his family. "The relationship between husband and wife, father and child, has been incredibly strained if not destroyed," Bumpers mourned. Understand, he insisted, that the president dissimulated to avoid "bring[ing] unspeakable embarrassment and humiliation on himself, his wife whom he adored, and a child that he worshipped with every fiber of his body and for whom he would have happily died to spare her or to ameliorate her shame and her grief." When Bumpers spoke, Mrs. Clinton watched the Senate trial for the first time on television. Fittingly, tragically, she watched it alone in the private dining room; her husband watched it alone in his office.[20]

The Senate's unwillingness to convict, and thus remove the president, along with the special prosecutor's ultimate unwillingness to indict the president or the first lady, left the Clintons feeling vindicated. They, their supporters, and even many historians would claim that "every official report on Whitewater exonerated the Clintons" and that "there was no evidence of wrongdoing in that matter."[21] That is a partisan political judgment, not an accurate legal or historical analysis. Kenneth Starr's successor, Robert Ray, found circumstantial evidence of perjury, tax evasion, and obstruction of justice. Deploying the prosecutorial discretion Clintonites claimed his office lacked, Ray chose not to prosecute because he doubted he could secure convictions. Still, in his final report, Ray denounced the president for labeling the process "bogus," noting that the "investigation resulted in the conviction of 12 defendants, including former Arkansas Governor Jim Guy Tucker, Jim and Susan McDougal, and former Associate Attorney General Webster L. Hubbell."

Although President Clinton ended up with a suspended law license because of his Lewinsky lies, the final report made Mrs. Clinton appear incompetent and possibly dishonest. Regarding the initial Whitewater investment, the prosecutor concluded the tax returns of these two intelligent lawyers "were not in full compliance with federal tax laws, [but] there was no intent to evade federal income tax."[22] There was also "insufficient evidence . . . to prove beyond a reasonable doubt" Governor Clinton's role in suspect loans Jim McDougal took out in Bill Clinton's name or for the Whitewater project's benefit.

Regarding Mrs. Clinton's role in representing Madison Guaranty, the prosecutors were convinced that insiders "used and misused her legal services to thwart federal examiners." Fearing the potential political embarrassment and civil liability connected to a bank failure "that ultimately cost the American tax payers about $73 million, Mrs. Clinton and the Clinton campaign made public statements regarding her representation that minimized her role." Here, too, "while the evidence did show that some of Mrs. Clinton's statements had been factually inaccurate, the evidence did not establish beyond a reasonable doubt that she knew that they were factually inaccurate when she made them." Moreover, "Mrs. Clinton's various descriptions of events about" Jim McDougal's retainer of her law firm "had substantial inconsistencies." Similarly, Mrs. Clinton's "claimed lack of memory" about the mysteriously elusive "billing records" was questionable, but illegality "could not be proven deliberately false beyond a reasonable doubt."[23]

Within the White House, regarding her role in the Travelgate firing, the independent counsel concluded, "Mrs. Clinton's sworn testimony that she had no input into . . . [the] decision or role in the Travel Office firings is factually inaccurate," but because there was no clear proof of her "intent," the evidence was insufficient to "establish the requisite elements of any criminal offense." Similarly, amid the chaos after Vince Foster's death, there was suspicious behavior but no smoking gun. Phone records showed hurried calls among Margaret Williams, Mrs. Clinton, Susan Thomases, and White House counsel Bernard Nussbaum. In particular, Thomases paged Nussbaum one minute after the completion of a three-minute call from the Rodham residence to Thomases'. All four "claim[ed] they were merely consoling each other," suggesting either a remarkable efficiency in transmitting emotional support or exchanges about some plans all agreed to conceal.[24] All in all, it was a humiliating spectacle, a replay of Ronald Reagan's embarrassing defense during the Iran-Contra scandal, when he preferred to be seen as incompetent and out of touch rather than venal. Any lawyer sunk in this morass of denials, oversights, forgotten conversations, and ethically questionable actions would be disgraced. Mrs. Clinton, however, benefited from an artificially high barrier. After years of hysterical charges, mounting costs, and a clever counteroffensive, only an indictment would have been devastating. Strong circumstantial evidence of sloppiness and even possible dishonesty now seemed like vindication. Moreover, the Monica Lewinsky affair upstaged Hillary Clinton's blunders. Once that ended, everything else seemed trivial.

Thanks, ironically enough, to the Lewinsky scandal, Mrs. Clinton entered the final years of her husband's tenure objectively more popular, perceived as more powerful, and feeling more empowered to speak out on her own. Critics and friends, Republicans and Democrats, agreed that she helped save the Clinton presidency. But personal anguish aside, this was not the policy victory or programmatic vindication she craved. The American people had not ratified her vision or given her a mandate to do much of anything beyond be a more sympathetic, less threatening first lady than she had planned on being.

After the Senate failed to convict her husband, Hillary Rodham Clinton seemed fed up—and oddly liberated. The flattering suggestion that she run for Daniel Patrick Moynihan's New York Senate seat quickly evolved into a "Hillary for Senate" boom. Mrs. Clinton tired of what she called her "vicarious role." After a quarter of a century of serving a self-centered, endlessly needy man with an all-consuming career, Hillary Clinton wanted to make her own mark as a "real person" clearly and unambiguously.[25] In the final recognition of her position's limitations, she would have to shirk her duties as first lady to find fulfillment—and succeed—as a senatorial candidate. In the final year of the Bill Clinton presidential saga, rather than serving as the indispensable first lady she had longed to be, Hillary Rodham Clinton ended up being the expendable first lady—and the republic survived.

Mrs. Clinton could contemplate running for Senate only by exploiting the personal politics she seemingly abhorred. The New York senatorial campaign extended the Clinton brand name, converting the first lady's name recognition, newfound popularity and iconic aura into political power. In this age of celebrity politics, with the professional wrestler Jesse Ventura still preening from his gubernatorial victory over Hubert Humphrey III in Minnesota, with the actor Arnold Schwarzenegger soon to capture the California gubernatorial chair, the first lady at least had political experience.

The "Hillary for Senate" boom did not just liberate Mrs. Clinton from servicing her husband's career; it also liberated her from her role's peculiar protocols and limitations. As her successes in the campaign and the Senate would demonstrate, a significant portion of the criticism she received as first lady had less to do with her personality, her policy, or her gender and more to do with her position's peculiarities and the difficult fit between her ambitions and the traditions of being first lady. Once freed from the gossamer shackles of being first lady, Senator Clinton—or Senator-to-be Clinton—was free to be as brainy and as policy-oriented as she wished to be. Barring a dramatic redefinition of the first lady's role—not simply the role of women in modern America—future first ladies would ignore this lesson at their peril.

Of course, it could not be a Clinton effort without some drama—and whispers about the spin and the counterspin. As the first lady publicly weighed her options, cynics wondered whether she was just playing coy. In fact, once Democrats such as Congressman Charles Rangel and Senator Robert Torricelli started boosting her candidacy,

Mrs. Clinton seemed quite taken by the idea. Still, in her memoirs, demonstrating her earnest, more cautious, and ever-evolving self, she wrote, "One benefit of my decision-making process was that Bill and I were talking again about matters other than the future of our relationship." And she attributed the final decision to a young high school athlete in New York City who met her at an event and whispered in her ear, "Dare to compete, Mrs. Clinton. Dare to compete."[26]

As she became the first first lady ever to plunge into her own electoral campaign, Mrs. Clinton succeeded in giving her rollercoaster years as first lady the happy ending she had craved. Win or lose, by ending on this bold, substantive note, Mrs. Clinton guaranteed that she would be judged more like an Eleanor Roosevelt than a Barbara Bush. Whatever compromises she made shrank to minor sacrifices along the way, deviations from a master plan to be a pioneering and independent first lady.

Before winning a single vote, Mrs. Clinton began to enjoy the fruits of her campaign. After one of her initial learning tours of New York, a vast state she barely knew, the Associated Press reported, "Historians say Clinton, a lawyer by training and a policy advocate by experience, has redefined the role of first lady to the extent that this political race is not so extraordinary." In listing Mrs. Clinton's accomplishments, the reporter—and presumably the historians—did not distinguish between Hillary's unambiguous successes in foreign travel and on the campaign trail, her failure with her "ambitious" health-care reform plan, and humiliations such as "testif[ying] before an independent counsel's grand jury, and advis[ing] the White House on strategy through a sex scandal and impeachment."[27]

Before plunging into the maelstrom of New York politics, Mrs. Clinton felt compelled to reassure voters that the state of her union with the president was strong. Even before officially announcing her campaign, she broke her year-and-a-half-long silence about her husband's infidelity. In a gift to her Hollywood patrons and her New York allies, she granted an interview to Lucinda Franks, the wife of legendary Manhattan district attorney Robert Morgenthau for the debut of Clinton enthusiast Tina Brown's new Disney-funded magazine, *Talk*. In an unintentionally self-damning admission, the woman who had long insisted on her husband's innocence, helping him squelch rumors of infidelity and often slandering his female accusers, admitted that her husband's "weakness" was a long-standing problem. "I thought this was resolved ten years ago," she said. "I thought he had conquered it."

The first lady gave New Yorkers what she thought they wanted. Using the psychobabble of the therapeutic culture more than the religious idioms of the Clinton marriage, she attributed her husband's compulsive infidelity to the fact that he was "scarred by abuses" when he was four—apparently his grandmother and his mother fought over him as the young child haplessly tried to "please each one." In this odd rendering, adultery was the result of childhood trauma—too much love—and the resulting cover-up tinctured with a patina of gallantry: "He couldn't protect me, and so he lied."

Still nursing her own anger—at her husband's "mean" opponents—Mrs. Clinton complained about their continued attempts to "strip away everybody's sense of dignity, of privacy." As she painted a portrait of a healing, loving couple who talked constantly—in the solarium, at the dining room table, in bed—she wondered, "Why do I have to talk about things no one else in politics does?" Yet she and her spokesperson voluntarily lifted the veil many Americans preferred to keep lowered.[28] "We've slowly seen a physical passion come back into their lives,"[29] her chief of staff, Melanne Verveer, reported a few years before "TMI"—too much information—became popular slang among teenagers. Once again, it seemed that the Clintons' zone of privacy was malleable and permeable, at their convenience.

Nevertheless, Hillary Clinton's bold exodus from the White House raised talk of a trial separation. "HILLARY DEMANDS DIVORCE—BILL GOES BERSERK!" the *National Enquirer* screeched. Clipped comments about future housekeeping arrangements fed the gossip. When reporters asked if the Clintons' new $1.7 million home in Chappaqua, New York, would be her husband's "primary residence" as well as hers, Mrs. Clinton responded: "That's a good question. I haven't really talked to him about that."[30]

The fact was that, as *Time* magazine noted, "the history of the Clinton Presidency . . . always has been the history of the Clinton marriage, which is why the distinction between public and private in this presidency has always been messy. From the start this union was a vessel not only of love but of ambition, a shortcut for two stars in a hurry to reach heaven."[31] And despite the depth of the Clintons' love for each other, the early days of White House life, which had genuinely helped revive their marriage, vanished, along with Hillary Clinton's faith that Bill Clinton had conquered his "weakness."

With his well-honed instincts for sensing popular sentiment, and with the clinical detachment of the master campaigner that he was, at one point during the campaign, the president turned to his wife and said, "Women want to know why you stayed with me." As staffers squirmed and looked down at their shoes, Hillary Clinton, without missing a beat, shot back, "Yes, I've been wondering that myself." "Because you're a sticker!" Bill Clinton exclaimed, saluting his wife's perseverance in their private life while publicly positioning her perfectly. "That's what people need to know—you are a sticker. You stick at the things you care about."[32]

President Clinton tried to appear bemused by his upcoming role as "first spouse." He laughed off the critics who began to perceive policy decisions or grants of clemency as bribes to New York voters. At times he seemed relieved that he could offer his long-suffering wife a tangible payoff. But his language was more prickly than Hillary Clinton's had been when she was his primary campaign cheerleader. Even if he did not yell—as the *National Enquirer* claimed he did—"There's no way I am going to be your First Lady," the president's language was detached:[33] "I'm very happy for her," he insisted twice at a press conference.[34] "I'm pretty good at flower arranging," he had joked earlier, anticipating his pending irrelevance, yet mocking his wife's seven-year attempt to make her role more substantive.[35] The president eventually warmed to the idea, which extended his legacy and helped balance the marital books.

At first, Hillary Rodham Clinton continued her delicate balancing act, this time trying to fulfill her first lady duties while advancing her candidacy. "Obviously, I'll be a full-time candidate for Senate and will spend the bulk of my time in New York," Mrs. Clinton insisted. "But I certainly will fulfill my duties here in Washington, whether it's following up on policy issues I've been involved in or hosting a state dinner."[36]

The contradiction, however, was apparent. The demands of both undefined yet seemingly infinitely elastic tasks were ultimately impossible to meet. The year before, Mrs. Clinton had taken five official foreign trips, hosted six state and official dinners, and averaged ten to fifteen White House events monthly. Moreover, she had positioned herself as a critical adviser in most major White House decisions and raised over $50 million for Democrats in the previous four years. The Democratic presidential nominee Vice President Al Gore both missed her assistance and suffered because of the millions of Democratic dollars diverted toward her campaign—feeding the growing alienation between the Gore and Clinton couples and camps.

Asking "Whither the First Lady?" as she began her "double life," Washington reporters said that "the loss will be subtle but real for Washington." The first lady's presence at, say, the twenty-fifth anniversary of the Hirshhorn Museum had elevated the event from a celebration of one museum to a celebration of the arts—with a much better chance of press coverage. The first lady's input in advancing what she considered her agenda—women, children, health—was unquantifiable yet irretrievable.[37]

Straying from the first lady's theoretically nonpartisan perch made Mrs. Clinton less popular and complicated her task. When the Palestinian first lady, Suha Arafat, libeled Israel in Mrs. Clinton's presence, campaign aides said that diplomatic imperatives justified the American first lady's silence. Nevertheless, supporters of Israel fumed, and Democrats worried about Mrs. Clinton's political tin ear. After seven years in the White House bunker—where aides handpicked her audiences and she carefully chose her battles—Mrs. Clinton found the three-dimensional nature of state politics treacherous. She could not support clemency for Puerto Rican terrorists without enraging New York City cops whom the terrorists had targeted; she could not march in the St. Patrick's Day parade with Irish Catholics without offending gays who were not invited. Moreover, to forge her own identity, she had to deviate from her husband's script. Alas, as vice presidents had learned on the campaign trail, and as first ladies had learned within the confines of the executive mansion, modern journalistic alchemy transforms mild assertions of independence into devastating criticisms.

Yet Mrs. Clinton could not simply resign from her post. By scaling back and moving north, she tried to shadowbox her way out of the elusive role she had struggled so hard to define. Still, as long as she was married to the president, she remained shackled as first spouse to a contradictory mix of burdens, duties, protocols, powers, and opportunities.

Unlike her husband, Hillary Clinton was not a natural on the campaign trail. But she was earnest, enthusiastic, and a fast learner. At one point, exhausted by the crowds, she told her friend, Harold Ickes, "I never realized how good Bill was at this until I tried to do it."[38] As much of a polarizing figure as her husband, Mrs. Clinton often winced as the media sought to reduce her to one of two mutually exclusive boxes. A *Newsweek* cover story had wondered whether she was a saint or a sinner; *Vanity Fair* deliberated between branding her "a crusader or a hypocrite."[39] At her worst, she, like her husband, tried to be all things to all people, a cynical, poll-driven reflection of what Americans seemed to desire. At her best, she, like her husband, was smart enough, creative enough, determined enough to transcend convention and hew a third way. And, like her husband, Hillary Clinton was blessed with incompetent enemies. The leading Republican candidate, Mayor Rudy Giuliani, self-destructed, fueled by his city-slicker contempt for upstate New York, his own extramarital affair, and a bout with prostate cancer. The eventual Republican nominee, Rick Lazio, was too young, too inexperienced, and too awkward with the national media to defeat a woman who had become an international superstar and a Democratic icon.

Always ready for a makeover, Mrs. Clinton allowed her celebrity to speak for itself—and she learned how to play against that aura to appear more humble, more approachable, and more pragmatic than her reputation suggested. Reporter Michael Tomasky would marvel at how Mrs. Clinton "presented herself to voters, especially in upstate New York, as their earnest problem solver who had traded in her once-grand crusades for more modest, and, as far as the voters were concerned, more useful ones."[40] She remained a formidable presence: "In addition to her genuine passion for the ideals she believes in, she is intelligent and studious, actively considerate of those who work for her, tough as reinforced steel, and has a will to succeed that is the strongest I've ever seen up close in an aspirant for office."[41] But over the course of her White House roller-coaster ride, struggling with the constraints of being a first lady and the occasional burdens of justifying her husband's hijinks, Mrs. Clinton had learned to reveal a softer side as well. Working hard, listening well, and learning how to be a candidate, Hillary Clinton did not just eke out a victory. On an Election Day when Al Gore and George W. Bush ended up in a virtual tie, she won in a landslide. It was now, Tomasky and others would acknowledge, "Hillary's Turn."

Indeed, it was "Hillary's Turn" to wield power and enjoy the spotlight. Her husband, the ex-president, globe-trotted in a dizzying, lucrative, but ultimately frustrating and somewhat meaningless round of speeches, book signings, and funerals, interrupted by the occasional do-gooding event. Meanwhile, George W. Bush's presidency made the junior senator from New York a very senior Democrat. Especially during the first Bush term, she was careful to avoid ruffling senatorial feathers. Just as she had charmed New York voters by appearing so down-to-earth, she charmed her less well known but more veteran colleagues by being solicitous and deferential. Still, once Senator John Kerry's 2004 candidacy failed, and as George W. Bush's second term bogged down in Iraq troubles, the Katrina catastrophe, soaring gas prices, whiffs of scandal, and plummeting poll ratings, the assumption became widespread that Senator Clinton would make a play to become another President Clinton.

Running for reelection in 2006, Hillary Clinton had the perfect cover to assemble a formidable campaign organization and amass millions of dollars. The fact that New York Republicans could not find a viable candidate to oppose her only highlighted the charade and fed the "Hillary for President" boom. Her Georgetown mansion, Whitehaven, became the center of the Democratic opposition, a hub of activity for those dreaming of a return trip to 1600 Pennsylvania Avenue. As more and more Clintonistas signed up as consultants, as more and more fund-raisers took place from coast to coast, as more and more national Republicans tried to mobilize their base by demonizing her, and as more and more reporters wrote glowing profiles, Hillary Clinton's position as the leading Democrat going into the 2008 presidential sweepstakes solidified.

The Hillary Clinton positioning for that run was a warmer, more self-assured, more agile public figure than she had been as first lady. Years of exposure to America's unrelenting media glare had simultaneously toughened and softened her. She seemed much less brittle and much more impervious to criticism, but she also seemed much

more centered and, frankly, much more fun. Yet as antiwar Democrats criticized her from the left for supporting the Iraqi war effort
and as conservative Republicans lambasted her from the right as the
ultimate big government liberal, just what her political identity
was—and what her campaigning or governing strategies might be—
remained quite elusive.

As Senator Clinton forged ahead with her political career, the position that had been her gateway into national politics remained en-
igmatic. Being first lady is the second hardest job in America, after
being president, because of the impossibly long list of things to do
in any given day, as well as the frustratingly long but only partially
visible list of dos and don'ts defining the role. Hillary Rodham Clinton demonstrated a first lady's potential political power, policy influence, and popular glow. Her tenure may have buried, once and
for all, the phrase, "No first lady ever did that before."[42] Future first
ladies now had a predecessor who raised money by the millions,
tried to reform one-seventh of the American economy, had an office
in the West Wing, often resisted invoking her husband's authority in
establishing personal and political standing, and ran for political office as her tenure was ending.

Yet despite all these precedents, Hillary Rodham Clinton failed to
make the office what she, many of her feminist friends, and many
journalists who cover the East Wing wanted it to be. Even in her memoirs, written in 2003, when she was already established as an influential senator and a potential presidential candidate, the legacy
she claimed for herself as first lady was derivative, not autonomous;
his legacy of peace and prosperity was her legacy. In assessing the
"two Clinton terms," she did not take personal credit for anything.
She did not emphasize any particular crusades, concerns, initiatives,
innovations, or ideas. "I supported his agenda and worked hard to
translate his vision into actions that improved people's lives,
strengthened our sense of community and furthered our democratic values at home and around the world," she wrote.[43] No one
would know, at first glance, where, if at all, her agenda, her ideology,
or her emphases differed from her husband's.

Moreover, although future first ladies undoubtedly will build on
Mrs. Clinton's activism, in the short term, this feminist trailblazer
blazed a trail for Laura Bush to follow quietly and effectively, without

controversy and with great popularity. The turmoil surrounding Mrs. Clinton led many Americans to appreciate Laura Bush's low-profile, calming approach. Mrs. Bush did not seem to be another Pat Nixon—the quintessential, long-suffering political wife whose passivity attracted journalistic contempt—but rather a softer, happier, more evolved version of her own mother-in-law, Barbara Bush.

Six months into the Bush presidency, nearly two-thirds of Americans polled approved of Laura Bush as first lady, and only 17 percent had a negative impression. Six months into the Clinton presidency, nearly a third of Americans had already soured on Mrs. Clinton. The words used to describe Mrs. Bush reflected her traditional aura: "Nice," "lady" or "ladylike," "classy," "intelligent," and "quiet." Most Americans, 61 percent, believed Mrs. Bush had less influence with her husband on policy issues than other first ladies, but 47 percent deemed the amount of influence she had on the administration just right, and 23 percent said it was too little, with only 6 percent saying too much. By contrast, 40 percent of those surveyed in May 1993 complained that Hillary Clinton was too influential.[44]

A decade and a half after Bill and Hillary Clinton's "two for one" campaign, power and popularity still tend to flow to those first ladies, like Laura Bush and Barbara Bush, who do not seem too eager, too interested in either public policy or grandstanding. Laura Bush's years in the White House demonstrated that the office was more effective as a center of calm, not controversy, as a bastion of tradition rather than a base for trend-setting. The office, in many ways, remains a throwback, a nineteenth-century ceremonial position set amid the rapid-fire pace of twenty-first-century life. It remains more fit for a queen, or at least a homegrown American aristocrat, than for a corporate go-getter or a political crusader. The fantasy of the feminist first lady remains unfulfilled. Women who want real power in the American political system need to learn the democratic lesson that Hillary Clinton ultimately learned: better to earn power via election than to assume it via marriage, even when your spouse is president of the United States.

NOTES

ABBREVIATIONS USED IN NOTES

BC   Bill Clinton
BC Mem   Bill Clinton, *My Life* (New York: Alfred A. Knopf, 2004)
HRC   Hillary Rodham Clinton
HRC Mem   Hillary Rodham Clinton, *Living History* (New York: Simon and
          Schuster, 2003)
NYT   *New York Times*
NR   *New Republic*
USNWR   *US News & World Report*
WasPo   *Washington Post*

PROLOGUE AND ACKNOWLEDGMENTS

1. HRC, "Remarks by Senator Hillary Rodham Clinton to the NYS Family Planning Providers," 24 January 2005. http://clinton.senate.gov/~clinton/speeches/2005125A05.html.

2. *NYT,* 25 January 2005.

3. *Washington Times,* 26 January 2005. http://www.washingtontimes.com/national/20050126-121258-1641r.htm.

INTRODUCTION: GOSSAMER SHACKLES: THE FEMINIST FIRST LADY'S DILEMMAS

1. *Vogue,* December 1998, 233, 231.

2. *Glamour,* August 1992, 269.

3. *Vanity Fair,* May 1992, 144.

4. Ibid.

5. *Newsweek,* 1 July 1996.

6. CBS News Transcripts, *60 Minutes,* Sunday, 26 January 1992.

7. George Stephanopoulos, *All Too Human: A Political Education* (Boston: Little, Brown, 2000), 24, 69.

8. *NYT,* 19 November 2001.

9. *NYT,* 22 September 2001.

CHAPTER 1: FROM PARK RIDGE TO LITTLE ROCK

1. *Miami New Times,* 18 March 1992.

2. David Maraniss, *First in His Class* (New York: Simon and Schuster, 1995), 257.

3. HRC Mem, 9.

4. Ibid., 9, 2.

5. Ibid., 3.

6. Ibid., 11.

7. Ibid., 20.

8. Ibid., 12.

9. HRC, *It Takes a Village* (New York: Simon and Schuster, 1996), 153.

10. HRC Mem, 12.

11. Alan Ehrenhalt, *The Lost City: Discovering the Forgotten Virtues of Community in the Chicago of the 1950s* (New York: Basic Books, 1995), 11.

12. HRC Mem, 21.

13. Rick Perlstein, *Before the Storm: Barry Goldwater and the Unmaking of the American Consensus* (New York: Hill and Wang, 2001), 474, 473.

14. HRC Mem, 23.

15. Ibid.

16. David Brock, *The Seduction of Hillary Rodham* (New York: Free Press, 1996), 22.

17. *WasPo,* 10 March 1992.

18. Miriam Horn, *Rebels in White Gloves* (New York: Times Books, 1999), xi–xii.

19. HRC, Wellesley College, 1969 Student Commencement Speech, 31 May 1969. http://www.wellesley.edu/PublicAffairs/Commencement/1969/053169hillary .html.

20. HRC Mem, 26.

21. *WasPo,* 12 January 1993.

22. HRC Mem, 37.

23. Ibid., 32.

24. Ibid., 37.

25. Roger Morris, *Partners in Power* (New York: Henry Holt, 1996), 127.

26. Ibid.

27. Ibid., 133.

28. HRC Mem, 38.

29. Horn, *Rebels in White Gloves,* 47, 46.

30. HRC, "Commencement Speech"; HRC Mem, 41.

31. HRC Mem, 40; Gail Sheehy, *Hillary's Choice* (New York: Random House, 1999), 59; Horn, *Rebels in White Gloves*, 47.

32. HRC quoted in Maraniss, *First in His Class*, 256–257.

33. Morris, *Partners in Power*, 125.

34. Maraniss, *First in His Class*, 265–257.

35. John Leo, *USNWR*, 31 August–7 September 1992.

36. Christopher Lasch, "Hillary Clinton, Child Saver," *Harper's Magazine*, October 1992, 80.

37. Daniel Wattenberg, "The Lady Macbeth of Little Rock," *American Spectator*, August 1992.

38. *Life*, 20 June 1969, 31.

39. HRC Mem, 53, 52.

40. Maraniss, *First in His Class*, 247, 246.

41. Ibid., BC to Carolyn Yeldell Staley, 342.

42. HRC in *Parade*, 11 April 1993.

43. *People*, 17 February 1992.

44. Judith Warner, *Hillary Clinton: The Inside Story* (New York: Signet, 1993), 75.

45. Virginia Kelley with James Morgan, *Leading with My Heart* (New York: Simon and Schuster, 1994), xvii.

46. Meredith L. Oakley, *On the Make* (Washington, D.C.: Regnery, 1994), 30.

47. BC Mem, 45.

48. Oakley, *On the Make*, 30.

49. Maraniss, *First in His Class*, 202.

50. BC in *Vanity Fair*, May 1992.

51. HRC Mem, 61.

52. Ibid., 69.

53. *WasPo*, 12 January 1993.

54. Sheehy, *Hillary's Choice*, 124–125.

55. Garry Wills, *New York Review of Books*, 5 March 1992.

56. Ernest Becker, *The Denial of Death* (New York: Free Press, 1973), 4; see also Maraniss, *First in His Class*, 345.

57. *WasPo*, 12 January 1993.

58. Sheehy, *Hillary's Choice*, 162.

59. HRC Mem, 85.

60. Ibid., 81, 91.

61. *Chicago Tribune*, 31 January 1992.

62. Joyce Milton, *The First Partner: Hillary Rodham Clinton* (New York: William Morrow, 1999), 119.

63. Ibid., 118.

64. Maraniss, *First in His Class*, 394.

65. *Time*, 27 January 1992.

66. Morris, *Partners in Power*, 115.

67. *People*, 17 February 1992.

68. Mary Ellen Guy, "Hillary, Health Care, and Gender Power," in *Gender Power, Leadership and Governance*, ed. Georgia Duerst-Lahti and Rita Mae Kelly (Ann Arbor: University of Michigan Press, 1995), 248.

69. Kelley, *Leading with My Heart*, 203.

70. *Vanity Fair*, February 1999.

71. Sheehy, *Hillary's Choice*, 171.

72. Pepper Schwartz, *Love between Equals: How Peer Marriage Really Works* (New York: Free Press, 1995), 111, 17.

73. Maraniss, *First in His Class*, 117.

74. *People*, 25 January 1993.

75. Connell Cowan and Melvyn Kinder, *Smart Women/Foolish Choices* (New York: C. N. Potter, 1985), 97; Schwartz, *Love between Equals*, 15.

76. *New Yorker*, 30 May 1994, 62.

77. James B. Stewart, *Blood Sport* (New York: Simon and Schuster, 1996), 70.

78. Cowan and Kinder, *Smart Women*, 105, 133.

79. *NYT Magazine*, 17 January 1993.

80. *WasPo*, 14 July 1992.

81. *Vanity Fair*, May 1992, 217.

82. *Newsweek*, 3 February 1992.

83. HRC, *It Takes a Village*, 43.

84. *Arkansas Democrat-Gazette (Little Rock)*, 28 February 1985.

85. HRC Mem, 95.

86. *Vanity Fair*, May 1992.

87. *Newsweek*, 28 December 1992.

88. Maraniss, *First in His Class*, 264.

89. David Brock, *Seduction of Hillary Rodham*, 74.

90. Ibid., 76.

CHAPTER 2: THE 1992 CAMPAIGN

1. BC, "Announcement Speech," 3 October 1991, in BC and Al Gore, *Putting People First* (New York: Times Books, 1992), 191, 187.

2. *Vanity Fair,* May 1992.

3. *WasPo,* 10 March 1992.

4. James T. Patterson, *Restless Giant* (New York: Oxford University Press, 2005), 247.

5. George H. W. Bush, 1988 Republican National Convention Acceptance Speech, 18 August 1988.

6. Judith Warner, *Hillary: The Inside Story* (New York: Signet, 1999), 185.

7. CBS News Transcripts, *60 Minutes,* 26 January 1992.

8. Ibid.

9. Ibid.

10. Ibid.

11. BC Mem, 385.

12. CBS News Transcripts, *60 Minutes,* 26 January 1992.

13. Tammy Wynette, lyrics, "Stand by Your Man" (Legacy/Columbia, 1968).

14. Christopher P. Andersen, *Bill and Hillary: The Marriage* (New York: William Morrow, 1999), 236.

15. Susan Faludi, *Backlash: The Undeclared War against American Women* (New York: Crown Publishers, 1991); Christina Hoff Sommers, *Who Stole Feminism: How Women Have Betrayed Women* (New York: Touchstone, 1994, 1995), 22.

16. Elizabeth Fox-Genovese, *Feminism Is NOT the Story of My Life: How Today's Feminist Elite Has Lost Touch with the Real Concerns of Women* (New York: Doubleday, 1995); *WasPo,* 18 December 1995.

17. EMILY's List, "Where We Come From." http://www.emilyslist.org/about/where-from.html.

18. Roger Morris, *Partners in Power* (New York: Henry Holt, 1996), 440.

19. *Time,* 27 January 1992.

20. George Stephanopoulos, *All Too Human* (Boston: Little, Brown, 1999), 60.

21. Peter Goldman et al., *Quest for the Presidency, 1992* (College Station: Texas A&M University Press, 1994), 630.

22. Ibid., 124.

23. Stephanopoulos, *All Too Human,* 66.

24. BC, "The New Covenant: Responsibility and Rebuilding the American Community," 23 October 1991, in Robert E. Levin, *Bill Clinton: The Inside Story* (New York: SPI Books, 1992), 289.

25. For a different interpretation, see Joe Conason and Gene Lyons, *The Hunting of the President: The Ten-year Campaign to Destroy Bill and Hillary Clinton* (New York: St. Martin's Press, 2000); "Minority Views of Senators Sarbanes,

Dodd, Kerr, Bryan, Boxer, Mosley-Braun, Murray and Simon," in *Investigation of Whitewater Development Corporation and Related Matters: Final Report*, U.S. Congress, Senate, Committee on Banking, Housing and Urban Affairs, Report 104–280, 104th Cong., 2nd sess., 1996, 395–664, which relies heavily on and confirms the Pillsbury Madison & Sutro law firm's independent report for the Resolution Trust Corporation absolving the Clintons.

26. James B. Stewart, *Blood Sport* (New York: Simon and Schuster, 1996), 213.

27. Stephanopoulos, *All Too Human*, 93.

28. Warner, *Hillary*, p. 185.

29. William Safire, "The Hillary Problem," *NYT*, 26 March 1992.

30. *NYT*, 18 May 1992.

31. ABC News and PBS/WGBH Boston, *Nightline/Frontline*, Paul Begala, in chap. 1, "The Clinton Years." http://www.pbs.org/wgbh/pages/frontline/shows/clinton/chapters/1.html#5.

32. HRC Mem, 110.

33. Peter Steinfels, *The Neoconservatives* (New York: Simon and Schuster, 1979), 287; Christopher Lasch, *The Revolt of the Elites and the Betrayal of Democracy* (New York: W. W. Norton, 1995), 6.

34. *Time*, 9 January 1984; Marissa Piesman and Marilee Hartley, *Yuppie Handbook* (New York, 1983). For Ralph Whitehead's critique and description of less-affluent baby boom "new collars," see *Chicago Tribune*, 9 July 1985.

35. George H. Gallup, *The Gallup Poll*, 3 vols. (New York: Random House, 1972), 3:2196.

36. *NYT*, 18 May 1992.

37. Julianne Malveaux, *Los Angeles Times*, 22 March 1992.

38. *NYT*, 28 April 1992.

39. *Life*, 20 June 1969, 31.

40. *Atlanta Constitution*, 31 January 1992.

41. *WasPo Magazine*, 1 November 1992.

42. *Seattle Post-Intelligencer*, 24 August 1992.

43. *Vanity Fair*, May 1992, 147.

44. Warner, *Hillary*, 188.

45. *Vanity Fair*, May 1992, 147.

46. Ibid., 144.

47. *People*, 17 February 1992; *Harper's Bazaar*, July 1992, 91.

48. Goldman et al., *Quest for the Presidency*, 702.

49. Ibid., 646.

50. *Boston Globe*, 14 September 1996.

51. *Seattle Post-Intelligencer,* 24 August 1992.

52. *Boston Globe,* 14 September 1996.

53. Stephanopoulos, *All Too Human,* 95.

54. Stan Greenberg, James Carville, and Frank Greer to BC, Mickey Cantor, and David Wilhelm, 27 April 1992, in Goldman et al., *Quest for the Presidency,* 664.

55. Ibid., 657, 663.

56. *Seattle Post-Intelligencer,* 24 August 1992.

57. Ibid.

58. *Washington Times,* 23 August 1992.

59. HRC, "Liz Carpenter Lecture Series, University of Texas," Austin, 7 April 1993, 2.

60. *Seattle Post-Intelligencer,* 24 August 1992.

61. Ibid.

62. Linda Bloodworth-Thomason in *People,* 20 July 1992.

63. Stan Greenberg to BC, 7 June 1992, in Goldman et al., *Quest for the Presidency,* 681.

64. *NYT,* 8 June 1992.

65. *Chicago Tribune,* 14 July 1992.

66. *NR,* 22 June 1992, 42.

67. *NYT,* 8 November 1992, 4:17.

68. *Christian Science Monitor,* 15 January 1993.

69. *NYT,* 18 July 1992.

70. *Seattle Post-Intelligencer,* 24 August 1992.

71. *WasPo Magazine,* 1 November 1992, 24.

72. Bob Schieffer, *CBS News,* 21 July 1992, quoted in "Media Watch." http://secure.mediaresearch.org/news/mediawatch/1992/mw19920801p5b.html.

73 *NR,* 15 February 1993, 6.

74. On commodification, see Robert Westbrook, "Politics as Consumption: Managing the Modern American Election," chap. 5 in *The Culture of Consumption: Critical Essays in American History, 1880–1980,* ed. Richard Wightman Fox and T. J. Jackson Lears (New York: Pantheon Books, 1983); on modern America's "show business discourse," see Neil Postman, *Amusing Ourselves to Death: Public Discourse in the Age of Show Business* (New York: Viking, 1985).

75. George Gallup, *The Gallup Poll: Public Opinion 1992* (Wilmington, Del.: Scholarly Resources, 1993), 194–197.

76. *NYT,* 30 October 1992.

77. "From feminist to homemaker, lawyer to moral crusader, Hillary Clinton knows to tailor her image for her audience. Now she's posing for Vogue," *Irish Times*, 4 December 1993; *Seattle Post-Intelligencer*, 24 August 1992.

78. *NYT*, 30 October 1992.

CHAPTER 3: COPRESIDENT

1. Judith Warner, *Hillary: The Inside Story* (New York: Signet, 1999), 171.

2. *Newsweek*, 23 January 1989.

3. *NYT*, 11 December 1988.

4. *WasPo*, 15 January 1989; *People Weekly*, 21 November 1988.

5. Judy Woodruff, interview with Barbara Bush, PBS-NBC, Republican National Convention coverage, 18 August 1992.

6. Sidney Blumenthal, *The Clinton Wars* (New York: Farrar, Straus and Giroux, 2003), 267.

7. Barbara Bush, "Family Values," 19 August 1992, in *Vital Speeches*, 15 September 1992, 7128.

8. Ibid.

9. Barbara Bush, *Barbara Bush: A Memoir* (New York: Charles Scribner's Sons, 1994), 275.

10. Barbara Bush, *Millie's Book* (New York: William Morrow, 1990).

11. *Newsweek*, 28 December 1992.

12. Ibid.

13. Gail Sheehy, *Hillary's Choice* (New York: Random House, 1999), 225–226.

14. Haynes Johnson and David S. Broder, *The System* (Boston: Little, Brown, 1996), 98.

15. *Courier-Mail*, 21 January 1993.

16. *Washington Times*, 20 January 1993, H10.

17. CNN & Company, 7 January 1993, Transcript 31.

18. ABC News, *Primetime Live*, 14 January 1993.

19. Ibid.

20. *People*, 10 May 1993, 83.

21. *Sunday Times (London)*, 20 June 1993.

22. Sister Souljah, BC, quoted in BC Mem, 411.

23. Elizabeth Drew, *On the Edge* (New York: Simon and Schuster, 1994), 38.

24. CNN, *Crossfire*, 22 January 1993, Transcript 752.

25. NYT, 10 February 1993.

26. FAIR [Fairness and Accuracy in Reporting], Veena Cabreros-Sud, and Farah Kathwari, "*New York Times* on Immigrants: Give Us Your Healthy, Wealthy

and 24-Hour Nannies," "Extra," April–May 1993. http://www.fair.org/extra/9304/nyt-immigration.html.

27. CNN, *Crossfire*, 22 January 1993, Transcript 752.

28. Debbie Price quoted in *Atlanta Journal and Constitution*, 20 January 1993.

29. CNN, *Crossfire*, 22 January 1993, Transcript 752.

30. Bob Woodward, *The Agenda: Inside the Clinton White House* (New York: Simon and Schuster, 2005), 110–111.

31. *NYT*, 26 January 1993.

32. Johnson and Broder, *The System*, 99, 98.

33. *NYT*, 27 January 1993.

34. Eleanor Clift, *Newsweek*, 1 February 1993.

35. *Ladies' Home Journal*, April 1993, 146.

36. Sally Quinn, 15 February 1993.

37. *Atlanta Constitution*, 9 February 1993.

38. Ibid.

39. *USNWR*, 25 January 1993.

40. *Time*, 4 January 1993.

41. *NYT*, 8 February 1993.

42. *NR*, 15 February 1993. The same poll found that only 43 percent of the men under 40 approved. *Atlanta Constitution*, 21 February 1993.

43. Mary Hoyt and Nancy Bingaman, "Report on the Functions and Organization of the Office of the First Lady," 6 January 1977, p. 1, Box 1, Daniel Malachuk Administration Files, Jimmy Carter Library, Atlanta, Ga.

44. Ibid., 28, 26.

45. Ibid., 26, 27.

46. See "Rosalynn's Staff," clipping, 21 February 1978, Box 29, Hugh Carter MSS, Jimmy Carter Library.

47. Public Law 95-570, 2 November 1978, in "Staff Offices Administration," Box 7, Malachuk MSS.

48. *Newsweek*, 15 January 1996, 22. See also *New Yorker*, 26 February 1996 and 4 March 1996, 125.

49. Deposition of Margaret A. Williams, 20 July 1994, in U.S. Congress, Senate, Committee on Banking, Housing and Urban Affairs, Depositions of White House Officials in Response to S. Res. 229, 103rd Cong., 2nd sess., 1994, 5:236–237.

50. Johnson and Broder, *The System*, 100.

51. BC, "Acceptance Speech to the Democratic National Convention by Governor Bill Clinton from Arkansas," New York, 16 July 1992.

52. BC and Al Gore, *Putting People First* (New York: Times Books, 1992), 107–108.

53. Johnson and Broder, *The System*, 82.

54. Theda Skocpol, *Boomerang* (New York: W. W. Norton, 1996), 109.

55. Ibid., 108.

56. Johnson and Broder, *The System*, 193.

57. Ibid., 104.

58. Ibid., 106.

59. Paul Starr to Ira Magaziner, 7 February 1993, Box 3308, Clinton White House, Interdepartmental Working Group, William J. Clinton Presidential Library, Little Rock, Ark.

60. George Stephanopoulos, *All Too Human* (New York: Little, Brown, 1999), 198.

61. David Gergen, *Eyewitness to Power* (New York: Simon and Schuster, 2000), 293–294.

62. Ibid., 308.

63. Ibid.

64. *Atlanta Constitution*, 21 February 1993.

65. Johnson and Broder, *The System*, 101.

66. *Newsweek*, 4 October 1993.

67. *Association of American Physicians and Surgeons, Inc. et al. v. Hillary Rodham Clinton et al.*, 997 F.2d 898, 902, 904 (U.S. App. D.C., 22 June 1993).

68. Gregory S. Walden, *On Best Behavior* (Indianapolis: Hudson Institute, 1996), 87.

69. *Boston Globe*, 26 February 1993.

70. *American Physicians v. HRC*, 813 F. Supp. 90 (D.D.C. 1993).

71. *American Physicians v. HRC*, 997 F.2d 905, 910–911. Eventually, in September 1994, the White House opened 230 boxes of documents from the working group to end the litigation.

72. Johnson and Broder, *The System*, 142.

73. *NYT*, 28 February 1993.

74. *Plain Dealer (Cleveland, Ohio)*, 2 May 1993.

75. *Boston Globe*, 15 March 1993, 13.

76. *Time*, 10 May 1993.

77. HRC to Julie Baldridge in James Stewart, *Blood Sport* (New York: Simon and Schuster, 1996), 91.

78. *Los Angeles Times Magazine*, 23 May 1993.

79. *Newsweek*, 24 June 1996.

80. *NYT*, 9 March 1993.

81. PBS, *Bill Moyers; The New American*, 9, no. 14, 12 July 1993. http://www.thenewamerican.com/tna/1993/vo09n014/vo09n014_hillary.htm.

82. Suzanne Dixon, "Conclusion—The Enduring Theme: Domineering Dowagers and Scheming Concubines," in *Stereotypes of Women in Power*, ed. Barbara Garlick, Suzanne Dixon, and Pauline Allen (Westport, Conn.: Greenwood Press, 1992), 222.

83. Marianne Means, *Seattle Post-Intelligencer*, 5 May 1993.

84. Eleanor Clift, *Newsweek*, 21 June 1993.

85. *Boston Globe*, 6 April 1992.

86. HRC, 6 April 1993 in *Tikkun*, May–June 1993, 8.

87. HRC, "Address at the Liz Carpenter Lecture Series on Civil Society, University of Texas, Austin," 7 April 1993.

88. *NYT Magazine*, 23 May 1993, 22.

89. *Life*, 20 June 1969, 31. See also the Port Huron Statement on "American values," "American virtue," "making values explicit," and the search for "a meaning in life that is personally authentic." "Agenda for a Generation," in *American Firsthand: Readings in American History*, ed. Robert D. Marcus and David Burner, 2 vols. (New York: St. Martin's Press, 1989), 2:296–299.

90. HRC, "University of Michigan Commencement Address," 1 May 1993.

91. HRC, "University of Pennsylvania Commencement Address," 17 May 1993.

92. Marianne Means, *Seattle Post-Intelligencer*, 5 May 1993.

93. Barbara Bush, "Choices and Change," *Vital Speeches of the Day* 56 (1 July 1990): 549.

94. *Parade*, 11 April 1993, 4.

95. *People*, 10 May 1993. See also *Time*, 14 January 1985, 24.

96. *Newsweek*, 26 April 1993.

97. Ibid.

98. *USNWR*, 31 January 1994.

99. *Newsweek*, 26 April 1993.

100. *NYT*, 7 May 1993.

101. *NYT*, 29 September 1993.

102. Magaziner to HRC in Johnson and Broder, *The System*, 16.

103. *NYT*, 29 September 1993.

104. Lloyd R. George in Meredith L. Oakley, *On the Make* (Washington, D.C.: Regnery Publishing, 1994), 285.

105. *NYT*, 29 September 1993.

106. Ibid.

107. CNN, 27 October 1993, 11:24 A.M., Transcript 237-4.

108. *Post-Standard (Syracuse, N.Y.)*, 17 October 1993.

109. Ibid.

110. BC Mem, 532.

111. *People*, 27 December 1993–3 January 1994.

112. Johnson and Broder, *The System*, 256.

113. *NYT Magazine*, 23 May 1993.

114. *Boston Globe*, 12 December 1993; Katha Politt in *NYT*, 3 October 1993.

115. *Harper's Bazaar*, January 1994, 39.

CHAPTER 4: BACKLASH

1. *American Spectator*, January 1994, 28, 22.

2. See David Brock, *Blinded by the Right* (New York: Three Rivers Press, 2002), 147–174.

3. Elizabeth Drew, *On the Edge* (New York: Simon and Schuster, 1994), 384.

4. *Boston Globe*, 22 December 1993.

5. HRC in *NYT*, 27 May 1993.

6. *Boston Globe*, 30 May 1993, 65.

7. David Gergen, *Eyewitness to Power* (New York: Simon and Schuster, 2000), 308–309.

8. Stephen L. Carter, *Integrity* (New York: Basic Books, 1996), 95. See also Thomas E. Patterson, *Out of Order* (New York: Alfred A. Knopf, 1993).

9. Rush H. Limbaugh III, *See I Told You So* (New York: Pocket Books, 1993), 143.

10. James Fallows, *Breaking the News* (New York: Pantheon Books, 1996), 92–93.

11. Haynes Johnson and David S. Broder, *The System* (Boston: Little, Brown, 1996), 277.

12. Ibid., 281; *Newsweek*, 15 November 1993; *Newsweek*, 1 November 1993.

13. Jack Farrell quoted in Kenneth T. Walsh, *Feeding the Beast* (New York: Random House, 1996), 239.

14. Howard Kurtz, *Hot Air* (New York: Crown Publishers, 1996), 4, 10.

15. Jim Johnson in Brock, *Blinded by the Right*, 177.

16. Ibid., 283.

17. Lori D. Ginzberg, *Women and the Work of Benevolence* (New Haven: Yale University Press, 1990), 216.

18. Arlene W. Saxonhouse, "Introduction—Public and Private: The Paradigm's Power," in *Stereotypes of Women in Power*, ed. Barbara Garlick, Suzanne Dixon, and Pauline Allen (Westport, Conn.: Greenwood Press, 1992), 7.

19. Suzanne Dixon, "Conclusion—The Enduring Theme: Domineering Dowagers and Scheming Concubines," in Garlick et al., *Stereotypes of Women*, 215, 218.

20. Mary Ellen Guy, "Hillary, Health Care, and Gender Power," in *Gender Power, Leadership and Governance*, ed. Georgia Duerst-Lahti and Rita Mae Kelly (Ann Arbor: University of Michigan Press, 1995), 254.

21. Brock, *Blinded by the Right*, 148.

22. *USA Today*, 26 April 1994.

23. *WasPo*, 14 June 1993.

24. Carl Anthony in *WasPo*, 31 January 1993; Blanche Wiesen Cook in *Los Angeles Times*, 17 January 1993.

25. *Los Angeles Times*, 17 January 1993.

26. *WasPo*, 8 December 1992.

27. *Redbook*, March 1993, 123.

28. George Stephanopoulos, *All Too Human* (New York: Little, Brown, 1999), 227.

29. Ann Compton in Walsh, *Feeding the Beast*, 159.

30. *Newsweek*, 21 March 1994.

31. Neil Eggleston to GAO, 6 April 1994, Draft Memorandum from David Watkins, undated, in Gregory S. Walden, "Recent Disclosures Regarding the First Lady," 11 January 1996, addendum to Gregory S. Walden, *On Best Behavior* (Indianapolis: Hudson Institute, 1996), 1, 3.

32. *NYT*, 29 February 1996.

33. *Boston Globe*, 3 April 1994, 63.

34. "Remarks in a Town Meeting in Charlotte, North Carolina," 5 April 1994, *Public Papers of the Presidents, William J. Clinton—1994* (Washington, D.C.: U.S. Government Printing Office, 1995), 1:587–588.

35. Ibid.

36. *Atlanta Constitution*, 11 March 1994.

37. Stephanopoulos, *All Too Human*, 226–228.

38. Stuart M. Butler, "Why the Clinton Health Plan Is in Trouble," *Heritage Foundation Reports*, Heritage Lectures, No. 452, 23 June 1993.

39. Theda Skocpol, *Boomerang* (New York: W. W. Norton, 1996), ix.

40. CBS, *CBS News Special Report*, 9:00 P.M. ET, 22 September 1993.

41. *Washington Times*, 2 October 1993.

42. *Washington Times*, 4 October 1993.

43. Brock, *Blinded by the Right*, 157.

44. *Rocky Mountain News*, 16 February 1994.

45. *WasPo*, 31 January 1994.

46. *NYT*, 29 March 1994.

47. *Los Angeles Times*, 25 January 1996.

48. *WasPo*, 16 November 1993.

49. HRC quoted in *WasPo*, 5 February 1994.

50. HRC, "Speech of the First Lady at National Education Association Convention, New Orleans, La.," 3 July 1994.

51. *WasPo*, 5 February 1994.

52. United Press International, 10 March 1994.

53. *Arkansas Democrat-Gazette (Little Rock)*, 13 March 1994.

54. *USA Today*, 5 April 1994.

55. James Stewart, *Blood Sport* (New York: Simon and Schuster, 1996), 418.

56. *Newsweek*, 21 March 1994, 35.

57. Joe Klein, "The Body Count," *Newsweek*, 7 August 1995.

58. *New Yorker*, 26 February–4 March 1996, 130.

59. *Atlanta Constitution*, 11 March 1994.

60. "Press Conference by the First Lady," 22 April 1994, in U.S. Congress, Senate, Committee on Banking, Housing and Urban Affairs, *White House Document Production in Response to S. Res. 229*, 103rd Cong., 2nd sess., 1994, 9:1590, 1587, 1588, 1591, 1596.

61. *WasPo*, 23 April 1994.

62. Stephanopoulos, *All Too Human*, 389.

63. Broder and Johnson, *The System*, 528.

64. Skocpol, *Boomerang*, 171.

65. Ibid., 10; *Los Angeles Times*, 14 August 1994.

66. Washington Newswire Association Inc., *PR Newswire*, 25 October 1994.

67. *NR*, 15 February 1993.

68. HRC quoted by Dick Morris in "Hillary's Choice," Gail Sheehy, *Vanity Fair*, February 1999, 172.

69. *Esquire*, March 1994, 52.

CHAPTER 5: A STRATEGIC RETREAT?

1. *Baltimore Sun*, 26 September 1994.

2. *Arkansas Democrat-Gazette (Little Rock)*, 26 June 1994.

3. *Plain Dealer (Cleveland, Ohio)*, 2 September 1994.

4. *NYT*, 13 July 2005.

5. David Gergen, *Eyewitness to Power* (New York: Simon and Schuster, 2000), 309.

6. *Commercial Appeal (Memphis)*, 8 October 1994.

7. *WasPo*, 30 September 1994.

8. *Commercial Appeal (Memphis)*, 8 October 1994.

9. Dick Morris, *Behind the Oval Office* (New York: Random House, 1997), 79–105.

10. Ben J. Wattenberg, *Values Matter Most* (New York: Free Press, 1995), 239–267.

11. *Newsweek*, 12 February 1996.

12. BC, "State of the Union Address of the President," White House, Office of the Press Secretary, 23 January 1996.

13. Don E. Eberly and George Gallup Jr., in Don E. Eberly, *The Content of America's Character* (Lanham, Md.: Madison Books, 1995), 6, ix. See also New York Times/CBS News Poll in *NYT*, 16 July 1996.

14. *USNWR*, 27 February 1995, 36.

15. *Atlanta Constitution*, 18 February 1995.

16. *Boston Globe*, 9 March 1995.

17. *New Yorker*, 26 February–4 March 1996, 126.

18. HRC, "Remarks to the United Nations Fourth World Conference on Women, Beijing, China," White House, Office of the Press Secretary, 5 September 1995.

19. *Good Housekeeping*, January 1993, 99.

20. HRC, "Remarks at Pentagon Celebration of Women's History Month, Washington, D.C.," White House, Office of the Press Secretary, 1 March 1995.

21. HRC, "Remarks by the First Lady to the Ninth Annual 'Women in Policing' Awards, New York, New York," White House, Office of the Press Secretary, 10 August 1994.

22. HRC, "Remarks at the Mother of the Year Awards, New York, NY," White House, Office of the Press Secretary, 13 April 1995.

23. *Newsweek*, 1 July 1996.

24. *Newsweek*, 16 January 1995.

25. HRC, "At Work on Issues: The First Lady of the United States," NARA, White House Web site ver. 3, July 2000. http://clinton3.nara.gov/WH/EOP/First_Lady/html/issues.html.

26. HRC, "Remarks Via Satellite to Children Now Conference," White House, Office of Press Secretary, 4 March 1994.

27. Ibid.

28. Ibid.

29. HRC, "Keynote Address by the First Lady at Scripps College," White House, Office of the Press Secretary, 26 April 1994.

30. HRC, "Remarks by First Lady HRC at the Greater Detroit Chamber of Commerce, Mackinac Island, MI," White House, Office of the Press Secretary, 1 June 1995.

31. HRC, "Remarks by First Lady HRC at Brooklyn College Commencement, Brooklyn, NY," White House, Office of the Press Secretary, 1 June 1995.

32. HRC, "Remarks by First Lady HRC at the Greater Detroit Chamber of Commerce, Mackinac Island, MI," White House, Office of the Press Secretary, 1 June 1995.

33. HRC, "Remarks by the First Lady at the Chicago Children's Museum, Chicago, IL," White House, Office of the Press Secretary, 18 February 1997.

34. Robert D. Putnam, *Bowling Alone* (New York: Simon and Schuster, 2000).

35. HRC, "Remarks at the Annual Meeting of the World Economic Forum," White House, Office of the Press Secretary, 2 February 1998.

36. HRC, "Remarks at the 150th Anniversary of the First Women's Rights Convention in Seneca Falls, New York," White House, Office of the Press Secretary, 16 July 1998.

37. James T. Patterson, *Restless Giant* (New York: Oxford University Press, 2005), 67.

38. HRC, "Remarks by the President and First Lady on the 25th Anniversary of the Legal Services Corporation," White House, Office of the Press Secretary, 27 July 1999.

39. HRC, "Column on Youth and Violence in the Media," *Talking It Over,* 2 June 1999.

40. HRC, "Remarks at the National Abortion Rights Action League's Anniversary Luncheon," White House, Office of the Press Secretary, 22 January 1999.

41. Ibid.

42. *Glamour,* August 1992, 269.

43. *New York Daily News,* 23 July 1995.

44. *NYT,* 10 August 1995.

45. HRC, "Remarks to the United Nations Fourth World Conference on Women, Beijing, China," White House, Office of the Press Secretary, 5 September 1995.

46. *People,* 25 December 1995–1 January 1996.

47. Michael Isikoff, *Uncovering Clinton* (New York: Crown Publishers, 1999), 246.

48. BC to Monica Lewinsky in Kenneth W. Starr, *The Starr Report* (New York: Pocket Books, 1998), 113.

49. George Stephanopoulos, *All Too Human* (Boston: Little, Brown, 1999), 32.

50. Evelyn Lieberman testimony, *Starr Report*, 64.

51. Monica Lewinsky in ibid., 49.

52. BC, "National Family Week," 15 November 1995.

53. Monica Lewinsky in *Starr Report*, 54.

54. *NYT,* 8 January 1996; see also *NYT,* 10 January 1996.

55. Bob Woodward, *Shadow* (New York: Simon and Schuster, 1999), 288, 309, 310.

56. BC Mem, 335.

57. Ibid., 336; Woodward, *Shadow,* 317.

58. Camille Paglia, "The First Drag Queen," Salon.com. http://www.salon.com/06/features/paglia.html.

59. *NYT Magazine,* 23 May 1993.

60. HRC, *It Takes a Village* (New York: Simon and Schuster, 1996), 11.

61. Ibid., 41, 50.

62. Suzanne Dixon, "Conclusion—The Enduring Theme: Domineering Dowagers and Scheming Concubines," in *Stereotypes of Women in Power,* ed. Barbara Garlick, Suzanne Dixon, and Pauline Allen (Westport, Conn.: Greenwood Press, 1992), 216.

63. John Brummett and HRC in *Mother Jones,* November–December 1993, 37.

64. *Los Angeles Times,* 25 January 1996, A1.

65. CNN, *Larry King Live,* Interview with HRC, 20 May 1996, transcript by Journal Graphics Inc., 8, 4, 7, 3.

66. Ibid.

67. Ibid.

68. *Time,* 28 December 1997–4 January 1998, 70.

69. *NYT,* 4 February 1997, 14.

70. HRC in ibid.

71. HRC, "Remarks on Democracy &Women, Sydney, Australia," White House, Office of the Press Secretary, 21 November 1996.

72. Morris, *Behind the Oval Office,* 79–105.

73. *Newsweek,* 12 February 1996.

74. Judith Warner, *Hillary Clinton: The Inside Story* (New York: Signet, 1993), 171.

75. ABC, *20/20*, "Barbara Walters Joint Interview with the Clintons," 20 September 1996.

76. Morris, *Behind the Oval Office*, 230.

77. Stephanopoulos, *All Too Human*, 387.

78. Morris, *Behind the Oval Office*, 164–165, 300.

79. Stephanopoulos, *All Too Human*, 419.

80. Morris, *Behind the Oval Office*, 300.

81. Stephanopoulos, *All Too Human*, 419.

82. Morris, *Behind the Oval Office*, 300.

83. Roger Simon, *Show Time* (New York: Times Books, 1998), 283.

84. Ibid., 284–285.

85. Ibid., 285.

86. Isikoff, *Uncovering Clinton*, 66.

87. Joe Klein, "The Politics of Promiscuity," *Newsweek*, 9 May 1994.

88. Simon, *Show Time*, 285.

89. Peter Goldman et al., *Quest for the Presidency 1992* (College Station: Texas A&M University Press, 1994), 649.

90. Simon, *Show Time*, 291.

91. Stephanopoulos, *All Too Human*, 415.

92. Simon, *Show Time*, 288.

93. Morris, *Behind the Oval Office*, 333.

94. Ibid., 335.

95. "Hillary Clinton and Elizabeth Dole—Separated at Birth?" *WOC Alert*, 15 August 1996. http://www.wlo.org/alert/96/815.html.

96. HRC, "First Lady Hillary Rodham Clinton Speaks at the Democratic National Convention," Chicago, 27 August 1996, *Newshour with Jim Lehrer*. http://www.pbs.org/newshour/convention96/floor_speeches/hillary_clinton.html.

97. CNN, *AllPolitics*, "Reinvented First Lady Speaks Tonight," 27 August 1996. http://cgi.cnn.com/ALLPOLITICS/1996/news/9608/27/hillary.watts/.

CHAPTER 6: MRS. CLINTON, MR. PRESIDENT,
AND MS. LEWINSKY

1. HRC, "Remarks by First Lady HRC at Brooklyn College Commencement, Brooklyn, N.Y.," White House, Office of the Press Secretary, 1 June 1995.

2. Stuart Taylor Jr., "Her Case against Clinton," *American Lawyer,* November 1996, 57, 58.

3. Evan Thomas with Michael Isikoff, "Clinton v. Paula Jones," *Newsweek,* 13 January 1997.

4. BC, "Inaugural Address of President William J. Clinton," White House, Office of the Press Secretary, 20 January 1997.

5. "New Documents Show White House's Desire For Campaign Money," CNN, *AllPolitics,* 2 April 1997. http://www.cnn.com/ALLPOLITICS/1997/04/02/ickes.documents/.

6. BC Memo, 5 January 1995, quoted in John F. Harris, *The Survivor* (New York: Random House, 2005), 271.

7. "Transcript of Vice President Gore's News Conference on Campaign Fund-Raising," *WasPo,* 4 March 1997.

8. Ibid.

9. Ibid.

10. Barry M. Goldwater with Jack Casserly, *Goldwater* (New York: Doubleday, 1988), 23–24.

11. Lanny J. Davis, *Truth to Tell* (New York: Free Press, 1999), 165.

12. Michael Isikoff, *Uncovering Clinton* (New York: Crown Publishers, 1999), 167, 168.

13. Davis, *Truth to Tell,* 12.

14. On the intensity of the opposition, see Joe Conason and Gene Lyons, *The Hunting of the President* (New York: St. Martin's Press, 2000).

15. "Excerpts from the Clinton Deposition in Jones Sexual Misconduct Suit," *NYT,* 16 March 1998.

16. Alan M. Dershowitz, *Sexual McCarthyism* (New York: Basic Books, 1998), 146.

17. Ibid., 20.

18. HRC Mem, 440.

19. Ibid.

20. *WasPo,* 28 March 1999.

21. *WasPo,* 3 October 1998.

22. Nancy F. Cott, *Public Vows* (Cambridge, Mass.: Harvard University Press, 2000), 201.

23. *Seattle Times,* 19 August 1998, A2. See also Davis, *Truth to Tell,* 38.

24. HRC Mem, 440, 441.

25. BC Mem, 800.

26. HRC Mem, 466.

27. Ibid., 469, 439, 442.

28. Sidney Blumenthal, *The Clinton Wars* (New York: Farrar, Straus and Giroux, 2003), 342–343.

29. Dick Morris quoted in *NYT,* 21 November 1999.

30. NBC, *Today Show,* 27 January 1998, AP, "Excerpts of Mrs. Clinton Interview," 27 January 1998, http://www.washingtonpost.com/wp-srv/politics/special/clinton/stories/excerpts012798.htm.

31. Ibid.

32. Jeffrey Toobin, *A Vast Conspiracy* (New York: Random House, 1999), 258.

33. BC, "State of the Union Address by the President," White House, Office of the Press Secretary, 27 January 1998.

34. HRC Mem, 466.

35. *NYT,* 14 August 1998.

36. *Newsweek,* 31 August 1998, 4.

37. HRC Mem, 471, 472.

38. Ibid., 476.

39. Claire Shipman, "Hillary's Hide and Seek," *George,* September 1998, 54.

40. *Time,* 28 December 1998–4 January 1998, 74.

41. *Vanity Fair,* January 1999, 39.

42. CNN, *All Politics,* 10 April 1997. http://www.cnn.com/ALLPOLITICS/1997/04/10/hillary/.

43. Barbara Kellerman, "The Enabler," *Presidential Studies Quarterly* 28 (Fall 1998): 890.

44. *Vanity Fair,* January 1999, 39.

45. Gail Sheehy, *Hillary's Choice* (New York: Random House, 1999), 168.

46. Karen Tumulty and Nancy Gibbs, "The Better Half," *Time,* 28 December 1998.

47. *Vanity Fair,* January 1999, 39.

48. *Newsweek,* 31 August 1998.

49. *NYT,* 19 August 1998.

50. *NR,* 14 and 21 September 1998.

51. *NYT,* 24 January 1998.

52. Diana Owen and Jack Dennis, "Kids and the Presidency: Assessing Clinton's Legacy Leadership and Values," 10, no. 3, 41, Roper Center for Public Opinion Research, *The Public Perspective,* April 1999–May 1999; for an opposing view, see Keating Holland/CNN, "Poll: Clinton Scandal Has Not Taught Young

Americans It's OK to Lie," 17 February 1999. http://www.cnn.com/ALLPOLITICS/
stories/1999/02/17/poll/.

53. *WasPo,* 8 July 1999.

54. CNN *Talkback Live,* 15:00 P.M. ET, 9 July 1999, Transcript 99070900V14;
WasPo, 8 July 1999; see *USA Today,* 16 November 2000.

CONCLUSION: SENATOR HILLARY: "COMPELLING PUBLIC FIGURE" OR "DEGRADED WIFE"?

1. HRC Mem, 469, 428.

2. BC, "Remarks of the President at Religious Leaders Breakfast," White
House, Office of the Press Secretary, 11 September 1998.

3. Senator Tom Harkin quoted by Shelby Steele in *Wall Street Journal,* 25 September 1998, in Gabriel Fackre, ed., *Judgment Day at the White House* (Grand
Rapids, Mich.: W. B. Eerdmans, 1999), 177–179.

4. *Newsweek,* 31 August 1998.

5. Alan M. Dershowitz, *Sexual McCarthyism* (New York: Basic Books,
1998), 221.

6. Reinhold Neibur, *Moral Man and Immoral Society* (New York: Charles
Scribner's Sons, 1932), xi–22, quoted by Betty Glad, "Evaluating Presidential
Character," *Presidential Studies Quarterly* 28 (Fall 1998): 862.

7. Kathleen Hall Jamieson and Sean Aday, "When Is Presidential Behavior
Public and When Is It Private," *Presidential Studies Quarterly* 28 (Fall 1998):
857–858.

8. Alan Wolfe, *One Nation After All* (New York: Viking, 1998), 54; George F.
Will, *Newsweek,* 30 August 1999, 68.

9. *Psychology Today,* July–August 1998, 35–36, 38.

10. BC Mem, 481–482.

11. *Newsweek,* 20 July 1998.

12. *New Yorker,* 24 and 31 August 1998, 50.

13. *Time,* 28 December 1998–4 January 1998.

14. *Newsweek,* 14 December 1998.

15. Gail Sheehy, *Hillary's Choice* (New York: Random House, 1999), 178.

16. *Vogue,* December 1998.

17. *Newsweek,* 19 October 1998.

18. BC, Mem, 489.

19. Dennis Kucinich, quoted in *Vanity Fair,* February 1999, 178.

20. *Newsweek,* 1 February 1999.

21. William H. Chafe, *Private Lives/Public Consequences* (Cambridge, Mass.: Harvard University Press, 2005), 362, 375.

22. Robert W. Ray, "Final Report of the Independent Counsel," 5 January 2001; "Text: Final Report of the Independent Counsel in Regards to the Whitewater Investigation," *WasPo,* 20 March 2002. http://www.washingtonpost.com/wp-srv/onpolitics/transcripts/whitewater_032002.html.

23. Ibid.

24. Ibid.

25. Claire Shipman, "Hillary's Hide and Seek," *George,* September 1998, 52.

26. HRC Mem, 501.

27. Marc Humbert, Associated Press report in *Montreal Gazette,* 8 July 1999.

28. Lucinda Franks, "Interview with Hillary Clinton," *Talk,* September 1999, 174.

29. Richard Cohen in *WasPo,* 3 August 1999.

30. Franks, "Interview with HRC," *Talk,* 173.

31. *Time,* 28 December 1998–4 January 1999.

32. John F. Harris, *The Survivor* (New York: Random House, 2005), 379.

33. See Drudge Report, 1 December 1999, http://www.rense.com/politics5/reap_n_sew.htm and Cox News Service, 5 December 1999.

34. *NYT,* 9 December 1999.

35. *Newsweek,* 30 August 1999, 4.

36. *WasPo,* 8 February 2000.

37. Ibid.

38. Harris, *Survivor,* 380.

39. *Vanity Fair,* June 1994, 104.

40. Michael Tomasky, *Hillary's Turn* (New York: Free Press, 2001), 16.

41. Ibid., 12.

42. *USA Today,* 28 January 2000.

43. HRC Mem, xi.

44. "Laura and Hillary Polls Apart," *Pew Research Center,* 24 July 2001. http://people-press.org/reports/display.php3?ReportID=6.

The literature regarding Hillary Rodham Clinton is vast but mostly unsatisfying. There is something about Mrs. Clinton that often brings out the worst in Americans and American politics. Sadly, many authors have succumbed to this Clinton Curse, suddenly preferring sensation to explanation, headlines to nuance, partisanship to insight, while seeking individuals' often unknowable secrets and tackling confusing psychological motives rather than assessing the public record.

This book, with its focus on Mrs. Clinton's tenure as first lady, is most concerned with that public record: what she accomplished, and how it shaped the Clinton administration and American history. This concern avoids the hysteria of the biographical hit men—and women—so anxious to draw blood from their subjects. This approach also eschews the hagiography of the acolytes, making a brief for their idol's ascension to sainthood. Those seeking a book indicting or exonerating Mrs. Clinton or her husband should look elsewhere. The focus on the public conversation and achievements also justifies publishing the work now, in 2006, even as the recently opened William J. Clinton Presidential Library is processing collections that by the end of the decade should yield fascinating archival finds. Yet before scholarship using these archival gems begins to work its magic and fill in the blanks, we need a less partisan, less judgmental, less emotional interpretive lens for viewing the first feminist first lady, which this book tries to offer.

This historical work tries to understand Hillary Clinton in the broader context of the American pageant, assessing her impact on the Clinton presidency and seeing where she fits in amid the changing definitions and phenomena of Puritanism, Progressivism, Populism, Methodism, consumerism, capitalism, feminism, individualism, conservatism, and liberalism, among other movements. This work of history also tries to understand Hillary Clinton's challenges within the peculiar constraints of the complex, extraconstitutional, formally undefined, yet politically potent and historically consecrated role of first lady.

Too many books about first ladies suffer from their own intellectual tics. Whereas a previous generation of tea-and-crumpets history spent too much time on ladies hosted and china purchased, this generation of first lady chroniclers seeks to make every first lady a feminist power-house, a nascent Eleanor Roosevelt, or a virtual copresident. Although Hillary Clinton at various points in her tenure fit all three molds, it is essential to understand the pressures that made it so difficult to operate as a policy partner, the intellectual and ideological delusions that led her to believe that the institutional momentum within the first lady's office favored such an approach, and just why it is that she achieved more success and popularity by following a different path. First ladies are not junior presidents, nor are they women politicians elected on their own terms, as Senator Clinton now is. Analysts and first ladies overlook these differences at their peril.

Historical interest in first ladies has increased lately, thanks especially to Lewis Gould, the editor of the series this book is a part of, who authored "First Ladies," *American Scholar* 55 (1986): 528–535, and "Modern First Ladies in Historical Perspective," *Presidential Studies Quarterly* 15 (1985): 537, while editing the encyclopedic *American First Ladies: Their Lives and Their Legacies* (New York, 1996). Together with his biographies of Lady Bird Johnson, these works have advanced the scholarly conversation considerably. As a leading presidential historian, Professor Gould suggests that it is time to end the ghettoization of first lady studies. Studying the history of first ladies together and individually opens an important window into understanding the modern presidency and individual presidents.

Studying the first lady exacerbates what Stephen Skowronek in *The Politics Presidents Make* (Cambridge, 1993) identifies as the presidential scholar's challenge: how to trace lines of development in a highly idiosyncratic institution. The presidency at least is constitutionally defined and has very specific mandates; it is that much more difficult to chronicle the ill-defined and idiosyncratic East Wing of the White House.

Still, this work has benefited from the many biographers, historians, and journalists who have tilled the same soil. This book especially relies on the increasingly intrusive press and the pressure on Mrs. Clinton, her husband, and their peers to be more forthcoming and accessible than their predecessors. The candor imposed on modern leaders helps compensate for the limited archival resources currently available. Modern presidents and first ladies submit to countless journalistic interrogations. As we all do, they develop pat answers and favorite stories. Often their phrasing and word choice will not vary from year to year or decade to decade. With so many of these interviews available, and with little prospect that I would succeed in freeing these practiced professionals from their conversational ruts, I did not attempt to interview Mrs. Clinton, her husband, or any of her colleagues. The limited potential gains did not justify the degree to which my historical distance might be compromised by using friendly intermediaries to secure an interview.

Both the Clintons' memoirs offer their versions of events in great detail. Hillary Rodham Clinton, *Living History* (New York, 2003) is more revealing; Bill Clinton, *My Life* (New York, 2004) is more encyclopedic. Hillary Rodham Clinton also wrote *It Takes a Village* (New York, 1996) and *Dear Socks, Dear Buddy* (New York, 1998).

Biographies of Mrs. Clinton include: Donnie Radcliffe, *Hillary Rodham Clinton* (New York, 1993); Judith Warner, *Hillary Clinton* (New York, 1993); David Brock, *The Seduction of Hillary Rodham* (New York, 1996); Roger Morris, *Partners in Power* (New York, 1996); Gail Sheehy, *Hillary's Choice* (New York, 1999); Joyce Milton, *The First Partner: Hillary Rodham Clinton* (New York, 1999); and Christopher Andersen, *Bill and Hillary: The Marriage* (New York, 1999). Valuable specific studies include Michael Tomasky, *Hillary's Turn: Inside Her Improbable, Victorious Senate Campaign* (New York, 2001) and Miriam Horn, *Rebels in White Gloves: Coming of Age with Hillary's Class—Wellesley '69* (New York, 1999), which is particularly useful regarding Hillary Clinton's college years.

See also Bill Clinton and Al Gore, *Putting People First* (New York, 1992); Virginia Clinton Kelley with James Morgan, *Leading with My Heart* (New York, 1994); George Stephanopoulos, *All Too Human* (New York, 1999); Lanny J. Davis, *Truth to Tell* (New York, 1999); Dick Morris, *Behind the Oval Office* (New York, 1997); and, most recently, John F. Harris, *The Survivor: Bill Clinton in the White House* (New York, 2005).

Other initial assessments of the Clinton years include: Michael Isikoff, *Uncovering Clinton* (New York, 1999); James Stewart's excellent book on Whitewater, *Blood Sport* (New York, 1996); the superb Clinton biography by David Maraniss, *First in His Class* (New York, 1995); Peter Goldman et al., *Quest for the Presidency: 1992* (College Station, 1994); Meredith L. Oakley, *On the Make* (Washington, 1994); and Elizabeth Drew, *On the Edge* (New York, 1994).

All the investigations the Clintons endured provided historians with many valuable primary source documents decades earlier than normal. See, for example, the deposition of Margaret A. Williams, 20 July 1994, in *Depositions of White House Officials in Response to S. Res. 229*, 5:236–237; "Testimony of Roger Altman," 2 August 1994, *Hearings Relating to Madison Guaranty S & L and the Whitewater Development Corporation—Washington, DC Phase*, 3:421; *White House Document Production in Response to S. Res. 229*, 9:1590, 1587, 1588, 1591, 1596, all three from U.S. Congress, Senate, Committee on Banking, Housing and Urban Affairs, 103rd Cong., 2nd sess., 1994; *The Starr Report* (New York, 1998); Merrill McLoughlin, *The Impeachment and Trial of President Clinton* (New York, 1999); and Gregory S. Walden, *On Best Behavior* (Indianapolis, 1996). The Court of Appeals decision regarding Hillary Clinton's status during the health care reform effort is *Association of American Physicians and Surgeons, Inc. et al. v. Hillary Rodham Clinton et al.*, 997 F.2d 898, 904 (U.S. App. D.C. 22 June 1993). For details regarding the final independent counsel reports, see Robert W. Ray, "Final Report of the Independent Counsel," 5 January 2001; and "Text: Final Report of the Independent Counsel in Regards to the Whitewater Investigation," *Washington Post*, 20 March 2002, available at http://www.washingtonpost.com/wp-srv/onpolitics/transcripts/whitewater_032002.html.

Arguments insisting that there was no basis at all in Whitewater, beyond a conservative vendetta, can be found in Joe Conason and Gene Lyons, *The Hunting of the President: The Ten-year Campaign to Destroy Bill and Hillary Clinton* (New York, 2000), and Sidney Blumenthal, *The Clinton Wars* (New York, 2003). See also "Minority Views of Senators Sarbanes, Dodd, Kerr, Bryan, Boxer, Mosley-Braun, Murray and Simon," in U.S. Congress, Senate, Committee on Banking, Housing and Urban Affairs, *Investigation of Whitewater Development Corporation and Related Matters: Final Report*, Report 104-280, 104th Cong., 2nd sess., 1996, 395–664.

The phrase "white glove pulpit" comes from Nancy Reagan, "Remarks for Associated Press Publisher's Luncheon," 4 May 1987, p. 6, F95-109, WHORM, Ronald Reagan Library, Simi Valley, California.

On family and marriage, see John Demos, *Past, Present, and Personal* (New York, 1986); David Hackett Fischer, *Albion's Seed* (New York,

1989); Steven Mintz and Susan Kellogg, *Domestic Revolutions* (New York, 1988); Pepper Schwartz, *Love between Equals* (New York, 1994); and Nancy Cott, *Public Vows: A History of Marriage and the Nation* (New York, 2002). On women and politics, see Paula Baker, "The Domestication of Politics: Women and American Political Society, 1780–1920," *American Historical Review* 89 (1984): 620–647; William Henry Chafe, *The American Woman* (New York, 1972); National Republican Congressional Committee, *Wives Manual* (Washington, D.C., 1972); Betty Friedan, *The Feminine Mystique* (New York, 1963); Linda Kerber, *Women of the Republic* (Chapel Hill, N.C., 1980); Ethel Klein, *Gender Politics* (Cambridge, Mass., 1984); Sheila Rothman, *Woman's Proper Place* (New York, 1975); Theda Skocpol, *Protecting Soldiers and Mothers* (Cambridge, Mass., 1992); and Barbara Welter, "The Cult of True Womanhood, 1820–1860," *American Quarterly* 18 (1966): 151–174.

On the presidency, see Barbara Kellerman, *The Political Presidency* (New York, 1984); Samuel Kernell, *Going Public* (Washington, D.C., 1986); Theodore J. Lowi, *The Personal President* (Ithaca, N.Y., 1985); Richard Neustadt, *Presidential Power and the Modern Presidents* (New York, 1990); Richard Pious, *The American Presidency* (New York, 1979); Stephen Skowronek, *The Politics Presidents Make* (Cambridge, Mass., 1993); Howard Gardner, *Leading Minds* (New York, 1995); and William Chafe, *Private Lives/Public Consequences: Personality and Politics in Modern America* (Cambridge, Mass., 2005).

On morality and rights, see Gertrude Himmelfarb, *The Demoralization of Society* (New York, 1995); George Lakoff, *Moral Politics* (Chicago, 1996); Michael J. Sandel, *Democracy's Discontent* (Cambridge, Mass., 1996); Ben Wattenberg, *Values Matter Most* (New York, 1995); *The American Scholar* (1993): 19; "Defining Deviancy Up," *New Republic*, 22 November 1993; and Robert Putnam, *Bowling Alone: The Collapse and Revival of American Community* (New York, 2001). See also George H. Gallup, *The Gallup Polls*, 3 vols. (New York, 1972).

On the New Class, see Peter Steinfels, *The Neoconservatives* (New York, 1979), 287; and Christopher Lasch, *The Revolt of the Elites and the Betrayal of Democracy* (New York, 1995), 6. On yuppies, see *Time*, 9 January 1984; Marissa Piesman and Marilee Hartley, *Yuppie Handbook* (New York, 1983). For an alternate view, see Ralph Whitehead, *Chicago Tribune*, 9 July 1985, C1.

On women and power, see Mary Ellen Guy, "Hillary, Health Care, and Gender Power," in *Gender Power, Leadership and Governance*, ed. Georgia Duerst-Lahti and Rita Mae Kelly (Ann Arbor, Mich., 1995); Barbara Garlick, Suzanne Dixon, and Pauline Allen, eds., *Stereotypes of Women in Power* (New York, 1992); and Lori D. Ginzberg, *Women and the Work of Benevolence* (New Haven, 1990).

On health care, see Theda Skocpol, *Boomerang* (New York, 1996); Haynes Johnson and David S. Broder, *The System* (Boston, 1996); and James Fallows, "A Triumph of Misinformation," *Atlantic Monthly*, January 1995. See also the documents from the task force at the William J. Clinton Presidential Library, under "Clinton White House: Interdepartmental Working Group."

On the Politics of Meaning, see Mrs. Clinton's speech of 6 April 1993 in *Tikkun*, May/June 1993; *NYT Magazine*, 23 May 1993; *Life*, 20 June 1969; see also the Port Huron Statement on "American values," and the search for "a meaning in life that is personally authentic."

On modern media and proportionality, see Stephen L. Carter, *Integrity* (New York, 1996); Rush H. Limbaugh III, *See I Told You So* (New York, 1993); James Fallows, *Breaking the News* (New York, 1996); Kenneth T. Walsh, *Feeding the Beast* (New York, 1996); and Howard Kurtz, *Hot Air* (New York, 1996). On Troopergate, see *American Spectator*, January 1994; David Brock, *Blinded by the Right: The Conscience of an Ex-Conservative* (New York, 2003).

On Clinton and values, see Don E. Eberly, *The Content of America's Character* (Lanham, Md., 1995); and Gary Aldrich, *Unlimited Access* (Washington, D.C., 1996).

Finally, this work has been blessed by the flourishing of the Internet, which was one of the defining achievements of the 1990s. The White House Web site, first developed in 1994, provided an extensive record of Hillary Rodham Clinton's activities and worldview, enabling the intensive analysis of her speeches and philosophy in the latter part of the book. The Clinton Presidential Library now has the Clinton Web sites back on the Web. In an interesting compromise between the fluidity of the medium and the rigidity of history, http://www.clintonlibrary.gov/archivesearch.html offers five snapshots of the Web site from the six years it was operational, which are, the library explains, now "historical materials, 'frozen in time,' which means that they are no longer updated and links to other sites will not work." Until more papers are processed, these Web sites will remain the most valuable and extensive windows into the Clinton presidency. In citing Mrs. Clinton's speeches as first lady, the notes provide the date and location of the speech, and with that information, they can then be found on the relevant Web site. All Internet addresses were accessed the first week of February 2006.

INDEX

The abbreviations BC and HRC refer to Bill Clinton and
Hillary Rodham Clinton, respectively.